PRINTING, WRITERS AND READERS IN RENAISSANCE ITALY

The spread of printing to Renaissance Italy had a dramatic impact on all users of books. As works came to be diffused more widely and cheaply, so authors had to adapt their writing and their methods of publishing to the demands and opportunities of the new medium, and reading became a more frequent and user-friendly activity. *Printing, Writers and Readers in Renaissance Italy* focuses on this interaction between the book industry and written culture. After describing the new technology and the contexts of publishing and bookselling, it examines the continuities and changes faced by writers in the shift from manuscript to print, the extent to which they benefited from print in their careers, and the greater accessibility of books to a broader spectrum of readers, including women and the less well educated. This is the first integrated study of a topic of central importance in Italian and European culture.

Brian Richardson is Professor of Italian Language at the University of Leeds. He is editor of Machiavelli, *Il principe* (1979) and *Trattati sull'ortografia del volgare* (1984) and author of *Print Culture in Renaissance Italy* (1994).

PRINTING, WRITERS AND READERS IN RENAISSANCE ITALY

BRIAN RICHARDSON

PUBLISHED BY THE PRESS SYNDICATE OF THE UNIVERSITY OF CAMBRIDGE
The Pitt Building, Trumpington Street, Cambridge CB2 1RP, United Kingdom

CAMBRIDGE UNIVERSITY PRESS
The Edinburgh Building, Cambridge CB2 2RU, UK http://www.cup.cam.ac.uk
40 West 20th Street, New York, NY 10011–4211, USA http://www.cup.org
10 Stamford Road, Oakleigh, Melbourne 3166, Australia

First published 1999

Printed in the United Kingdom at the University Press, Cambridge

Typeset in Baskerville 11/12.5 pt [VN]

A catalogue record for this book is available from the British Library

Library of Congress cataloguing in publication data

Richardson, Brian.
Printing, writers and readers in Renaissance Italy / Brian Richardson
p. cm.
Includes bibliographical references and index.
ISBN 0521 57161 8 (hardback) – ISBN 0521 57693 8 (paperback)
1. Book industries and trade – Italy – History. 2. Printing – Italy – History. 3. Authors and publishers – Italy – History. 4. Books and reading – Italy – History. I. Title.
Z340. R53 1999
306. 4'88'0945'09024 – dc21 98–30354 CIP

ISBN 0521 57161 8 hardback
ISBN 0521 57693 8 paperback

Contents

Figures

Following page 104

Preface

The introduction of the printing press to Italy in or shortly before 1465 had profound consequences for all users of the written word. Books now became available in much larger quantities than before, they cost much less, and texts could thus be disseminated more quickly and more widely. The sale of copies of a text could also be controlled, in principle, to the benefit of its author. Texts in printed books were presented differently in some respects from those in manuscripts, and new texts were produced with new sorts of readers in mind.

My aim in this book is to provide an introduction both to this revolutionary means of diffusing the written word and to its impact on writers and readers. The first part describes the production and circulation of books. Chapter 1 summarizes the techniques of the printing process; chapter 2 outlines the wider contexts in which presses operated: the financing and selling of books, and the regulation of printing by states and by the Church. I then turn to the influence of print. Part II is concerned with writers: with the differences which printing made to the process of publication (chapter 3), and with the relations between writers and the world of print (chapter 4). The focus in Part III is on the public who read or who wished to read. After assessing the extent of literacy in the period, chapter 5 considers the affordability of printed books and the effect of the relative abundance of books on personal and public libraries. The final chapter looks at developments in the forms and the contents of the printed texts which were provided for readers.

The time seems ripe for a broadly based survey of this kind. In the past few decades, increasing attention has been paid to the need to build bridges between the study of the book itself and the study of the contexts in which texts were written, reproduced, bought, kept and read. D. F. McKenzie has argued persuasively in *Bibliography and the Sociology of Texts* that there should be no border between bibliography and textual criticism on the one hand and literary criticism and literary history on the other. Historians of the book are alert to the danger of divorcing books from their intellectual contexts, of allowing – to use a phrase of Roger Chartier's in *The Order of Books* – their subject to become a history with neither readers nor authors. Especially since the publication in 1958 of *L'apparition du livre*, the pioneering work conceived by Lucien Febvre and written by Henri-Jean Martin, there has been a more widespread awareness of the technological and economic aspects of book production and consumption. As Luigi Balsamo stressed in an important article of 1973, 'Tecnologia e capitali nella storia del libro', a book is not just a 'content' but also an 'object', to be manufactured and traded alongside other commodities. Historians of Italian literature, including textual critics, have recognized that their subject is poorer if it is a history of authors unconcerned by who was going to read their works, what rewards they might receive for them, and how these works were going to be read, or a history of texts divorced from the processes by which they were diffused and the material forms in which they were received and interpreted – if, in short, they ignore Carlo Dionisotti's call (in the memorable opening passage of his essay 'Chierici e laici', included in his *Geografia e storia della letteratura italiana*) for the study of the real conditions in which that literature was created and transmitted.

My warmest thanks are due to those who helped in the making of *this* book. Foremost among them is Conor Fahy, himself one of the most skilful of bridge-builders between bibliographical and literary studies. He has generously offered valuable advice, information and constructive criticism from the earliest stages. Without his guidance and encouragement, and his expertise both in the techniques of printing and in the broader field of Renaissance culture, this book might never have been written and would certainly have been much the poorer. Richard Andrews was kind enough to read drafts of parts of the work and to offer stimulating suggestions. For help in obtaining information I am indebted to Christopher Challis, Franco D'Intino, Lotte Hellinga, Mario Infelise, Angela Nuovo and Oliver Pickering. Josie Dixon, Linda Bree and Jane Van Tassel of Cambridge University Press have piloted the enterprise with skill and tact. Finally, I am deeply grateful for the unfailing support of my family, especially my wife, Catherine.

A note on currency

The basis of the monetary system in central and northern Italy during the Renaissance was 12 denari = 1 soldo, 20 soldi = 1 lira. However, coinage differed greatly from state to state. Florence, Milan, Rome and Venice all had a gold coin of similar value, weighing about 3.5 grams. That of Florence was called the fiorino (florin), while Milan, Rome and Venice each had a ducato (ducat). In the sixteenth century, these and other Italian cities began to mint a gold or silver scudo of slightly lower value; in Florence and Rome, for instance, the gold scudo began to replace the florin or ducat in 1530. The rates of exchange between the lira and the florin or ducat varied over time. The florin had a value of between 5.5 lire (in 1471) and 7.5 lire (in 1531). The Venetian ducat was worth 6.2 lire in the early sixteenth century but 10 lire at the end of the century.

There was also a wide range of coins of lesser value made of silver (for example, Venice had a silver soldo and a silver marcello, worth half a lira), and there was a varied petty coinage in base-silver or copper. The lira was simply a money of account until a silver coin of this value was minted, first in Venice under Doge Niccolò Tron in 1472 and then in other cities.

Abbreviations

ASV, ST	Archivio di Stato, Venice, Senato Terra
BMC	*Catalogue of Books Printed in the Fifteenth Century Now in the British Museum*, 9 vols. (London: British Museum, 1909–49)
EDIT16	*Le edizioni italiane del XVI secolo: censimento nazionale* (Rome: Istituto centrale per il catalogo unico, 1985–)
GJ	*Gutenberg Jahrbuch*
GSLI	*Giornale storico della letteratura italiana*
GW	*Gesamtkatalog der Wiegendrucke* (Leipzig: Hiersemann, 1925–)
IGI	*Indice generale degli incunaboli*, 6 vols. (Rome: Libreria dello Stato, 1943–81)
IMU	*Italia medioevale e umanistica*
ISTC	*The Illustrated Incunable Short-Title Catalogue on CD-ROM* (Reading: Primary Source Media in association with the British Library, 1997)
LB	*La Bibliofilìa*

PART I

Printing and book production

CHAPTER I

The arrival of printing and its techniques

I THE SPREAD OF PRINTING IN ITALY

In about 1466 Leon Battista Alberti described how he and a friend in Rome had talked of a wonderful technique of reproducing texts which had recently been introduced to the area. 'It happened', he wrote, 'that we greatly approved of the German inventor who in these times has made it possible, by certain pressings down of characters, to have more than two hundred volumes written out in a hundred days from an original, with the labour of no more than three men; for with only one downwards pressure a large sheet is written out.'[1] In order to appreciate how great would have been Alberti's sense of enthusiasm and awe at the power of the new process of printing books, we can recall that just ten years earlier the Florentine bookseller Vespasiano da Bisticci had needed the work of forty-five scribes and a period of twenty-two months in order to copy out two hundred manuscripts commissioned by Cosimo de' Medici for the library of the Badia di Fiesole.[2] Strange and foreign though the technique of printing was, Alberti and his Italian contemporaries were quick to realize that it provided a means of production so much more rapid and economical than the pen that, for better or for worse, it would revolutionize their written communication.

The 'German inventor' of printing is traditionally identified as Johann Gutenberg of Mainz, a goldsmith by profession. His interest in such procedures went back as early as 1436, when he was residing in Strasburg. He was not alone in experimenting with the mechanical production of books: another goldsmith was teaching an 'art of writing artificially' ('ars scribendi artificialiter') in Avignon in the mid 1440s. But the weight of evidence strongly suggests that it was Gutenberg who, after returning to Mainz by 1448, began to produce books by using the key invention of printing with movable metal types, as opposed to making an impression from a fixed block of wood or metal. By 1452 he must have been working on his great forty-two-line Bible. During the 1450s several other printing houses probably began to operate in Mainz, and the first dated volume appeared in 1457.[3] But the spread of the industry beyond Mainz did not occur until towards 1465, when presses were set up in two other German cities and when two German printers, Conrad Sweynheym and Arnold Pannartz, began to work in Italy.

This first printing venture outside Germany was most probably promoted by a German cardinal, Nicholas of Cusa, and it took place in a Benedictine monastery in which the majority of monks were German, at Subiaco, about fifty miles east of Rome. The press here produced four books between 1465 and 1467. One was an elementary Latin grammar, for which there would be a certain demand from schools, but the others were aimed at a cultured elite of humanists and clerics: Cicero's *De oratore* and works by the early Christian writers Lactantius and Saint Augustine. Printing very soon moved from such a peripheral setting to Rome itself, where editing and marketing would have been much easier. There is evidence that a 'company to print books' combining German technical skill and Italian finance had been set up in the city by the autumn of 1466, and Sweynheym and Pannartz moved there in 1467, printing at least forty-eight more books together before their partnership broke up in 1473. Other Germans introduced printing to Venice in 1469 and to Foligno and nearby Trevi in 1470. Then came a sudden expansion of print: presses began to operate in 1471 in cities such as Ferrara, Florence, Milan, Bologna, Naples, Perugia and Treviso, in 1472 in Padua, Mantua, Parma, Verona and Perugia, and in the following year in Brescia and Pavia. By the end of the century, printing had taken place in nearly eighty towns or cities in Italy, many more than in Germany or France.[4]

Printing took root so fast and so widely in Italy because, once ecclesiastical patrons had given it a crucial initial impetus in Subiaco and then in Rome, the peninsula provided the fertile terrain which was essential to nourish and support it, in spite of the disunity of its states and the political instability of the period. On the one hand, printing needed a context of literacy and culture. Italy had in plenty the writers and scholars who would provide the industry with its raw material, the texts to be set in type, and it had urban populations sufficiently large, literate and well-to-do to provide the demand for the products of the industry: books for use in schools, books for personal study, entertainment or devotion, and books connected with professions or vocations, as in the cases of lawyers, doctors, clerics, teachers and university students. On the other hand, printing also required suitable economic conditions: the support of individuals or groups willing to take the initiative of promoting printing (for reasons of idealism, profit or both), and a good trade network which would provide access to supplies of paper and which would then distribute and sell the finished books efficiently. Many Italian cities were well placed to provide these contexts, especially those from Rome northwards; of the southern printing centres, only Naples was of any importance.

The city which offered the best conditions of all was Venice. Intellectual life flourished in the city and in its subject towns of Padua, with its important university, Verona and Vicenza; its government and territory were relatively stable, apart from the temporary setback of the battle of Agnadello in 1509; and it had a thriving mercantile system whose links reached throughout the Mediterranean and north of the Alps. Venice thus soon came to dominate the Italian printing industry, indeed for a while the European printing industry. The extent of this dominance is reflected in the results of two estimates of the percentages of books printed in the major Italian centres. One, by Ennio Sandal, focuses on books printed before 1501, known as incunables or incunabula.[5] In this period Italy may have produced, in at least seventy-six places of printing, some twelve thousand editions, a total which would represent some 45 per cent of the European output. The estimated production of the centres, in round figures, is shown in table 1. Another analysis, carried out by Amedeo Quondam, covers the period up to 1600 and is based on the holdings of the British Library (which, extensive though they are, represent of course only a sample of all the editions printed). The percentage figures shown in table 2 for the output of the eight major centres of the whole period (Pavia has now yielded its place to Ferrara), as proportions of the production of all Italy, suggest that Venice produced over half of all the editions overall and at one point, between 1526 and 1550, produced nearly three-quarters of the editions printed in Italy.[6]

2 THE CONTINUITY BETWEEN MANUSCRIPT AND PRINT

Just how revolutionary was this new means of communication which spread so rapidly through Italy? The initial development of the various media of mass communication – most notably the printed book, the newspaper, recorded sound, telecommunications, film – has characteristically involved a two-part scenario. In the first place, a set of

Table 1. *Sandal's estimates of editions printed before 1501*

	No. of editions	% of total
Venice	5,000	41.32
Rome	2,000	16.53
Milan	1,200	9.92
Florence	800	6.61
Bologna	650	5.37
Naples	300	2.48
Pavia	280	2.31
Brescia	260	2.15
Others	1,610	13.31
Total	12,100	100.00

Table 2. *Quondam's estimates of editions printed 1465–1600* (percentages of total output)

	1465–1600	1465–1500	1501–25	1526–50	1551–75	1576–1600
Venice	52.4	42.7	48.9	73.7	61.6	40.7
Rome	11.4	15.0	16.8	7.8	4.3	13.8
Florence	8.7	7.7	8.0	5.2	8.8	12.3
Milan	5.1	9.0	8.8	1.9	2.6	3.1
Bologna	3.6	4.6	5.8	3.3	3.1	1.7
Brescia	2.0	3.0	0.7	0.7	3.3	1.6
Naples	1.7	1.8	1.2	1.3	1.6	2.5
Ferrara	1.7	1.2	0.9	0.7	1.6	3.3

favourable social, economic and cultural circumstances provides a context in which a new medium can flourish. Secondly, this new medium is developed as a result of a perfection and synthesis of existing technical and commercial know-how, in other words a combination of continuity and innovation. In the case of the birth of printing in western Europe in the fifteenth century, long-term factors, such as urbanization, the rise of the cost of labour, and the development of universities and hence of lay culture, came together to foster a demand for cheaper and more plentiful reading matter. This demand was met by Gutenberg's invention; but we must bear in mind that the transcription of texts in type and their distribution to the public built in several respects on foundations laid during the age of manuscripts.[7]

From the thirteenth century, techniques had been evolved to promote the manufacture and circulation of books in order to satisfy the needs of the teachers and students of the new universities, a development described by Petrucci as an 'embryonic process of industrialization of book production'.[8] Entrepreneurial booksellers co-ordinated the work of those who prepared the animal skin on which the texts would be written, of the scribes who copied the texts, and of the various people who gave the product its finished appearance: illuminators (who embellished the text with decorative letters at its main divisions or with elaborate vine-stem motifs in the margins of the first page), rubricators (who painted simple initial letters, book and chapter headings, and paragraph marks), flourishers (who added red or blue flourishes to capital letters), and binders (who sewed together the separate gatherings or quires of leaves and added a covering to the resulting book). Manuscripts of a text in heavy demand could be turned out in a process resembling mass production: a group of manuscripts of Dante's *Commedia* copied by professional scribes in the mid fourteenth century is known as the 'gruppo del Cento' after the story of one such scribe who married off his daughters thanks to his earnings from writing a hundred Dantes.[9] In the thirteenth and fourteenth centuries some large universities, such as Bologna and Padua, had a system to regulate and expedite the rapid diffusion of correct copies of set texts. A *stationarius*, or stall-keeper who had sworn to obey university statutes, hired out an authorized *exemplar* (master copy) of each work, provided not as a complete unit but by the separate *pecia* (piece or gathering, consisting of four or more written sheets), to be copied by professional scribes or by teachers and students themselves. The tariff was fixed by the university, and the bookseller could be fined if his master copy contained errors.[10] Multiple copying itself, then, was by no means a new concept; printing simply increased the scale on which it could take place, and to a large extent ensured that copies would be uniform.

Furthermore, for all the justified admiration aroused by Gutenberg's invention, he was essentially adapting technology and materials which had been in use previously, though not necessarily in the context of book production. The printing press itself, which will be described in section 4 of this chapter, shared the mechanical principles of the wine press. Ink had of course been used for centuries, though printer's ink had to be thicker than that made for use with a quill and was oil-based rather than water-based.[11] The two materials on which the printed impression was normally made, paper and vellum (treated animal skin, also known as parchment), were likewise inherited from the manuscript age, though vellum was far less commonly used in printing. Paper was much the younger material, in European terms, since it had arrived in Italy from China, via the Arabs, early in the twelfth century and had been used widely in place of vellum only since the late fourteenth century. There was a flourishing industry of paper mills in many parts of Italy, notably at Fabriano in the Marche and around Salò on Lake Garda. Without an adequate supply of paper, the spread of print would not have been possible. Paper is more fragile than vellum, but it was also several times cheaper (being made at that time from linen or hempen rags, which were allowed to rot, then pulped, diluted with water, and drained in rectangular wire moulds); it was much lighter and therefore less expensive to transport; and unlike vellum it offered a perfectly flat surface.[12] The movable metal types, consisting of printing, alphabetical and other signs cast in relief at the end of metal stalks, were of course new; but even these were, as will be shown in section 3, produced with tools – the punch and the matrix – which were in everyday use in making coins, medals and seals and in hallmarking metal. Gutenberg, we have noted, was a goldsmith, as were several early Italian printers.[13]

The appearance of the printed book was, naturally and necessarily, intended at first to be as similar as possible to that of the only existing model, the handwritten book. We shall see below that printed books could be individually hand-finished in the same way as manuscripts. We shall see in more detail in chapter 6, too, that typefaces imitated the main current forms of script; that, like manuscripts, early printed books did not have title pages; and that printers and publishers continued for many years to provide information about their identity and the place and date of printing by adapting the device of the concluding 'colophon', which scribes might use to give equivalent information about themselves. Many of the Italians involved with printing in its early years had been connected in one way or another with manuscript publication. The *cartolai*, who dealt chiefly in book materials and made bindings but who sometimes dealt in handwritten books, also supplied printed books, and they were among those who financed and organized printing enterprises.[14] Some scribes, too, learned to use the new technology. Clement of Padua, probably the first native Italian printer, taught handwriting, binding and illumination in Lucca before 1470 and, after working in the printing industry in Venice, was invited to return to Lucca in 1472 in order to exercise 'his art of printing letters, binding, and illuminating', the last two activities now to be carried out also in the context of printed books.[15] Others who were concerned with the production of both manuscript and printed books include, in the fifteenth century, André Belfort in Ferrara and Francesco del Tuppo in Naples, and, in the first half of the sixteenth century, Bartolomeo Zanetti and Ludovico degli Arrighi.[16] The circulation of books in manuscript certainly declined once printing had become established in the 1470s but by no means came to an end: there was still a demand for manuscripts of texts not yet in print or of choir books, or for de luxe manuscripts for presentation or collection.[17] Both the court of the Este in Ferrara and the Aragonese court in Naples continued to pay scribes to copy manuscripts up to the turn of the century.[18] Some authors, we shall see in chapter 4, were reluctant to commit their works to print. The copying of manuscripts from printed editions was quite common, and it shows that some readers still preferred the traditional medium, or perhaps found it impossible to obtain copies of some printed texts.[19] Even a student might need to commission a manuscript, as one sees from an order for a work by Albertus Magnus placed in Naples in 1475.[20]

The transition from manuscript to printed book was in some respects, then, a process of evolution. But the production of a printed book also required technical innovation, and we must now turn to examining its various stages. We can then go on in chapter 2 to examine the financial and institutional frameworks within which the printing industry operated.

3 COMPOSITION, IMPOSITION AND PROOFREADING

The crucial innovation in the printing process was, as has been mentioned, the use of a fount (that is, a set) of type.[21] Three devices were needed in order to cast this. First and most important was the punch (*punzone* in Italian), made originally of bronze or brass and then of steel, on the end of which was cut by hand a relief pattern, in mirror image, of an alphabetical or other symbol. The elegance of the type depended on the skill with which this cutting was done, and the contribution to type design made by punch-cutters such as Francesco Griffo, who worked for Aldo Manuzio, was thus fundamental.[22] The punch was hammered into a small block of softer metal (at first lead, then copper) in order to create a hollow image of the symbol; this was the matrix (*matrice*). In order to cast a type, the matrix was clamped in a mould (*forma*) of two parts, made of steel and clad in wood so that it could be held comfortably in the hand during the moulding process. The type-caster then poured into the mouth of the mould a molten alloy which solidified very rapidly. The principal metals used appear to have been lead, tin and antimony, but the proportions are uncertain.[23] In the early decades, some printers would possess their own punches and matrixes and would employ a specialist to cast founts of type for them, and it is thus often possible to use the typeface in order to identify the press at which a book was printed. During the sixteenth century, individuality in type design from press to press gave way to the purchase of punches, matrixes and types, first within states, then internationally, and some specialized type-founding companies developed.[24] But type remained expensive, and printers could therefore afford to keep only a limited number of characters in stock.

Types were kept in a case (*cassa*), a wooden tray divided into separate compartments (sing. *cassettino*) for each symbol, with capital letters at the top (hence the terms 'upper case' and 'lower case'). The process of assembling type for printing is known as composition (*composizione*), and was carried out by a compositor (*compositore*). His (or occasionally her) working day probably lasted from twelve to fourteen hours.[25] He set up his 'copy', the source text or exemplar, over the case on a clip known in Latin as a *visorium*. The text might have been previously corrected by an editor and might have been marked with instructions concerning layout.[26] Sitting before the case, which was propped up at an angle, the compositor picked out types one by one and assembled them in a composing stick (*compositoio*), a small hand-held tray with a slide adjustable according to the length of line desired (see fig. 2). As each line of type was completed, he ensured that the right-hand margin was even (or 'justified') by altering the space between words or by introducing or expanding abbreviations, using hyphenation or (most significantly from the point of view of the nature of the text) alternative spellings where these existed. When the composing stick was full, the few lines of type in it were transferred to a tray called a galley (*vantaggio*) which eventually came to hold a mirror image of a whole page of text. At this point the compositor tied the page of type with string and would probably mark in his copy-text the place at which the printed page ended (this mark would also be useful later when carrying out corrections). Composition was thus an intricate job which demanded both dexterity and enormous concentration; yet it was carried out in distracting conditions, in the same room as the creaking press, and at times by candlelight.

Books were printed on sheets which were large enough to contain at least two printed pages on each side. In the early years of printing, vellum was used not uncommonly for works of devotion, such as breviaries and missals, perhaps partly because the exclusiveness of the material appealed to customers who were as wealthy as they were pious, partly because its durability made it a sensible investment in the case of works which would receive frequent handling.[27] Thereafter vellum was used only occasionally for a few de luxe copies of an edition, destined to be presented as gifts or collected by bibliophiles (see chapter 3, section 1), and, as has been mentioned, the normal support was paper. The four sizes of the paper sheet (*foglio*) on which the great majority of early books were printed were, in decreasing order of surface area but in increasing order of frequency of use, imperial (*imperiale*, about 74 × 50 cm), royal (*reale*, about 61.5 × 44.5 cm), median (*mezzana*, about 51.5 × 34.5 cm) and chancery (about 45 × 31.5 cm). This last, presumably because it was the size normally used, was generally known as *comune* in Italian, but the term *rezuta* was used in the Bolognese paper-manufacturing regulations of 1389 (*rezuta* apparently means 'cut in half', the surface area being just over half that of royal).[28]

Once the number of pages of type sufficient to cover one side of a sheet had been composed, they were put together in a process known as imposition (*imposizione*). (Some manuscripts, too, appear to have been written page by page on a large sheet, and this technique was used in the fifteenth century for their mass production.)[29] The compositor arranged the pages so that they would follow in the correct sequence once the paper was folded and cut. He fixed them in a rectangular wooden or iron frame called a chase (*telaio*), locking them firmly with screws or wedges. Each set of pages thus imposed for printing on one side of a sheet of paper is called a forme (*forma*, to be distinguished from its other sense of 'mould'). Of the two formes required to print a sheet on both sides, that containing the first and last pages of the sequence of pages was the 'outer' forme, the other the 'inner' forme (for an example, see fig. 3). If it was felt that page divisions could be predicted, for instance in the case of poetry, the compositor might set the text 'by formes' (*per forme*), in other words setting all the pages of one side of the sheet rather than in their natural text sequence. This meant that the types could be reused without waiting for the second forme to be composed, and that more than one compositor could work simultaneously on the same forme. Setting by formes can be detected when faulty type was reused or when the 'casting off', or calculation of the number of pages, was inaccurate and consequently the second forme to be composed had pages of an irregular length in order to fit in with what had already been set. Another means of reducing (approximately by half) the quantity of type required was half-sheet imposition (*imposizione a mezzo foglio*) or

Format	Leaves per sheet	pages per sheet
2°	2	4
4°	4	8
8°	8	16
12° and long 12°	12	24

'work and turn'. In this method the number of *consecutive* pages of the text which would fill one side of a sheet (e.g. four pages in quarto format) was imposed in one forme, instead of being divided equally between outer and inner formes together with the other pages destined to fill the sheet. This forme was printed on one side of a sheet and then, after the heap of paper had been turned over, on the other side; finally, each sheet was cut in half to give two identical sets of half sheets.

Once printed on both sides, each sheet was eventually folded to form a gathering or quire (*fascicolo*). The different arrangements of pages on the sheet of paper, and the corresponding foldings of the printed sheet, give rise to different book formats (*formato*). The choice of format, we shall see in chapter 6, depended to some extent on the genre and the readership of the book. Page size depended partly on the size of the sheet and partly on how the sheet was folded. The most common formats were, in decreasing order of size: folio (abbreviated as 2°, Italian *in folio*), in which sheets were folded once along the shorter dimension of the rectangle; quarto (4°, *in quarto*), in which a second fold was made along the longer dimension; octavo (8°, *in ottavo*), in which a third fold was made along the shorter dimension; duodecimo or twelves (12°, *in dodicesimo*), in which the sheet was folded twice along the shorter dimension and three times along the longer; and long duodecimo or long twelves (long 12°), in which it was folded once along the longer dimension and five times along the shorter. (See fig. 3 for the example of quarto format.) The consequent numbers of leaves or folios (Italian *carta* or *foglietto*) and of pages (one side of a leaf, Italian *pagina*) per sheet are as shown in the table. One can also find unfolded broadsheets (1°, Italian *foglio atlantico*) and smaller formats such as sixteens (16°), twenty-fours (24°), thirty-twos (32°) and so on down to a tiny 128°. If folded more than once, the sheet had to be cut along the folds at the edges of the pages in order to be legible.

Printed sheets in folio format would normally be folded one inside the other to form a gathering of up to six sheets; it was then easier to sew together the sheets when the book was bound. A gathering of five sheets, for instance, would have ten leaves and twenty pages, and the format is termed, after the number of leaves in the gathering, 'folio in 10s'. In quarto format, two sheets were often folded together to give 'quarto in 8s', each gathering having eight leaves and sixteen pages. It follows that identification of format must take account not only of the number of leaves per gathering but also of the dimension of the leaf and, in particular, of features of the paper which can be seen when viewed against the light and which show how the book was imposed: the chain lines (Italian *filone*), which are marks left by the broader brass wires of the paper mould and which run along the shorter dimension of the sheet at intervals of about 30–35 mm, and in some cases a watermark (*filigrana*), a symbol which was originally the trade mark of an individual paper manufacturer, which, when present, normally appears in the centre of one half of the oblong sheet. At some point, perhaps in the second half of the fifteenth century, a small countermark (*contrassegno*), usually based on the initial or initials of the paper-maker, began to appear in the other half. Chain lines are vertical in the leaves of books printed in 2°, 8° and long 12°, and horizontal in those printed in 4°, 12° and 16° (see fig. 3 for the example of quarto format).[30]

The compositor, we have seen, had to put the made-up pages of type within the forme in the correct sequence, and at a later stage printed sheets would have to be ordered and folded in order to compile a complete copy of the book. Two systems were used in order to assist in one or both of these complicated tasks. (Neither system involved continuous numbering of the leaves or pages, and we shall see in chapter 6 that such numbering was introduced only gradually.) The more important of the two systems used the signature (*segnatura*), an identification mark inserted by the compositor normally at the bottom right-hand corner of the recto of a leaf (the right-hand page when the book is open for reading). In Italian books, almost without exception, only the leaves of the first half of each gathering were signed; since the leaves of the second half of each gathering were joined to those of the first, it was felt that they did not need signatures. The use of signatures increased steeply in the 1470s, and probably about nine out of ten printed books had them by the 1490s.[31] Most signatures consisted of two elements: the first was a sign such as one of the twenty-three letters of the Latin alphabet (no J, U or W), running from A to Z or a to z, then if necessary further sequences such as AA–ZZ, AAA–ZZZ; the second was the lower-case roman or arabic number of the leaf within the gathering, though this second element might be omitted for the first leaf. Thus the first five leaves of the second gathering of a folio in 10s might be signed B or Bi, Bii or Bij, Biii or Biij, Biiii or Biiij (Biv was less likely), and Bv (or B1, B2 etc.; for other examples, see figs. 2, 3, 5, 6, 10 and 13). Preliminary items such as dedications, letters to the reader and indexes were normally printed last, and the gatherings in which they were contained were often signed with non-alphabetical symbols such as an asterisk or a Maltese cross. The other device used more sporadically to identify the order of components was the catchword (*richiamo*), an indication of the first word of a page set at the foot of the preceding page (see fig. 2). In Italy catchwords might be used to indicate only the order of gatherings, in which case they are found on the verso (left-hand page when the book is open) of the last leaf of each gathering, or also to indicate the order of pages when imposing, in which case they are found on every page; occasionally they are found on the verso of every leaf.[32]

At the end of the book there would then often be a register (*registro*) or statement of the order of the components of the volume.[33] The first registers appeared in Italy about 1470 and contained lists of the first word of each leaf in the first half of each gathering. Then registers began to list simply the signatures identifying each gathering; this saved a considerable amount of space. The first such register occurs in an edition printed in Venice in 1483. Registers sometimes indicated the number of pairs of leaves joined at the back in each gathering: *duerni* had two such 'conjugate pairs', *terni* had three, *quaderni* had four, *quinterni* had five, *sesterni* had six (see fig. 11). The *Orlando furioso* of 1532, for example, a quarto in 8s, has a register which runs from A to Z, then from a to h, followed by the statement that all these gatherings have four pairs of leaves: 'Tutti questi sono quaderni.'

The work of a compositor naturally needed to be checked. Correction was presumably not left to him alone, especially if he was being paid as a piece-worker rather than by the hour and was therefore in a hurry to get his job finished. Another person often involved would be the master printer or foreman (*proto*). If the text required special attention, for instance if it was a scholarly work, then an appropriately qualified person might come into the printing house to carry out corrections in return for some remuneration. Thus for example a Milanese contract of 1499 for the printing of a Greek work stipulated that a corrector was to be paid at 5 ducats a month.[34] A priest called Marsilio tells us in his dedication to Petrarch's *Trionfi* (Venice, 1513) that he came into the workshop of Bernardino Stagnino to correct books on the day of printing, and Antonio Blado refers to proof correction being carried out by 'his priest' and himself in 1539.[35] The Dutchman Arnoldo Arlenio was recruited by Iacopo Giunti in the 1560s to come in twice daily to correct Greek texts at the rate of 20 soldi a sheet.[36] Paolo Manuzio, who never had more than two *correttori*, distinguished them as two sorts: the theologians who were to edit religious texts and others who needed to be of only moderate learning but of great vigilance.[37] Proofs might also be sent out to be checked: the Florentine contract of 1484 concerning Ficino's translation of the works of Plato specified that the printers were to send the sheets ('facce') at least once a day to the house of one of the two men paying for the edition, so that correction could take place at their expense.[38] It was unusual for an author to be involved from day to day in the correction of proofs, unless he was particularly keen and would be available during what could be a long process. Ariosto, for example, seems to have corrected proofs of the 1532 edition of the *Furioso*, and the agreement between Filippo Giunti and Scipione Ammirato for the printing of the latter's *Istorie fiorentine* in 1600 stated that the author would carry out a second correction.[39]

But how was correction carried out? In some documents one finds the phrases 'leggere in piombo' or 'ascoltare in piombo' (literally, to read or listen in lead), and from this it is reasonable to deduce that the first check, which was probably all too often the only one, involved a comparison of the typeset text and the copy-text which was carried out, not by one person making a visual comparison, but with the compositor reading one text aloud while a second person (the master printer or a corrector from outside) verified that it conformed with the other.[40] Reading a reverse image of the text in this way would be another obstacle on the path to accuracy; furthermore, the 'accidentals' of the original – its spelling and use of capitals, punctuation and any diacritic accents – could easily be passed over. Once imposition had taken place, the forme could be taken to the press so that a proof (*bozza*) could be made, using a piece of defective paper in order to save expenditure on a commodity which was relatively precious (see chapter 2, section 1).[41] The proof might even be taken outside the printing house. For example, members of the College of Apostolic Secretaries stipulated in a contract of 1586 that the printer Paolo Blado was to send a proof on paper to be corrected by one of their two deputies; this person would add marginal notes and would then see a second proof in order to correct any errors in these notes. The two deputies were to receive thirty copies of the book, at Blado's expense, as their reward.[42]

However, unlocking a forme in order to alter the setting of type, let alone sending a proof out for correction, would be relatively time-consuming, and financial and technical constraints would have tempted many printing houses to hasten through or even omit the proofreading stage. Neglect of proofreading must have been one of the factors behind the perceived decline in the quality of the output of Venetian presses which led the state to lay down rules in 1603 for a three-stage process of control over compositors' work: what they had set 'in lead' had to be read by the master printer or other qualified person; a sheet was then to be printed and read by a corrector who had been approved by the University of Padua and whose name would appear at the end of the volume; finally a second proof was to be run off in order to check that all corrections had been made.[43] In reality, procedure must often have been very different. A forme would often have had to be printed as soon as possible after composition, probably within twenty-four hours, and then stripped in order to eke out the type. If a sheet had already been printed on one side, the other side had to be printed while the paper was still damp (see below). In mid-sixteenth-century Venice, it was claimed by a well-known editor, Girolamo Ruscelli, that there was normally no check that compositors had corrected errors noted during proofreading, and that the first reading itself was carried out too hastily. The over-worked pressmen might well begin printing the forme before a proof had been fully checked; if errors were spotted, printing would then have to be halted while stop-press corrections were made, and only the sheets printed subsequently would contain the corrected text.[44] Given the high cost of paper, it was often considered too expensive to print extra sheets in place of the incorrect ones. Some editions were even corrected systematically by stamping or by pen. Often a list of errors ('errata') noticed after printing, together with their corrections, would be inserted, usually at the end of the volume.[45] Some of these lists contain second thoughts as well as corrections of printing errors, and must therefore have been compiled by authors or editors. So, while authors were not normally involved in proof correction, it seems to have been common practice for the printer to send sheets to writers after they had been printed off but before the book was finally issued. When Marsilio Ficino's translations from Iamblichus and other Neoplatonic commentators were being printed by Aldo Manuzio in 1497, Ficino asked only to see all the gatherings so that he could compile a list of emendations which would be printed and included in the books before they were sold.[46]

4 PRESSES AND THEIR OPERATION

When a forme was considered ready for printing, it was taken to the press (*torchio*; see figs. 1 and 2). This comprised two sets of moving parts. The impression assembly, contained in a vertical wooden frame up to about two metres high, consisted of a wooden or bronze spindle whose upper part was cut as a screw, a wooden-handled iron bar (*mazza*) attached below the screw in order to turn the spindle, and, below the toe of the spindle, the platen (*piano*), a flat-bottomed block which in sixteenth-century Italian documents is described as being made of *bronzo*, that is bronze or possibly brass. When the bar was pulled, the spindle turned through about ninety degrees and pressed the platen down some 15 mm. The wooden frame was only strong enough to permit the use of a platen a little larger than half the size of a sheet of paper, with the longer dimension of the platen running parallel to the frame of the press. The more important printing houses could have had a bigger press intended for printing the larger sizes of paper.[47] Lying horizontally across the frame, about 75 cm above the ground, was the other set of moving parts, the carriage assembly. The carriage (*carro*) included a shallow wooden box which in English has the macabre name of 'coffin', but is called *forziere* (coffer) in eighteenth-century Italian sources. The forme was laid inside the coffin on what is now known as the press stone, *pietra* (stone) or *marmo* (marble) in Italian, but which was made of bronze, according to sixteenth-century Italian documents. Hinged to one end of the coffin was the tympan (*timpano*), and hinged to the other end of the tympan was the frisket (*fraschetta*). The tympan was a wooden and iron frame covered on its upper side (when open) with parchment, behind which were layers of cloth or paper; the frisket was an iron frame covered with parchment or thick paper in which windows were cut corresponding with the areas to be printed. From about 1472, Roman and then other Italian printing houses adopted a new kind of press with a moving carriage which was slid to and fro under the platen by means of a handle called the rounce (*molinello*) which turned a winch underneath. At first the forme had been of the same size as the platen, covering half a sheet, but the moving carriage meant that the size of forme could be doubled to contain two folio pages, four quarto pages and so on. This speeded up the rate of printing, but it also made the setting of pages in type more complicated, since they were normally imposed in the forme out of their numerical sequence.[48]

The press was operated by two pressmen (*torcoliere*), each with a distinct role. Their repetitive work lasted from early morning until late in the evening. One man acted as inker, beating the type in the forme (as his Italian name, *battitore*, implies) with a pair of ink balls (*mazzo*), which were covered in leather and stuffed with wool, horsehair or dog hairs and had wooden handles. The rocking motion he used could pull types out of the forme, and there was a risk that the pressmen might replace them wrongly or not at all.[49] The other pressman, the puller (*tiratore*), had a more complex and physically taxing job. He reached across the carriage and took a sheet of paper from a heap which had previously been wetted in order to help the absorption of ink, fitted this sheet over the parchment of the tympan, folded the frisket over the paper so that it was held firmly in place, and then folded tympan and frisket together, with the paper sandwiched between them, down and over the forme. With his left hand, the puller turned the rounce anticlockwise so that the first part of the forme slid under the platen, reached across with his right hand to grasp the bar, and pulled it towards himself, pushing with his foot against a footstep beneath the carriage. The platen pressed the paper down against the inked forme; the frame formed by the covering of the frisket which lay beneath the paper protected the margins of the paper from being soiled; and the padding of the tympan above the paper improved the impression of the types on the paper. Once the change, mentioned above, to a press with moving carriage and to a larger size of forme was made, the first pull brought the platen down on only the first half of the forme; now a second pull was needed in order for the platen to cover the rest of the type area. The puller therefore allowed the bar to spring back, turned the rounce again so that the other half of the forme moved under the platen, pulled and released the bar once more, turned the rounce clockwise in order to withdraw the carriage from under the platen, opened tympan and frisket, removed the printed sheet and placed it on a second heap alongside the first. When the pressmen had worked through their heap of white paper, normally containing as many sheets as there were to be copies of the edition, they replaced the first forme with the second, adjusting its position so that its pages would fall exactly on the backs of those of the first forme, and then printed the heap of paper on its other side. This needed to be done while the paper was still damp, for example in the afternoon if the first forme had been printed in the morning, or the next day if the edition was to be a large one. The printed sheets were hung to dry on ropes beneath the ceiling. As soon as a forme had been printed off, it was liable to be dismantled, its types being washed and distributed back into the case for immediate reuse.

In theory each pressman might act as puller in turn, but there seems to have been a tendency to specialize: those working in Florence in 1484 and in Rome in the 1560s were identified as either *battitore* or *tiratore*, and the latter was paid at a higher rate.[50] As for compositors, they were quite well rewarded, with salaries near those of the lower part of the range for teachers, though their work does not seem in general to have been valued more highly than the pressmen's manual labour. A compositor in Padua in 1475 was paid at a monthly rate of 3 ducats plus 1 ducat's worth of books which were doubtless intended for him to resell.[51] In Milan, two compositors were employed in 1477 for 22 lire imperiali, the equivalent of 2.75 Milanese ducats each, but they too received some of their pay in the form of books and only 12 lire in cash.[52] In Florence in the 1480s, compositors could be paid 4 florins a month, pressmen only 1–1.5 florins.[53] But printers working in Parma and Bologna in 1474 were paid at rates similar to those which compositors would expect, from 2.5 ducats per month plus board and lodging up to 5 ducats if there was a shortage of specialized labour.[54] In Rome in the 1560s, by which time the scudo had replaced the papal ducat, Paolo Manuzio even paid his two pressmen rather more than his two compositors, who received 5 scudi a month.[55] Printers took on apprentice compositors in their teens, typically giving them a salary, plus perhaps board and lodging (in which case the salary might be no more than about one-tenth of what a professional earned) over a period of three years.[56]

An edition (*edizione*) is defined by Gaskell as 'all the copies of a book printed at any time (or times) from substantially the same setting of type'.[57] We have seen, however, that the setting of type in a forme might be altered during printing, either unintentionally through the dislodging of type, or intentionally because corrections were requested (by a proof-reader, author or editor) after some sheets had been printed. When such stop-press corrections occurred, they are said to create a further 'state' (*stato*) of the forme in question. Different states may also result from changes resolved upon after the printing of a sheet had been completed.[58] If it were decided to increase the size of the edition, but the type for the sheets already printed had been distributed, it would be necessary to reset the formes. In this process, both deliberate corrections and accidental errors might be introduced. It might also be decided to delete or to insert one or more printed sheets or individual leaves; and deletion might be followed by replacement of the discarded unit with a cancel (Italian uses the Latin *cancellans*, plural *cancellantia*, for a replacement leaf, and *cancellandum*, plural *cancellanda*, for a discarded leaf). The aim of cancels might be to improve the text or to provide alternative material such as a second dedication (see chapter 3, section 1). Within an early printed edition one may also find more than one 'issue' (*emissione*), a subset of copies which are made up mainly but not entirely of sheets deriving from the original setting of type and which are offered for sale as a distinct publishing unit. Separate issues might be put on the market simultaneously, for example if the printing costs had been shared by two publishers and two title pages were printed, each with the name of one publisher. If many copies of the first issue of an edition remained unsold, they were commonly put on the market as reissues at a later date. The trick used here was to substitute a cancel for the opening leaf or leaves, including the current year on the new title page.[59]

Contracts between a financer and a printer sometimes specified that the sheets of each gathering were to be delivered to the financer as soon as they were printed.[60] Otherwise, individual copies of the book were assembled when printing was complete. The sheets, once dry, were laid one on top of the other, with the last at the bottom, then folded in half and baled for storage or for immediate distribution.[61] Books normally arrived at the point of sale unbound, and might then be sold unbound by the retailer: transport costs were thus kept down and binding could be carried out according to the tastes and financial resources of the purchaser. Another process which might take place after printing, in the years when the influence of manuscript production methods was still strong, was the addition by hand of the initial letters, and even the headings, of sections of books: a space was often left by the printer for this purpose, with perhaps a small guide letter to avoid ambiguity (see fig. 5). Such hand-finishing would be carried out by the illuminators, rubricators and flourishers whose functions were mentioned in section 2 above.[62] Like binding, hand-finishing might be commissioned by the customer, but on some occasions it was organized by the printer. Jenson in Venice must have ordered the rubrication and some illustration in the vellum copies of the *Breviarium romanum* printed in 1478, and the journal of the Florentine press which two enterprising friars, Domenico da Pistoia and Piero da Pisa, set up in the convent of the Dominican nuns of San Iacopo di Ripoli in via della Scala (1476–84) records that the press often commissioned, on its own initiative rather than that of a customer, the decoration (probably simple rubrication) of up to fifteen copies of an edition.[63]

5 THE OUTPUT OF PRESSES

The print run or press run (*tiratura*), in other words the number of copies printed, of the earliest Italian books might be as low as 100 or 200. John of Speyer cautiously produced only 100 copies of his first Venetian edition of 1469, Cicero's *Epistulae ad familiares*, and then of Pliny's *Natural History*; and Bartolomeo della Fonte chose the same total when he commissioned an edition of Statius' *Silvae* in 1480 from the Ripoli press. But the early Venetian norm seems to have been about 300–400 copies. John of Speyer's second edition of Cicero's letters, which came out within three months of the first, consisted of 300 copies, and his brother Windelin printed 400 copies of the Latin historian Sallust in 1470. In Rome, Sweynheym and Pannartz said that they printed four works in 300 copies and that the rest of their editions averaged 275 copies, and the editions published by Giovanni Filippo De Lignamine in this period were probably similar in size.[64] Florentine print runs seem to have been of the same order at least until the mid 1480s. The figure could occasionally rise to over 1,000, as when Cristoforo Landino had 1,200 copies printed of his 1481 edition of Dante's *Commedia.*[65] In Venice, print runs began to rise from the mid 1470s, helped no doubt by the doubling in the size of the forme which took place around this time. We have figures of 930 copies for a Latin Bible of 1478, 1,300 and 2,300 for legal texts of 1490–1, and probably as many as 3,000 for an edition of three Latin poets brought out by Aldo Manuzio in 1502.[66] But, having reached four figures, print runs remained on a plateau in the following century. In Venice and Florence, the norm was about 1,000 copies, rising to 2,000 or even 3,000, in Venice at least, if publishers were confident of sales.[67] The Milanese bookseller Niccolò Gorgonzola commissioned 550 and 650 copies of religious texts in the early 1500s, but these were intended for a chiefly local market, and the inventory of his warehouse in 1537 suggests that he normally ordered 1,000 copies from printers.[68] Boiardo's epic poem, *Orlando innamorato*, was printed in 1,250 copies in 1495. As we shall see in chapter 4, the 1516 edition of Ariosto's sequel, *Orlando furioso*, was probably of similar size, but the popularity of the poem seems to have led Ariosto to double the run for the 1532 edition.

While we have a fair amount of evidence about the output of printing houses in terms of the size of editions, it is not so easy to gauge how quickly printing was carried out. One must distinguish here between two ways of measuring output: the rate at which a book could go through a printing house, and the rate at which one fully served press could operate.

The rate of progress on a text appears to have been quite slow in the early printing houses. The compositors working for Sweynheym and Pannartz at Subiaco in 1467 completed only about two folio pages, or one side of a sheet, per day, and even this rhythm was not kept up consistently, perhaps because some of the work was allocated to monks, who would have had other calls on their time.[69] In the sixteenth century, however, the average rate was probably one sheet per day. This was the rhythm specified in a Florentine contract of 1505 concerning a book of sermons by Girolamo Savonarola: the printers Antonio Tubini and Andrea Ghirlandi were to print and deliver on each working day the agreed number (1,100 copies) of at least one whole printed sheet ('almanco uno foglio intero, cioè fogli millecento').[70] This pace was being followed when the priest Marsilio was preparing his edition of Petrarch for Stagnino in 1513 and had to deliver to the printers a *quaderno* of text, four pairs of quarto leaves (or two sheets), every two days. The same applied when a work by Ruscelli was being printed in 1559.[71] One sheet per day was also the rate specified in a contract made by the Blado company in Rome in 1583.[72] However, the rate might be slower or faster. Although the second (1521) edition of Ariosto's *Orlando furioso* was printed at this rate, the first and third editions (1516 and 1532) took longer (and, perhaps as a consequence, contain fewer errors).[73] The first edition of Equicola's *De natura de amore*, a quarto in 8s, was printed in 1525 at the rate of two sheets daily, since the printer was asked to provide a gathering to be proofread every evening before printing the next day.[74] Filippo Giunti's agreement with Ammirato, mentioned in section 3 above, envisaged a possible minimum daily production of one forme, that is one side of one sheet, whereas the first edition of Vasari's *Vite* (1550) was at one point advancing at three formes per day.[75]

It seems that, in order to keep up with this pace, two compositors would often have had to work on a text simultaneously. The work rate expected of a compositor in Padua and Milan in the 1470s was only two folio pages a day, and one can calculate that compositors in Florence in 1484 completed only about three octavo pages in a working day, or a forme every 2.67 days.[76] True, there must have been occasions when one compositor sufficed for one press: for example, if the number of copies to be printed was high, or if the typeface was large. The editor of a work printed by Vitus Puecher in Rome in 1475 talks of its being produced by three men, though one cannot be sure that he meant one compositor and two pressmen.[77] Contemporary depictions of printing houses show sometimes one compositor (the *Grant danse macabre* of 1499 and Scriverius' etching of 1628), sometimes two (see fig. 2).[78] But it must have been common for two compositors to work simultaneously on a text, setting separate formes or sharing their work more closely. Moreover, the printing of different sheets of a book might in the larger printing houses be shared out between more than one press, each with its compositor or compositors. The inventories of the property of Pierre Maufer (1478), Paolo Blado (1594) and the Tipografia Vaticana (1595) included respectively five, four and six presses, and one can see that it required very good organizational skills to co-ordinate the regular supply of paper and the work of composition, correction and printing when running an operation of this size.[79] Printers might well have had more than one book in hand at a time, so work on one text was not necessarily continuous. All these practices naturally increased the risk of inconsistency in the transfer of a text into print.

The question of the rate of output of one press is complicated by the transition made from the fixed, one-pull press to the press with mobile carriage; this speeded up output, since the sheet of paper laid on the press could now be printed on the whole of one side, albeit with two pulls of the press. We know that this change had become general in Italy by the 1480s, but until then one cannot always be sure which type of press was in operation. Another element of uncertainty stems from the fact that, even if we have evidence about the output of a printing house, we do not always know how many presses were operating in it. Furthermore, before 1480 it seems likely that houses with more than one press could have had one-pull and two-pull presses operating side by side.[80] A chronicle printed in 1474 says the first Germans working in Rome turned out 300 *cartae* daily.[81] This probably means 300 copies of a sheet printed on both sides, and this was the average rate achieved by Puecher in the edition of 1475 mentioned above (each copy consists of 183 sheets, and its editor says that 300 copies were produced in three months). But was this output achieved on just one press? A Ferrarese contract of 1473 envisages printing taking place at a minimum of only about 150 sheets daily.[82] However, it seems that one press crew could process 300 sheets daily: in Padua in 1477 a commentary on Avicenna was printed at the rate of 600 copies of two sheets per day, probably using four presses for the 2,400 impressions (printings of one side of a sheet) required, and Michael Pollak has estimated that a daily rate of 250–300 sheets per press was indeed achievable.[83] Yet a century later this would have seemed snail-paced. There was constant pressure to step up the speed of work: the number of copies in each edition was rising, and although pressmen could be paid by the month, the workshop could be paid according to its output of printed paper.[84] By the second half of the Cinquecento, pressmen had been expected to increase their output by about four- or fivefold with the same equipment. Those in France turned out between 1,250 and 1,675 sheets daily; that is, from 2,500 to 3,350 impressions, at an average rate of about one impression, each requiring two pulls of the bar, every fifteen seconds in a twelve-hour day. Paola Blado undertook in a contract of 1583 to print 1,125 sheets per day, and in 1593 a pressman in Rome testified that it was normal to print 1,500 sheets of Latin texts on each side in a day.[85]

The speed of production which made printing so welcome to Alberti in the mid 1460s had thus become even greater by the end of the sixteenth century, partly because of the introduction of the two-pull press, partly because, with experience, print workers achieved admirably high levels of skill. The transformation which Gutenberg's ingenious combination of devices had brought about in book production had been made even more remarkable by the craftsmen and workers who followed him. At the same time, it must be remembered that printing in this period, as well as a rapid operation, could also be a hasty one, involving as it did a relentless cycle of often complex activities which did not always enjoy full quality control. Once the required number of pages had been composed and the pages had then been imposed into the forme, there was too little time to check proofs carefully. The pressmen had to print off the forme as quickly as possible so that its types could be reused; they also had to complete printing of both formes while the sheets of paper were still damp. Compositors in their turn had to work as quickly as possible so that the press did not stand idle. For all the excitement that the new medium rightly caused on its arrival in Italy, proneness to inaccuracy in the printing procedure was one of the factors which could undermine confidence in it, especially, as we shall see in chapter 4, among writers.

CHAPTER 2

Publishing, bookselling and the control of books

1 PUBLISHING

Those who worked in or for the printing house were not the only ones on whom the creation of a book depended; indeed, in most cases they could not even have begun their tasks without the help of others. The most obvious and essential kind of support needed was financial. As Giovanni Andrea Bussi, bishop of Aleria and editor of twenty-four of the books printed by Sweynheym and Pannartz in Rome, put it bluntly in a dedication to Pope Sixtus IV in 1471: 'the expense needed to carry out the art of printing is very great'.[1] There is a wealth of documentary evidence to bear out this claim. For example, two legal texts printed in Modena in 1475 and 1476 in about 500 copies, consisting of 95 and 74 sheets respectively, cost 404 and 614 lire, equivalent to about 100 and 150 ducats; a Bible printed in Venice in 1478 (228 sheets, 930 copies) would have cost about 450–500 ducats for paper and labour; a Latin translation of the works of Plato printed in Florence in 1483 (281 sheets, 1,025 copies) would have required about 250 florins for paper and labour; and a breviary of nearly 50 sheets printed in the same city in the following year in 300 copies required an investment of 284 florins. (To provide ourselves with a yardstick here, we can remember that a compositor might hope to earn 50 or 60 ducats in a year.) A Venetian printer, requesting state protection for sales of his edition of the Bible in 1492, claimed that the project would cost over 4,000 ducats; even if he had been quadrupling the real cost in order to gain sympathy, his investment was still huge.[2] A century later, costs were still high: a work in five volumes printed in Venice in 1580–1 in 1,125 copies, and containing 565 sheets in each set of volumes, required an outlay of 1,920 ducats.[3] Production costs would certainly have included printing equipment, paper, labour in the printing house, the premises used (the workshop, and a warehouse for storage) and distribution; and they would often have included the purchase of the exemplar to be used by the compositor and fees for an editor or translator.

The press itself represented a fairly small proportion of expenditure. One was sold, together with its accessories, in Florence in 1497 for 5.5 florins, and in Modena in 1539 another press was given a similar value, 38 lire, or under 10 per cent of the total value of the contents of the printing establishment. One could also hire a press for a moderate sum: a Roman contract of 1473 set a fee as low as five copies of each edition produced on three presses. Matrixes and types were more expensive. The Ripoli press in Florence paid 10 florins for matrixes in 1477. Types represented 60 per cent of the value of the Modenese sale in 1539. To hire them was also costly: 140 lb of types were rented for 1 florin a month in Florence in 1497, with a fine of 20 florins if they were not returned.[4] Paper prices varied according to quality and the place of manufacture, but a ream (500 sheets, of which some 50 might be too spoiled for printing) cost about 2.5 lire for the smallest size and 6.4 for the largest.[5] The paper for the Florentine breviary of 1484 cost 40 florins, only about 14 per cent of the total bill; however, in other cases paper costs made up a much higher proportion of the investment and could outstrip labour costs. In the Modenese volume of 1476 mentioned above, 51 per cent of expenditure went on paper, 25 per cent on salaries, the rest on board and lodging for the workers and on minor expenses. A Roman contract of 1526 concerning the printing of 500 copies of a book of songs estimates the total cost at 27 ducats, including 10 ducats for 11 reams of *carta mezzana* and 16 ducats for the wages and living expenses of the printer and his apprentice for two months.[6] Estimates for Venice and Florence put the ratio of paper to labour costs at between 2:3 and 3:2.[7] Compositors, pressmen and correctors had to be paid a fairly respectable wage, as was seen in chapter 1. Editors could also command quite high rates of payment in cash or kind.[8]

The profits from these investments were potentially high, perhaps as much as 50 to 100 per cent even if only 300 or 400 copies were printed: small print runs were profitable as long as fixed costs (such as composition, correction, rent, the press) were low in proportion to those costs that varied according to the number of copies produced (paper, ink, presswork).[9] However, the return on investment was uncertain and slow, and a high proportion of presses went out of business after producing just one or two editions. In the first years of printing, the market quickly became saturated with copies of works by classical authors and Church Fathers; in Rome, an appeal for help on behalf of

Sweynheym and Pannartz had to be made to Pope Sixtus IV in 1472 because their house was 'full of quires, empty of necessities', and in 1473 there was a 65 per cent drop in the output of Venetian presses.[10] There could be a considerable delay before copies were sold and the income from sales was recovered. This point was made by a Venetian publisher in a petition for copyright protection in 1496: the works in question would be expensive to print, he said, 'and furthermore, once printed, they cannot be sold off so quickly'.[11] A request from the Florentine firm of Filippo and Iacopo Giunti in 1563 talked of unsold books frequently ending up 'standing guard over the warehouses and after a while being used to wrap groceries'.[12] After Girolamo Strozzi had made the venture into publishing which will be mentioned below, he had to instruct his agent in 1477 to drive the booksellers with spurs ('sollecitarli cholli sproni') and get the cash out of their hands.[13] Unpredictable hazards might be lying in wait, including 'pirated' or unauthorized copies of an edition made by other printers, real piracy and other mishaps as books were being transported, fire in the warehouse, warfare, or outbreaks of plague such as those which hit the Venetian state in 1478 and 1576 or Milan in 1524.

Given, then, that printing was an expensive and uncertain business, who was prepared to give it the initial financial support and protection which it needed? To a limited extent, such help might come from the state: either indirectly, by granting the 'privileges', to be discussed in section 3 below, which gave publishers, authors and so on protection against competition, or directly, by giving commissions to print on behalf of the state or of the Church. However, both courts and republics were slow to offer direct support. The senate of Lucca invited Clement of Padua to come to print in the city in 1472 (see chapter 1, section 2), offering him a small subsidy of 3 florins a month (an improvement on the 2 florins he received for other work in 1470), and we shall see later in this chapter that both Venice and Milan offered exclusive printing rights to individuals in 1469–70. But these offers were not repeated. When in November 1470 Clemente Donati, an early financer of printing who was based in Rome, asked the Ferrarese state for a loan to enable him to operate eight presses there for three years, he received the brusque reply that, if printing was as lucrative as he claimed, he should find private sources of capital, namely partners and merchants ('socios et mercatores').[14] The Church, in contrast, was quick to perceive value in using the press both as a means of diffusing official documents and as a weapon of propaganda, just as it took early action against the dangers which the press might represent in diffusing heresy or immorality (see section 3 below). Pope Sixtus IV rewarded Jenson for services to the Church by making him a count palatine in 1475.[15] In Rome, Antonio Blado and Francesco Calvo were designated printers of the Apostolic Camera, which administered papal properties and revenues, and among Roman presses instituted by the Church in the second half of the Cinquecento were the Tipografia del Collegio Romano, the Stamperia del Popolo Romano, the Tipografia Apostolica Vaticana and the Stamperia Camerale. For similar reasons, Florence had a ducal printer from 1547 to 1563, and Turin and Bologna had equivalent appointments from the 1570s and 80s.[16]

Much more important as a source of support were the private 'partners and merchants' in whose direction Donati was pointed by council members in Ferrara in 1470. The Ferrarese would probably have known by hearsay, and Donati would certainly have known by direct experience, that from the earliest years finance for printing in Italy had come from citizens who had acquired their wealth from a variety of sources. In the first place, authors, editors and educated professionals – physicians, notaries, teachers and so on – might all have wanted to see certain texts published and have had sufficient cash to realize their wish. Alliances between such men and printers were of the greatest importance in overcoming any prejudice against the press and in establishing the medium of print as one from which the world of learning could derive both intellectual and material benefits. Secondly, the promotion of printing could be seen as a lucrative strand to be added to existing commercial operations. Those who took this opportunity might already have interests directly related to books. Owners of bookshops were important sources of commissions for printing throughout the Renaissance. Examples from Venice include Francesco de Madiis in the 1480s, the Florentine Luc'Antonio Giunti the elder, whose partnership with his brother Filippo was worth the huge sum of nearly 20,000 florins in 1510, the Brescian Nicolò Garanta from 1525 to 1530, and Giovanni Battista Pederzano from 1522 to 1554.[17] Stationers (*cartolai*) in Florence formed partnerships with the Ripoli press.[18] It was similarly natural for paper manufacturers (*cartai*) to have an interest in publishing, and early examples of those involved are Giovanni da Legnano, who financed printing in Milan and Pavia as well as selling books, Federico Corner, who promoted printing in Padua, Giovanni da Verona, who signed the first surviving printed book from Verona, and Michele Manzolo, who printed in Treviso.[19] When Donati made his Ferrarese application in 1470, printing had recently been established in Venice, doubtless with the favour of a group of patricians, while in nearby Bologna a contract for printing had been signed in October 1470 by a banker as well as two university professors.[20] In Rome, the earliest known contract for printing, signed at some time before the autumn of 1466, provided for the financing of German technical know-how by a consortium of investors including Donati himself and the merchant Simone Cardella of Lucca, who was to go on to lend his support to the printer Ulrich Han in 1471–4. Sweynheym and Pannartz had set up their Roman press in 1467 in the *palazzo* of the noble Massimo family, and in August 1470 there had appeared the first of the editions underwritten by the Sicilian gentleman Giovanni Filippo De Lignamine.[21] The motivation for the support of these men would often have been solely speculative; but on occasion they will have wished also to promote their own works, or to obtain a stock of books which could be distributed as gifts, or to promote a cause which might have been philanthropic or, as has been suggested in the case of early printing in Venice, part of a political programme.[22] In the context of the Renaissance, any such investor in printing can be termed a publisher (*editore* in Italian). Some publishers who were giving their support to authors could be described as patron-publishers, as we shall see in chapter 3. Even the most successful commercial publishers traded simultaneously in other commodities: Luc'Antonio Giunti the younger, for instance, shipped barrels of herrings out of Yarmouth just as he shipped his books around the Mediterranean.[23]

The backing of a publisher might be signalled at the start or end of a book by the presence of his name preceded by a phrase such as *ad instantia di* (at the request of) or, in Latin, *impensis, sumptu* or *sumptibus* (at the expense (of): see fig. 11). The Italian and Latin prepositions *per* and Latin *apud* are ambiguous: they normally precede the name of the person by whom a book was printed, but may occasionally refer to the publisher for whom it was printed.[24] However, publishing was often carried out anonymously as far as the general public was concerned, just as printing might be.[25] One reason for this may have been that the association formed in order to print a book was ephemeral, ad hoc, and may even have been unstable enough to change during the course of printing.[26] We can, though, get at least a partial picture of the alliances formed between printers and their financers, particularly in the fifteenth century, from archival evidence such as contracts, legal disputes, privilege requests and wills. Such contracts as survive can be divided into two broad categories. In the first, one or more editions were produced on commission, with printers working to the instructions of others and receiving only whatever payment had been agreed in advance. In the second, printers contributed to the cost of production, sharing in profits in proportion to their investment. The two powerful syndicates which dominated Venetian printing in the 1470s belonged respectively to the first and second type: on the one hand, the combination of two Germans, John of Cologne and John Manthen, neither of whom probably had technical skill in printing but who took over and managed the press of Windelin of Speyer in the crisis of 1473 when there was, as we saw, a sudden slump in the industry; on the other hand, the joint venture into which the French printer Nicholas Jenson entered, probably in late 1473, with Johann Rauchfas and Peter Ugleheimer and in which Jenson appears to have had a status comparable with that of the two Germans. When the two companies merged in 1480 to form a supersyndicate of five years' duration, Jenson again seems to have had a major share in the partnership, of which the working capital has been estimated at between 7,000 and 10,000 ducats.[27]

Early Venetian printing provides other examples of the type of association in which the printer worked at the behest of another man. Jenson himself was commissioned in 1476 by two Florentines, the brothers Girolamo and Marco Strozzi, to print a new vernacular translation (also commissioned by them) of Pliny's *Natural History*. The same two entrepreneurs employed another Frenchman working in Venice, Jacques le Rouge, to print translations of the Florentine Histories of Leonardo Bruni and Poggio Bracciolini.[28] At other times Le Rouge worked with Jenson in an association in which the latter was probably more patron than partner.[29] A Venetian contract of 1478 made it clear that the printer was servant of the publisher: the German Leonard Wild was employed by Nicholas of Frankfurt to print a Bible at the rate of 5 ducats per quire, payable on delivery of each quire, plus twenty free copies, and in Padua in the same period the Frenchman Maufer was to deliver his printed output quire by quire to the gentleman employing him, Bartolomeo Valdezocco.[30] In Milan, similarly, the priest Giuliano Merli employed in 1471 the brothers Antonio and Fortuna Zarotto and another priest, Gabriele Orsoni (who was probably acting as corrector), to print 300 copies of Cicero's *Epistulae ad familiares* on a press owned by the physician Panfilo Castaldi, at the rate of 25 soldi per copy, with Merli providing paper, paying up to 30 ducats for expenses and keeping all proceeds from sales.[31] Cristoforo Valdarfer worked under similar terms for Filippo Lavagna in the same city in 1473 and 1477.[32] The account book of the Ripoli press in Florence shows that 42 of the 101 editions which it brought out between 1476 and 1484 were produced for individuals or syndicates. The importance of these one-off publishing commissions varies from Ficino's Latin translation of the works of Plato (1484–5), which two gentlemen subsidized with 90 florins, to, at the other end of the market, an *Operetta di Erode* (Little work about Herod) ordered in 1481 by someone identified as 'il Pigro ciermatore' (Lazybones the charlatan), who paid the final amount outstanding on his bill with a bedsheet.[33] In the contract of 1505 which the notary Lorenzo Violi made with the company of Tubini and Ghirlandi, Violi agreed to provide the paper and to pay the printers the sum of 2.25 lire per printed ream in weekly instalments; but the printers were liable for a fine if they made any copies beyond the 1,100 to be delivered to Violi.[34]

A printer could also be bound to work for others over a period of several years. In 1508, for example, the physician Ludovico Bonaccioli drew up a contract in Ferrara which obliged the humanist Ludovico da Ponte (Pontico Virunio) and his brother-in-law Andrea de' Baldi to carry out printing for him for six years: Ludovico was to control the choice of texts, characters and format, while the others were to do 'whatever I see fit' ('quanto parerà a me').[35] An unusual contract from Messina in 1520 engaged two booksellers to pay 20 ducats to Pietro Spira, another bookseller who was also a printer, so that Spira could purchase two sets of characters in Naples; Spira was to repay his debt by printing for the two booksellers over the next four years.[36]

The second broad category of contracts covers a range of agreements in which a printer contributed to the capital costs, and therefore had some say in what was published and how it was presented. As we shall see in more detail in chapter 3, section 2, when we look at contracts between printers and writers, this category can be subdivided into those in which the printer paid a proportion of costs, typically half, and those in which the printer paid all costs, sometimes even paying the author for his manuscript as well. Several contracts from the fifteenth century show printers sharing costs with others. A tripartite contract signed in Trevi in 1470 stipulated that a German printer was to receive 50 per cent of the profits of the partnership's first book, that the two Italians involved, a notary and a lawyer, were each to receive 25 per cent, and that on future occasions each partner would receive one-third of the profits.[37] In the 1470 contract from Bologna mentioned above, which was to run for two years, the banker Baldassarre Azzoguidi was to provide premises and to pay for paper, ink and compositors, the humanist Francesco Dal Pozzo (Puteolano) was to provide corrected exemplars and to promote sales of the literary and legal works concerned, while Annibale Malpigli was in charge of printing on three presses; Dal Pozzo was to receive one-third of the books or one-third of the profits from sales.[38] This pattern of dividing costs, responsibilities and profits was reproduced with variants in examples from Perugia, 1471 (Braccio de' Baglioni, three other investors and two German craftsmen form a partnership to print books which lasted nearly two and a half years); Milan, 1472 (in May, the printer Antonio Zarotto and the two partners in his press, an editor-corrector and a compositor, contract to work four presses for three years in partnership with the humanist Gabriele Paveri Fontana and two noblemen; in September, Filippo Lavagna undertakes an edition of 400 copies of a medical work in conjunction with two physicians); and Modena, 1475 (Johann Vurster forms an equal partnership with the *cartolaio* and notary Cecchino Morano which ends unhappily with the German being imprisoned for debt).[39] Two other 'town and gown' contracts drawn up in 1499 linked a leading scholar with a printer for the production of a single work. In one case, Demetrius Chalcondylas joined with two other investors (former pupils of his) and two printers in Milan with the intention of printing and selling 800 copies of the Greek dictionary called *Suda*; in the other, Filippo Beroaldo signed a contract with Benedetto di Ettore Faelli in Bologna for the printing of 1,200 copies of *The Golden Ass* by Apuleius with Beroaldo's own lively and lengthy commentary. Both scholars had edited the texts concerned and were partly responsible for selling the volumes; Beroaldo was to give extra publicity to his edition by lecturing on the text at the local university.[40]

Also important were the longer-term alliances between financers and scholars or writers who brought out books under their own imprint. In the mid sixteenth century, there are the cases of Antonio Brucioli, a Florentine exile in Venice, who set up a press 'al segno della Speranza' (at the Sign of Hope) in partnership with his brothers and Giovanni Centani in 1540, and Francesco Sansovino, whose company 'all'insegna della Luna crescente' (at the Sign of the Crescent Moon) began operations in 1560 with partners such as Nicola Tinto.[41] But the best-known example, and a most influential one in its contribution to the winning of respectability for printing, was the Venetian company established in 1495 between Pierfrancesco Barbarigo, son and nephew of successive doges; the printer, publisher and bookseller Andrea Torresani; and the scholar and teacher Aldo Manuzio. Capital and profits were divided equally between Barbarigo, as one party, and Torresani and Manuzio, as the other, with Manuzio probably holding one-fifth of this half share. Aldo seems to have had a considerable degree of independence both in editorial and typographical matters and in the day-to-day running of the company: in 1499, for instance, he spent the large sum of 42.25 ducats on paper and was later reimbursed for his expenses. He undertook some printing on commission (such as the *Hypnerotomachia Poliphili* of 1499: see chapter 3, section 2) and some as a joint venture with others (such as the *Epistole* of Saint Catherine of Siena in 1500). But to some extent he would have depended on his partners to provide his running costs, and in the end would have had to tailor accordingly his decisions on what to print.[42]

Another means by which a printer could obtain help in providing capital costs, and at the same time share the risks of publication, was to form a co-operative consortium with one or more other printers and publishers. Thus in Venice in 1507 Battista and Silvestro Torti, Giorgio Arrivabene, Luc'Antonio Giunti, Amadeo Scotti and Antonio Moreto agreed on a five-year plan according to which Giunti and Scotti were to provide financial backing and the Torti brothers and Arrivabene were responsible for the supply of paper, which was to be of the largest sizes (royal or imperial), and for printing on at least two presses each. The company also drew up a list of legal works to be published and stipulated that no member could print these works on large paper for himself, thus ensuring that they would not be competing against each other while undertaking this expensive venture (the paper would cost 4 lire a ream). All the volumes were to appear under the name of Battista Torti, a very prestigious one in the context of legal printing.[43]

This example bears out what was said earlier in this chapter about the difficulty of identifying, from the sole evidence of a book, all the parties responsible for it. Nor, as one can see from the dual roles which were to be played by the Torti brothers and Arrivabene, is it always possible to draw a sharp distinction between those who helped to finance printing and those who executed it; indeed, the Renaissance book industry in general is characterized by fluidity and a lack of rigid specialization, so that the same person could be both a bookseller and a printer, a printer might work on commission for publishers but might also finance some of his own editions, and someone such as Benedetto Faelli of Bologna could be a bookseller, a printer and a publisher. However, the activities of printing and publishing must be clearly distinguished, even if one person could combine both roles. Bearing this in mind, one can suggest that those directly or indirectly involved in book production can be classified into three broad categories:[44]

1. The publishers (*editori*) who supported printing financially but did not own or operate presses. Examples include some men whom we have already encountered, such as Giovanni da Legnano and Niccolò Gorgonzola in Milan and Luc'Antonio Giunti the elder in Venice, or others from sixteenth-century Venice such as the Sessa family, Giovanni Battista Pederzano, Stefano Alessi and Pietro da Fino. Their operations could range from the small-scale and occasional, as in the case of Pietro da Fino, to those which involved a continual investment of large sums, as in the case of Giunti. Very often these men were also involved in selling books and can therefore be termed bookseller-publishers (*librai-editori*); examples are Giunti, Gorgonzola, Pederzano, Alessi and Pietro da Fino. Further subcategories are made up of two kinds of non-professional publishers: the civic and ecclesiastical authorities which could commission printing from time to time, and the authors, editors and performers who contributed to printing costs.

2. The printers who owned a press and contributed to the financing of most of their own printing activities, and who could thus be termed printer-publishers (*tipografi-editori*) if one takes this to refer to *self*-financing. Antonio Zarotto in Milan comes into this category, while the major examples in Venice are the firms of Nicholas Jenson, Aldo Manuzio and his descendants, and Gabriele Giolito. But here too categorization is complicated by other factors. Such men might be supported by the capital of others, and they might derive some income from bookselling, or from commissioning work from other presses, or from both sources, as in fifteenth-century Venice in the cases of Nicholas of Frankfurt and Andrea Torresani, or in that of Ottaviano Scotti, who gave up printing for publishing and bookselling after 1484.[45]

3. The printers who worked solely or predominantly as craftsmen commissioned by others: 'practical printers', in Scholderer's phrase, or *tipografi puri*, in Veneziani's. Many of the German and French printers working in the early years of the industry come under this heading, but Christopher Valdarfer is an example of one who accumulated enough resources to print on his own account as well as for others.[46] An example from sixteenth-century Rome is probably that of Baldassarre and Girolama Cartolari, a married couple active from 1540 to 1559.[47] Comin da Trino, operating in Venice from 1539 to 1574 and probably the most prolific printer of his day, is estimated (from a sample of about one-third

of his work) to have produced about 76 per cent of his editions as a printer working on commission from publishers, 10 per cent as co-publisher with booksellers, and about 10 per cent as the sole bearer of technical and commercial responsibility. The work of printers such as Comin can be hard to identify, because their books may contain the device of the publisher but be unsigned by the printers themselves.[48]

2 THE BOOK TRADE

As we saw at the start of this chapter, there could be no successful publishing without successful selling. We now need to look at how books were distributed and sold, and at the problems which publishers faced in obtaining a return on their investment.[49]

Bookshops and bookstalls might be run by the publishers and printers themselves and could be found at or near the place in which the books were printed (except in Venice, where the areas given over to shops were too crowded to allow other activities). Thus for instance Ulrich Han applied for permission to set up a bench to sell books in front of his house in Rome, Jenson had a bookshop in the Mercerie in Venice, and Mattia Cancer's books were on sale at his printing house in Naples and in the shops of other booksellers in this city.[50] But books had to be distributed as widely as possible within Italy and often abroad in order to speed up the return on investment. Those published by Lazzaro Soardi and Luc'Antonio Giunti the younger, for example, were available from booksellers throughout the peninsula and overseas, with Soardi giving them a commission of 10 per cent.[51] The same rate was offered by Venetian bookseller-publishers to booksellers in sixteenth-century Brescia.[52] Of the 1,275 copies of a Greek work printed in Rome in 1542, nearly 300 were sent on commission to other booksellers from Lyons to Naples.[53] The largest Venetian publishers would also have their own shops, or agents selling books on commission, in other cities as well as in Venice. We know, for instance, that John of Cologne was operating in Brescia by 1473, that Jenson had a shop in Pavia and agents in France, that the company formed by John of Cologne and Jenson had stocks of books in cities in Tuscany and Umbria, that Gabriele Giolito had shops in Ferrara, Bologna and Naples, and that relatives of Giovanni Varisco ran shops in Rome and Naples. Some Venetian sales networks were wider still: Melchior Sessa the younger had booksellers working on commission as far away as Genoa, Calabria, Sicily and Spain, and Vincenzo Valgrisi declared to the Inquisition that he had outlets in Padua, Bologna, Macerata, Foligno, Recanati, Lanciano, Frankfurt and Lyons.[54] Even booksellers who were publishers would most probably also stock books from other publishers: thus for instance the selection offered by Francesco de Madiis in Venice included titles from Milan, Parma, Reggio Emilia, Florence and Rome, while in Niccolò Gorgonzola's Milanese shop one could buy titles from his fellow-publisher Alessandro Minuziano.[55] Booksellers might occasionally be given exclusive rights to sales in certain areas, for example when the Church wished to regulate the diffusion of liturgical manuals and catechisms.[56]

Booksellers tended to concentrate in certain areas of cities: in Venice, for example, along the Mercerie (between Piazza San Marco and Rialto) and the Frezzeria (to the east of the Piazza), in Florence around the Badia, or in Rome in the Parione district and Piazza Campo dei Fiori. Their shops would have had a display open to the street, as well as the interior shop to which we are accustomed nowadays. A French illustration of 1499 shows a counter giving on the street, with shelves inside.[57] Francesco de Madiis notes, though, that on certain feast days his shops are half shut 'and things are not put outside in the window'.[58] Outside, there would normally be a sign with an emblem specific to the shop; Gorgonzola's, for example, was a star, still visible today.[59] Inside the shops, books would be displayed on shelves and tables.[60] Bound copies may have been laid flat, as in the 1499 woodcut, but in any case most copies were unbound. The larger shops offered the services of a binder working on the premises or would at least organize binding from someone working on their behalf. Ready-bound copies cost nearly twice as much as those which were unbound.[61] As inventories from this period show, the number of books in stock could run to many thousands of copies (see chapter 5, section 2). Inventories can also contain books printed many years before the date on which they were compiled; this suggests that, unless the books had been very slow to sell, second-hand books were on offer alongside the newer ones.[62]

Bookshops were not the only places in which one could buy books. Informal stalls dealt in whatever volumes their owners could lay their hands on, sometimes together with other second-hand goods. Some illegal trading in stolen books went on, as allegedly in the case of 'a big man with a dirty grey overcoat and a black beard' who ran a second-hand bookstall in Campo dei Fiori in 1600.[63] One could buy books from many *cartolai*. All cities and towns would have had pedlars or chapmen selling pamphlets from trays or baskets hanging from their necks. There is a reference of 1539 to works being carried around displayed on the end of a stick.[64] Of the 252 people who registered their names in order to sell printed products in Florence between 1490 and 1600, 7 were printers, 97 were *librai*, 90 were *cartolai* and as many as 58 were itinerant sellers or *ambulanti*.[65] These might include street performers who could augment their income by selling copies of the poems or scenes which they had recited (though in doing so they were also, in the longer term, contributing to the demise of their own performing traditions), or even a figure such as the *cerretano* (charlatan, mountebank) Jacopo Coppa of Modena, who in the 1540s appeared in *piazze* selling soap or patent medicine alongside booklets commissioned by him and containing short works by himself or others such as Aretino and Ariosto.[66] Also very important as outlets for book sales, both retail and wholesale, were the fairs held in Italy – such as the Ascension fair in Venice, the twice-yearly fair of Lanciano, those of Recanati, Foligno and Naples – and abroad, particularly those of Frankfurt and Lyons. The amount of trade generated by fairs encouraged larger publishers and booksellers to set up stores in the towns in which they were held, as we have seen, and other booksellers would engage men as agents to 'go round the fairs' on their behalf.[67]

Selling books was certainly no easier, and in some respects more difficult, than trading in other merchandise. An initial problem was presented by the need for publicity. Publishers produced catalogues which could be given to booksellers, to their agents or to their customers. Of the few catalogues which survive, the earliest are broadsides, sheets printed on one side only, but in the sixteenth century they began to be issued as booklets made up of two or three sheets folded in folio, quarto or octavo format. At the end of the century, the Aldine press made some use of spare pages in its books in order to advertise its titles and prices.[68] Once books were packed into cases or bales, transport was costly and hazardous. There were tolls and duties to pay when moving them from state to state, with books being valued by weight just like any other commodity.[69] Sea transport was about four times cheaper than transport by land, but there was the danger of loss through shipwreck and, even when the cargo was books, through piracy. Whatever means of transport was used, and especially during winter, there was a risk of damage by water. Some of these problems are pointed out in a note written by the printer Benedetto Giunti in September 1550: to send a pack-animal load (*soma*) of books from Rome to Lyons would cost 18 scudi by land and 4 by sea, but 'we are entering a bad period to send books around both by sea and by land, because we are going into winter and they run the risk of getting wet'.[70] Then there were commercial problems. There was no straightforward system of invoicing followed by a transfer of cash. There was a tradition of making payment by barter: Francesco de Madiis was sometimes paid in wine, oil or flour; pedlars left objects such as bedsheets or tablecloths with the Ripoli press as security until they had sold their batch of books; a bookseller's debt to Giovanni Giolito was settled by granting him the use of warehouses for a certain period; and booksellers could arrange an exchange of stock with their counterparts in Italy or in other countries.[71] Distance and the existence of different currencies created further problems. Archival records provide abundant evidence of difficulties arising when people tried to extract payment with bills of exchange or when large debts remained unpaid.[72] Aldo Manuzio complained in 1502 that a merchant, probably Jordan von Dinslaken, was bulk-buying his books, exporting them to Germany and undercutting Aldo's prices there.[73] It was even difficult for a publisher to control the selling of his books within Italy: when Gabriele Giolito sent Giovanni Battista Capello to take over the running of his bookshop in Naples in 1563, he was doubtful whether the previous agent would hand over the company's property there, and he later complained that Capello was no more trustworthy than his predecessor had been.[74] The misadventures of Giolito's Neapolitan branch also illustrate yet another problem faced by booksellers in the second half of the Cinquecento: the risk of punishment or financial loss as a result of stocking books prohibited by the Inquisition, a subject on which more will be said at the end of this chapter. In view of all these obstacles to success, one can sympathize with a Brescian bookseller who drew up a list of money owed to and by him in 1568, noted that most of the debts in his favour dated from eight or ten years previously, and then lamented: 'God knows when they will pay. I wish to point out to your excellencies that the book trade is a slow business, and every few days books get banned, and those that are in use this year, next year are good only to throw to the fish.'[75]

3 THE CONTROL OF PUBLISHING AND BOOKSELLING

From the early years of printing, both individual Italian states and the Church – popes themselves and local representatives such as bishops – exercised a degree of control over what was printed and what was available from booksellers. Such control had two broad aims: first, to encourage commercial and intellectual activity by protecting the interests both of those responsible for the production of books and of the customers who wished to buy them; second, to regulate the contents of books with regard particularly to religious orthodoxy, morality and, to a lesser extent, political opinion.

The main means of achieving the first aim, while at the same time providing a state with an additional means of control over content, was the system of privileges which gave exclusive rights in a process or a product for a certain number of years.[76] Those who petitioned the state for a privilege included anyone who invested money or time or both in books. They might be publishers who were not responsible directly or indirectly for any aspect of the text but who were paying the costs of printing, or they might be connected in various ways with the provision of the text: editors, translators, those who had paid translators, those who had paid for the manuscript to be used as the exemplar, and of course the authors and relatives and descendants of authors, to whom we shall return in chapters 3 and 4.

Both Venice and Milan initially offered to individuals a monopoly over all printing in the cities, in 1469 and 1470 respectively. However, neither privilege came into effect, in the first case because the beneficiary, John of Speyer, died soon afterwards, in the second because Antonio Planella chose for unknown reasons not to make use of his opportunity. As presses multiplied, such monopolies were not normally granted, though in 1533 Genoa did offer to Antonio Bellone exclusive rights for twenty-five years, and the terms of the Florentine privilege of ducal printer, established in 1547, specified that no one else could print in the city without his permission. Some of the Venetian petitions concern typographical innovations in either technique or design: for instance, new systems of printing Greek characters (Aldo Manuzio, 1496, and Gabriele da Brisighella, 1498), systems to print music (Ottaviano Petrucci, 1498 and 1514, and Iacomo Ungaro, 1513), or the italic typeface used for the first time by Aldo Manuzio (1501).[77] But most requests concerned the reproduction and sale of one or more works within the state concerned. Such protection began, it seems, in Milan in 1481, when a six-year privilege was awarded by the duke to Antonio Zarotto for the printing of Simonetta's *Sforziade*. The first Venetian book privilege was granted in 1486, but the main body of applications dates from 1492 on. No book advertised the fact that it benefited from a privilege until in 1488 Bettino da Trezzo decided to versify his privilege and include it in the Milanese edition of his *Letilogia*, an experiment fortunately not repeated by others. The edition of the works of Giovanni Antonio Campano which was edited and published by Michele Ferno in Rome in 1495 advertised a privilege granted by the Duke of Milan, but it appears that no Roman book claimed a privilege for the Papal States until 1498. Publishers in Florence probably had to wait until 1516 before they could claim protection.

A typical application for a privilege began with a preamble explaining the innovation and the reasons for the request, such as the effort and expense devoted by the applicant, his fear of competition and loss, and the public benefit which would result from the product. Then came the request itself. In the case of an application for protection of a title, this would specify that nobody else should be allowed to print it, cause it to be printed, bring it into the state for sale, or cause it to be brought in for sale, for a certain period, under pain of a fine and possibly other penalties, and it would end by indicating who was to receive any money paid as a fine. The period for which privileges were granted might be as short as one year but was generally much longer: the average in Venice and Rome at first was ten years, and it rose towards twenty-five by the end of the sixteenth century, with some privileges being granted for as long as thirty years. The fine for infringement of the copyright might be set at so much per book or, more commonly, a lump sum, which could be as high as 1,000 ducats (as in the case of Ariosto's Venetian privilege for the first edition of the *Orlando furioso*, granted in 1515), or exceptionally even higher (2,000 ducats was fixed in the case of a work written by the theologian Silvestro Mazzolini da Prierio as part of the campaign of the Catholic Church against Luther and printed in Rome in 1520). Fines were usually to be divided between the state and the beneficiary, and perhaps the accuser as well. There could also be a threat of confiscation of the offending volumes and, in privileges granted in Rome, of automatic excommunication on perpetrating the crime ('latae sententiae'). Venetian sanctions occasionally included a short prison sentence or even a long period of exile. In order to underline the risks which offenders ran, the text of privileges was sometimes included in the books concerned, but more often the book would simply display, usually on the title page, a warning phrase such as 'con privilegio' or 'con gratia et privilegio' (see fig. 12). This type of warning might be a bluff: in 1552 Curzio Troiano Navò and Giovita Rapirio were given relatively minor fines, 15 and 10 ducats respectively, for using 'con gratia et privilegio' on a title page without authority to do so.[78]

Naturally, a privilege was valid only within the jurisdiction of the issuing state. If one wanted wider protection, one had to make separate petitions to the authorities concerned. Because Ariosto was extremely anxious to prevent the *Orlando furioso* of 1532 from being printed without his permission, he obtained, and included in the book, privileges from the pope, the emperor, Venice and Milan, and he alluded to others from Ferrara, Mantua, Urbino and other powers. However, at least in the second half of the Cinquecento, Venice protected its own printing industry by awarding few privileges to books which were not produced in that city.[79]

As an example of a privilege application and its acceptance, here is the text of one made by Aldo Manuzio to the Venetian Collegio (the body which prepared the business of the Senate) for the protection of works by Pietro Bembo which he intended to print:[80]

1505, 17 Marzo. Serenissimo principi suoque pio et excellentissimo Consilio. Per che in ogni luogo hoggimai se è introdutta una pessima usanza, che i stampadori molte volte, per schivar faticha et spesa, stampano senza alcuna diligentia et animadversion molte cose, contendandose solamente de far numero de libri per guadagnar, onde le opere escono fuora et se hano incorrette et vitiade cum dano de i studiosi et cum vergogna de i auctori loro; havendo Aldo Romano, stampador in questa cità, tolto a stampar do opere et composition del nobile homo messer Piero Benbo del magnifico messer Bernardo el kavalier, una in latina lengua *De coruptis poetarum locis*, l'altra in materna, el titolo de la quale è le *Asolane questione*, et volendo in esse non sparagnar alcuna faticha o spesa perché le vegnano in man de i homeni non corrotte et non guaste, come infinite volte suol venir; per tanto el prefato Aldo suplica ala Serenissima Signoria vostra che in questa cità et in tute altre terre et luogi sottoposti al dominio suo altro che lui non possa stampar le antedite do opere del prenominato messer Piero Benbo, over parte de quelle, per anni X proximi futuri, sotto pena de ducati 500 e perdida delle opere, et che, se in altri luogi fusseno stampade, non possino esser vendute ne li soprascritti luogi sotto pena de ducati 50 per ogni una de le opere che se vendesse, et perdida de le non vendute, le qual pene siano scosse per li magnifici Avogadori de comun, un terzo de le qual habi l'accusador, l'altro dicti magnifici Avogadori, et el terzo sia dell[a Signoria].

Quod suprascripto supplicanti concedatur prout petit.
Consiliarii: Ser Franciscus Barbadico, Ser Marcus de Molino, Ser Nicolaus Foscareno, Ser Andrea Gritti

(1505, 17 March. To the most serene Doge and his loyal and most excellent Council. Whereas everywhere nowadays there has grown up a very bad custom of printers often, in order to avoid effort and expense, printing many things without any diligence and attention, being content merely to turn out quantities of books in order to make a profit, as a result of which the works come out and are published incorrect and corrupted, to the detriment of scholars and to the shame of their authors; Aldo of Rome, printer in this city, having undertaken to print two works and compositions of the noble gentleman Pietro Bembo, son of the magnificent Bernardo, one in Latin, *De corruptis poetarum locis* [On corruptions in the texts of the poets], the other in the vernacular, entitled the *Asolani*, and wishing not to spare any effort or expense over them so that they may not be published corrupted and blemished, as so often happens; therefore the aforesaid Aldo begs your most serene Lordship that in this city and in all other towns and places under your dominion no one other than him may print the aforesaid two works by the aforementioned Pietro Bembo, or any part of them, for the next ten years, on pain of 500 ducats and loss of the works, and that, if they were printed elsewhere, they may not be sold in the aforementioned places on pain of 50 ducats for each of the works sold, and loss of those unsold, these fines to be collected by the magnificent Avogadori de comun [the public prosecutors], and a third to go to the accuser, a third to the said magnificent Avogadori and a third to the Council.

Granted to the abovementioned petitioner as he requests.
Council members: Francesco Barbadico, Marco Molin, Nicolò Foscarini, Andrea Gritti)

It was natural for petitioners to portray themselves, as did Aldo here, as working in a world of cut-throat competition. A Venetian request by a printer in 1498 spoke of 'the treacherous rage of competition habitual among this wretched profession'. Fears of double-dealing were by no means unfounded. In another request of 1496, a Venetian bookseller complained that some merchant printers were engaged in espionage ruinous to others, wheedling printed sheets out of pressmen while a work was going through the press and then using a large number of presses in order to rush copies onto the market in advance of the original investor. When Niccolò Gorgonzola was accused in 1517 of stealing four gatherings of an edition of Ovid's *Metamorphoses* while it was being printed in Milan by Giovann'Angelo Scinzenzeler, it emerged that another printer, Agostino Vimercate, had lured an apprentice into stealing them in return for a copy of a book.[81] But Giovann'Angelo's father Ulrich and another Milanese printer, Leonard Pachel, had themselves been in the habit of carrying on another underhand practice, that of issuing books with counterfeit imprints of other cities (in their case Venice, Siena and Naples), probably in the hope of attracting purchasers there.[82] Aldo Manuzio had to repeat his petition for protection of his copyright on printing with an italic fount in 1502, complaining of counterfeits produced in Lyons, with his own name on them, and of an edition copied in Brescia with a fictitious Florentine imprint. In Florence itself, the press of Filippo Giunti was producing editions under its own name but which plagiarized Aldo's texts and his characteristic combination of italic typeface and an octavo format, and again Aldo had to take action against such unfair competition, apparently by means of a lawsuit in 1507.[83]

Yet the privilege system was on occasion undoubtedly abused. In the absence of competition, prices could be kept at a high level, and paper and presswork could be of poor quality. The granting of privileges for vast projects would prevent others from venturing into certain areas of publication for long periods, while the original beneficiaries might be unable to achieve what they had claimed, ingenuously or disingenuously, to want to achieve. There was also ambiguity over what constituted an edition sufficiently original to be worthy of protection: it was easy to make some slight changes to a text or to add a small amount of material and then claim that a work was new. In Venice, the printing industry was important enough in terms of commerce and prestige for the state to try to sort out these problems. In 1517, in order to stem an exodus of printers from the city, it was decided that all existing privileges should be revoked and that future privileges would go only to works not previously printed. Further legislation of 1534 and 1537 introduced time limits within which privileges had to be used and controls over prices and paper quality, reiterating that 'new' works were only those previously unpublished in their entirety. There may also have been an unwritten convention that editions needed a minimum print run of 400 in order to obtain a privilege.[84]

The growing power of the printed word meant that what was printed had to be policed.[85] Before the 1540s, ecclesiastical authorities, and to some extent secular ones, made some attempts to control the content of printed works by screening them before publication or by listing works whose sales were prohibited. Papal bulls of 1487, 1501 and 1515 called for prepublication approval by the Church and for the burning of harmful books. In the same period, senior churchmen in Treviso and Venice decreed that books on religious matters should not be printed without permission, and also tried to prevent the printing of illustrations considered obscene and descriptions of 'shamefulnesses both of women and otherwise'. In the case of the illustrations, a compromise seems to have been reached: the printer did not have to throw away what had been printed, but the parts which gave offence were inked over.[86] It was proclaimed in Rome in 1525 that works had to be submitted to the Master of the Sacred Palace, the pope's theologian, before printing, but a political motive seems to have lain behind this, because the decision arose out of the appearance of an anonymous poem 'in which were things to bring the pope and the emperor to blows'.[87] Venice, too, was sensitive to the political damage which could be inflicted by the press. In 1515 the Council of Ten gave access to state papers to two citizens engaged in writing histories, on condition that the Council had the right to veto publication. But it was because the Franciscan order had been offended in print, in a work by Alvise Cinzio de' Fabrizi, that the same Council decided in 1527 that no new works could be printed without a licence issued by itself.[88] The Milanese state was acting specifically against Protestantism when it ordered the surrender of Lutheran books in 1523 and when in 1538 it issued the first Index of Prohibited Books to appear in Italy. The Florentine state established prepublication censorship with laws of 1507 and 1527, and the penalties decreed for transgressors in 1507 were severe: a fine of 25 florins, torture (ten drops on the strappado) and five years' imprisonment.

Sweeping and sometimes threatening as all this early legislation was, little attention seems to have been given to its application. In the 1540s, however, as hopes of reconciliation between Catholics and Protestants receded, the Church in Italy became harsher in its repression of books suspected of spreading heretical doctrine. Such repression was one of the aims of the tribunal known as the Roman Inquisition, established by Pope Paul III in 1542. Italian states made some efforts to reconcile ecclesiastical pressure with their desire for independence and with thc commercial interests of bookmen, but they had to be seen to be working in collaboration with the Church. From 1543 onwards, several states introduced new legislation against unauthorized printing and bookselling and issued their own Indexes of books which were not allowed to be sold or owned. The two methods of censorship adopted before 1540 – prepublication censorship and the listing of banned books – were now used more severely, and to them was added a third method, the inspection of bookshops and of books being imported into a state. The Index of Pope Paul IV, published in 1559, included not only works considered heretical but also those held to be anticlerical or immoral, including all the writings of Aretino and Machiavelli and even (on account of its perceived anticlericalism) the most popular and most imitated work of fourteenth-century vernacular prose, Boccaccio's *Decameron*, unless it were expurgated. However, this Index was not enforced, because Pope Paul died in August. Protestant literature had to be smuggled in and distributed clandestinely, avoiding controls on imports and inspections of bookshops, through the efforts of men such as Pietro Perna, a Lucchese who exported books from Basel from the mid 1540s, and Pietro Longo, who in 1588 became one of the few on whom the Inquisition inflicted the ultimate penalty for heresy, drowning at sea under cover of darkness. Public burnings of prohibited books were organized: on 18 March 1559 there were two burnings in Florence, one before the cathedral and another in Piazza Santa Croce, and on the same day a huge bonfire in Venice destroyed between 10,000 and 12,000 volumes.[89]

From the 1560s, conditions for all those concerned with books became even more difficult. The Index prepared by Pope Pius IV, and approved in 1564 by the Council of Trent (hence called the Tridentine Index), was more moderate than the Pauline Index of 1559 in that it allowed for the publication of certain works in expurgated form, but it gave no guidelines for expurgation and provided for no body which could implement censorship efficiently. In 1562, the Venetian state introduced its own procedures: every new manuscript was to be read before printing by a clergyman and two laymen, each of whom had to testify that it did not contain 'anything against religion, or against princes, or against good customs'. The process of obtaining permission to publish, Grendler estimates, took one to three months, and was costly, since the publisher had to pay each of the three readers a ducat for every 160 manuscript leaves read, and, following a further decision in 1569, had the expense of providing two manuscript copies, one to serve eventually as printer's copy and another, a bound copy, to be kept by the state for purposes of comparison with the printed version.[90] Elsewhere there were similar bureaucratic obstacles to publication. Even an abbot, writing from Naples in 1583, felt obliged to complain that he had paid a printer fifteen months earlier but that his work was still in the hands of the Master of the Sacred Palace, awaiting scrutiny before publication.[91] The link between bookseller and reader was kept under surveillance by the 1562 decision of the Holy Office that within the Papal States, but in principle also in other states, the names of all customers had to be recorded.[92] After the booksellers of Florence had been instructed by the Inquisitor of the city in 1570 to present inventories of their bookshops within a fortnight and not to buy any books from the estates of those who had died recently unless they had permission to do so from the Inquisition, they complained to the Grand Duke's secretary that, because of the fear aroused by the Inquisition, 'no more books are being sold', nobody wanted to run bookshops, and employees could be found only among the riff-raff.[93] Similarly, a Neapolitan bookseller lamented in 1577 that many of his kind were being driven into poverty by the long delays in producing the expurgated editions envisaged by the Tridentine Index, even though the papacy had in 1571 established the Congregation of the Index for the purpose of overseeing expurgation.[94] Measures which had been intended primarily to prevent the spread of Protestantism thus undoubtedly had a wider depressing effect on print culture. As well as hindering those involved in publishing and selling books, they must also have inhibited writers. Even reading could, in some cases, arouse suspicion: the simple fact that a silkworker in Venice read 'all the time' was enough for a priest to denounce him to the Holy Office in 1565.[95]

PART II

Writers and print culture

CHAPTER 3

Publication in print: patronage, contracts and privileges

We can begin our examination of the impact of print on writers (including in this term the authors of original works and the translators, editors, anthologizers or adapters of the works of others) by asking how far it made a difference to their involvement in the process of publication – that is, the issuing of a version of a privately created work for the consumption of the public at large. We will consider first the means by which, before the press established itself in Italy, writers could try to direct the initial diffusion of their works and to benefit from it; then we will assess the extent to which these 'old' methods continued to be used when writers published in print. But the context of print publication was, as we saw in Part I, in many respects different from that of scribal publication, mainly because of the requirement for capital investment; and we will thus need to go on in the second and third sections of this chapter to inquire what arrangements writers would have to make, or consider making, if they wished to take advantage of the new medium.

I WRITERS' USE OF DEDICATIONS AND GIFTS

The concept of authors publishing their work was perfectly familiar to Italians in the manuscript age. The Latin verb *publicare* was adopted into the vernacular at an early stage in order to express this action: Boccaccio used it in the 1350s when he explained that Dante used to send a few canti of the *Commedia* to Cangrande della Scala, lord of Verona, before giving copies to whoever wanted them, but that Dante died 'before he could publish it all'.[1] Petrarch made the same distinction between giving out parts of a work to others and formally issuing the complete work. On sending his *Bucolicum carmen* to Jan, bishop of Olmütz, he wrote that 'no one except you has had [it] in its entirety, although many have seen it'.[2] Publishing was also differentiated from circulating a draft of a work among friends; but if this led to a wider diffusion without the author's consent, he might accept the necessity of publishing an official version of the work, as Petrarch did when he sent a copy of his *Epistole metrice* to their dedicatee, Barbato da Sulmona, so that they could be used as 'norms'.[3] Fifteenth-century humanists could identify as the 'archetype' or 'original' of their work a manuscript prepared by them in order that other copies might be derived from it (see fig. 11).[4]

The author was not, however, the only person involved in the making public of works in manuscript. In the first place, it was likely that someone else would have copied all or most of the work, even if the author had then corrected it. Armando Petrucci has argued that, between the eleventh and fourteenth centuries, some authors had become more closely involved in the material production of their own texts, both at the drafting stage and in the creation of the 'author's book' ('libro d'autore'), the definitive manuscript written out and perhaps later revised by the author, which would in turn become the source of other copies. A prime example of such an author was Petrarch, influenced no doubt by the three generations of notaries from whom he descended.[5] But even Petrarch acknowledged reluctantly that learned men usually had to entrust copying to less enlightened professionals. When he wanted to send his *De vita solitaria* to its dedicatee, Philippe de Cabassoles, he commissioned a copy from a priest whom he fully expected to do a poor job; scribes, in his view, were ignorant, lazy and deceitful.[6] He warned his brother Gherardo in 1374 that the books of noble intellects were more incorrect than those of others, because such people did not concern themselves with writing, illumination, binding and so on but aspired to higher things.[7] He may have been saying this with some regret, but he accepted it as a fact.

Secondly, authors would regularly use other people as initial diffusers of their work in manuscript. These others would be friends or patrons and, unlike scribes or booksellers, would not have a professional involvement in the process of diffusion. Petrarch, we have seen, used Barbato da Sulmona, a member of the Neapolitan court, in this way when he published his *Epistole metrice*. Boccaccio made similar use of prominent Tuscan acquaintances: he sent his *Comedia delle ninfe fiorentine* to Niccolò di Bartolo del Buono, comparing him with Maecenas and other classical Roman protectors of writers, and he turned to Andreola Acciaiuoli and Mainardo Cavalcanti in order to issue respectively his *De mulieribus claris* and *De casibus virorum illustrium*. Such figures would not only promote the circulation of a work but would also add their own 'authority' to that of the author and help to defend him from possible criticisms. Boccaccio's first request to Cavalcanti – in accordance with the conventional modesty used by classical Latin writers such as Pliny the Younger when making dedications or gifts of books – was for him to read and correct the *De casibus*. Then Boccaccio asked Cavalcanti to send it forth in public among their common friends, so that it should bring some fame to them both. He told Andreola Acciaiuoli that, if the *De mulieribus* was sent forth to the public under her auspices, it would be protected from the insults of the malicious, while also making her famous.[8]

In the fifteenth century, examples multiply of authors taking advantage of a developing system of patronage and offering their works or their services to members of the ruling families of the Italian states, to patrician households (especially in the larger cities such as Milan or Venice, where the signorial or ducal household was not the only source of patronage), or to leading figures in the hierarchy of the Church.[9] In return, authors could hope for some material reward in the form of gifts, money, or occasionally even a sinecure or a stipend; they could also hope that the patron would use his or her influence to assist and protect them and that the patron's name would lend prestige to their work in the eyes of fellow-authors, readers, and other potential patrons. Authors were occasionally paid while writing their works. The lists of those salaried by the Sforza court of Milan include, in 1466, the humanist Francesco Filelfo, engaged in the composition of the *Sforziade*, a Latin epic on the military career of Francesco Sforza, and, in 1499, Tristano Calco and Donato Bossi, both writing histories. Bernardino Corio, too, was assigned an 'honesto stipendio' from Duke Lodovico Sforza while writing his history of Milan.[10] Antonio Cornazzano obtained the salaried post of 'poeta' at the Ferrarese court in 1475.[11] However, while the patronage of fine art and of architecture usually depended on an initial commission, in most cases literary patronage involved authors approaching patrons speculatively.

The author's aspirations to receiving patronage were expressed, above all, in a dedication placed at the start of the work, either in the form of a letter of presentation or woven into the opening lines of the text itself. The author might also be able to glorify the patron, and perhaps the patron's family, within the text, especially in the genres of historiography and epic poetry. A further important token of the author's allegiance was the presentation to the patron of a copy of the work prepared especially for this purpose, using high-quality materials, so that the gift consisted not only of the work itself but of an object of commercial value. The elements of decoration sometimes included a miniature showing the act of presentation, and here the author's inferior status could be signified by his posture, bowed or on bended knee before a dedicatee seated at a higher level.

The dedication would, of course, sing the praises of the generosity of the patron, precisely because this generosity was what the author hoped for. And generosity could indeed be shown. To take one example from many, when Cornazzano presented two manuscripts (one in Latin, one in the vernacular) of his poem *De excellentium virorum principibus* (On the most prominent of excellent men) to Borso d'Este, duke of Ferrara, in 1465–6, he was well rewarded with sixty gold ducats and some seven metres of crimson velvet.[12] Yet often the patronage system failed to fulfil an author's expectations. At least forty-one humanistic works were dedicated to Cosimo de' Medici, and in return he was undoubtedly generous to men of letters, giving them books, money, houses and jobs in the Florentine chancery, the university and the Church; but this liberality was to some extent motivated by self-interest, in that it helped him to control key posts and public opinion, and his reputation as a generous Maecenas depends at least in part on wishful declarations by poverty-stricken and equally self-interested poets.[13] Even when an author managed to obtain a reward, his success might conceal frustrations of one kind or another. Although Cornazzano no doubt hoped that his presentation to Duke Borso would lead to a post in the Estense court, he appears not to have received employment there until four years after Borso's death. Poggio Bracciolini received nothing at first from King Alfonso I of Naples in return for the dedication of his Latin translation of Xenophon's *Cyropaedia* (1447), because of warfare between Naples and his native state of Florence, and he was given a sum of money only in 1450. Alfonso's heir, Ferdinand I, offered employment to humanists but expected them also to perform some useful service such as teaching or secretarial work.[14] In Milan, the patronage of the Sforza dukes could be more generous in appearance than in reality. Most of the salaries offered to historians remained unchanged between 1466 and 1499, even though the currency in which they were paid had lost about one-fifth of its value, and Corio had problems in obtaining his stipend.[15] Filelfo, we saw, appeared on the 1466 list of *salariati*, but in practice he and other colleagues remained unpaid – by 1467 he was apparently owed nearly 5,000 ducats for seventeen years' service – and in any case his stipend was cut heavily in 1468. He survived by cultivating the favour of other members of the Sforza court and by being continually on the lookout for support from the rulers of other states.[16]

Filelfo's career in Milan bears out the unstable and fragile nature of the patron–client relationship. On the one hand, it was informal and therefore prone to misinterpretation or deliberate failure to keep one's promises. On the other hand, the intellectual solidarity and admiration declared by the client towards the patron tended to conflict with the real asymmetry of the pairing, the inequality of power and wealth which existed between them, and the potentially demeaning effect on the client. Given these circumstances, there was an inherent potential for manipulation and deceit on the part of the patron, for hypocrisy and (if better opportunities arose) disloyalty on the part of the client, and for rancour on the part of the would-be client who failed to achieve reward.[17] Drawing on evidence from the Florence of Lorenzo de' Medici, Lauro Martines has argued that the feeling of the client towards the patron could be expressed in the language of love and also in that of anxiety and anger, and that the rivalry between contenders for patronage could have its outcome in the language of vituperation.[18]

To sum up the consequences of the system of scribal publication, an Italian author who wished a work to be diffused in manuscript, but did not want this diffusion to be uncontrolled and unrewarded, could accept a collaboration between himself, a professional scribe and a more highly placed person. This triangular system involved some sacrifice of autonomy, but one can see in it the tenuous beginnings of the idea of the literary property of the author: he did not simply send his work forth at random, but could control the creation and the physical appearance of the version of the work from which copies were to be taken and decide on the person through whom the initial diffusion was to be directed, and he could sometimes hope to reap benefits from this person. However, because of the nature of the patronage system, any gains for the author other than literary renown were, to say the least, uncertain.

How far was there continuity with this scheme of publication after the arrival of printing in Italy?[19] There might be a superficial similarity in so far as the author still often made a financial contribution towards the costs of reproduction; but, as we shall see later in this chapter, such costs were of a much larger order than before. The main element of continuity lay in the fact that the writer would still usually choose to involve a dedicatee in the process of sending the work forth to the general public and to present him or her with a gift copy of the work, a practice still illustrated in the books themselves, as in Francesco de' Lodovici's *Triomphi di Carlo* of 1535 (see fig. 4).[20] This preservation of traditional practices in the new context allowed writers to maintain literary and social decorum. Both gifts of books and dedications had a distinguished tradition going back to classical Latin verse (from Lucretius onwards) and prose. Although these gestures might be – indeed were usually – intended to curry favour, they could be interpreted as entirely altruistic acts on the part of gentleman amateurs and in any case could lead only to voluntary displays of gratitude. They thus conferred on print publication an aura of courtly disinterest, effectively masking any commercial taint which it might bear.

There may initially have been some hesitation about whether the gift of a printed book had the same status as that of a manuscript. Some authors of printed works preferred to offer handwritten copies to patrons.[21] There is no doubt, however, that printed books were considered prestigious gifts from the start, and that print therefore encouraged an extended use of books for presentation. Writers could now take advantage of the possibility of giving copies of their work to several people, not just a single copy to a dedicatee. Marsilio Ficino added handwritten dedications to printed copies of his works, but such a compromise was not normally felt necessary. A Venetian privilege request of 1503 concerning a speech delivered to the doge stated that it had been printed beautifully 'to sell and to present' ('per vendere et per donare'). As Erasmus put it frankly in a letter of 1518, if you present a work to someone powerful, you get a higher price than if you were selling it.[22] Ortensio Lando sent two copies of an unidentified work in 1554 or 1555 to Cardinal Cristoforo Madruzzo and his brother Nicolò, members of a family which provided several bishop-princes of Trento between 1539 and 1658 and favourite targets for letters of dedication, and on the strength of these gifts he was able to ask for two favours: he wanted Nicolò to send him a gift of money so that he could pay his printing expenses before he was arrested for debt, and he wanted the cardinal to use his influence to lift the ban imposed by inquisitors on his books – something which was a particularly grave blow for one who lived by his pen.[23] The gift of a book would, of course, be all the more appreciated if it were made special by having a more costly support than the rest of the edition – vellum, or at least large paper with wider margins – and by being decorated by hand. If a small proportion of an edition were printed on vellum, such books would have value as collectors' items.[24]

As for dedications in print, there were several reasons why they continued to have at least as much importance as those in manuscript. Just as before, the act of linking a work with a highly placed figure lent it authority, as Filippo Calandri acknowledged when addressing in 1492 his *De arithmetica* to Giuliano de' Medici, then aged twelve (see fig. 10). Dedications diminished the risk to the author of seeming vain or self-important by fostering the illusion that he was engaged, at least in the first place, in a private conversation with a single figure, and one to whom he cast himself as inferior. One must remember, too, that dedications did not benefit the writer alone. As with other forms of sponsorship, a positive response to a dedication could also be to the advantage of the benefactor: if given due publicity, it could bring recognition of his or her generosity as a promoter of culture. One of the advantages of the printed book was that it had much greater potential for providing such publicity. Dedicatees could be mentioned by name on the title page, giving them an apparent role in the production of texts alongside those of the author and the printer or publisher. For instance, the first item of information given in the third book of Pietro Aretino's letters (1546) is that the work was directed 'to the magnanimous lord Cosimo de' Medici, prince of goodwill'.[25] The title page might even display the dedicatee's coat of arms, as in the 1503 edition of Iacopo Filippo Foresti's *Supplementum chronicarum*, which uses this technique to give further prominence to Cardinal Antoniotto Pallavicino.[26] Dedications could also be seen as beneficial by the reader: they were 'signs of celebrity endorsement', albeit misleading ones, as Arthur Marotti has commented, which conferred a social and intellectual status on the book and established a context in which it could be read.[27]

But, beneath the veneer of social propriety, dedications in print were also important to writers because they offered them the opportunity to seek gifts in cash or in kind. When Orazio Toscanella drew up his will in 1578, he asked his executor and his brother-in-law to do their best to have his *Historia universale* printed and dedicated to the grand duke of Tuscany, Francesco de' Medici. His desire was not only for the work to be published but for it to be exploited as a potential source of income: he stipulated in the will that, if any profit was derived from the dedication, it was to be shared among his heirs.[28] The benefit sought by the writer might be financial assistance with the printing of the book, in which case he was of course obliged to negotiate with the dedicatee beforehand. The Florentine author Gabriele Simeoni tried unsuccessfully in 1546 to obtain the hundred ducats needed to see through the press his history of Venice, Milan, Mantua and Ferrara (*Comentarii sopra alla tetrarchia*), first from Cardinal Ercole Gonzaga, then from Duke Cosimo I de' Medici, before the Venetian doge, Francesco Donato, eventually offered the sum.[29] A dedication in print might also bring benefits through the exercising of the patron's influence. One example concerns Pietro Andrea Mattioli's translations, with commentary, of the work on the medical properties of plants by the Greek physician Dioscorides. Mattioli dedicated the Italian versions which were printed in Venice from 1544 onwards (with a new illustrated version appearing in 1555) to Cardinal Cristoforo Madruzzo. On the strength of this dedication, Mattioli successfully requested Madruzzo to intervene with a fellow-cardinal, Ercole Gonzaga, in the hope of preventing the work being reprinted in Mantua by someone who had obtained a privilege for that state. Mattioli, in other words, was using a traditional means of seeking advantage from his work, namely the dedication, in order to try to block the use by someone else of one of the new means of seeking advantage from printing, namely the privilege. Even more important for Mattioli, his dedication of an internationally orientated Latin translation (1554) to Archduke Ferdinand of Tyrol led to his being summoned to Prague and appointed doctor to one of the emperor's sons.[30]

Another advantage which printing offered over manuscripts was that it made it relatively easy to dedicate a work to more than one person simultaneously. One had only to have the type reset for the text of the dedication, including an alternative name. But dual dedication was a procedure which could irritate both of the dedicatees and thus backfire, and it was rarely used.[31]

Far from demoting the use of dedications, then, printing initially had the effect of giving them even more significance. There was obvious potential here for conflicting, not to say contradictory, motives when making dedications. That this situation could create anxiety is shown by a dialogue by Giovanni Fratta which was printed in Venice in 1590: *Della dedicatione de' libri, con la correttion dell'Abuso, in questa materia introdotto* (On the dedication of books, with the correction of the abuse introduced in this matter).[32] Fratta's main concern, that dedication had become a mercenary matter, is revealed in his own dedication, where he complains that many contemporary authors did not use this device unless certain of reward. In the dialogue, the character Critone shows his anxiety that the mentality and language of commerce is no longer taboo for men of letters, indeed that profit was taking over from altruism as their motivation for writing. Among authors, he says, the laudable aim of benefiting others is being replaced by an aim which is merely mercantile; and anyone who dedicates books 'with the intention of trading in them [tener mercato di quelli] reveals himself more desirous of gain than eager for virtue' (ff. B3v–B4r). A little later, a certain 'dauber of paper' ('impiastra carte'), identifiable as Anton Francesco Doni, is attacked as one of those writers who promise more on their title pages than their books contain, in order to extract from their dedications more reward ('emolumento') than their works deserve (f. C3v). Another character, Eugenio, criticizes printers who remove a dedication when printing a work so that they can gain a double income ('rendita') from it by dedicating it to someone else (f. D2v). Francesco Porta, a character who is himself a printer, replies by attacking in turn those writers who send their work to someone they consider generous, but obtain nothing in return and so 'tear up their dedicatory letter and put one or more others in its place', until they find someone suitable. They then have the work reprinted with a new dedication in order to gain reward ('emolumento') from it (ff. D2v–D3r). Porta accuses Mattioli of having done just this with his Dioscorides, even though the first Italian editions had been richly rewarded by Madruzzo: various editions of the Latin and Italian versions were dedicated in fact not only to Archduke Ferdinand, as we have seen, but also between 1559 and 1568 to other members of the imperial family and to all the princes of Germany. Fratta himself incorporated his dedication in the work itself rather than in a separate letter, a technique which, as Eugenio points out, prevented one from changing the dedicatee if the work was reprinted (ff. F2v–F3r). Towards the end of the work, Eugenio and Porta discuss the questions of to whom and how one should dedicate. Eugenio considers that an author can offer a work to a prince, as long as it corresponds with his interests; the courtesan Veronica Franco should not, he feels, have dedicated her letters to a cardinal, Luigi d'Este. Porta extends the list of acceptable dedicatees to include academies, colleges, noblewomen and rich merchants. But Eugenio (whose name is presumably meant to signify noble birth) has reservations about merchants because, he says, 'the intention of honouring them in terms that are beyond their ken is deliberately mechanical' ('espressamente mecanica', f. E3r–v).[33] In conclusion, Eugenio calls for moderation. He condemns both flatterers and those who dedicate 'indifferently, with the intention of gain' (f. F1r); for mercenaries of this sort, friendship ends as soon as they have finished their business. Fratta's dialogue shows the continuing importance of dedications from the point of view of writers who published in print, but at the same time it confirms that in the course of the Cinquecento – his examples range over the previous half century – they had been used in an increasingly mercenary spirit.

2 WRITERS AND PRINTING CONTRACTS

There were, we have seen, good reasons for writers to continue to use, in the context of print publication, the non-contractual mechanisms of dedications and gifts traditionally associated with scribal publication. However, whereas publication in manuscript could be an informal matter handled by amateurs (indeed, the writer himself or herself could transcribe the original exemplar from which other copies were to be taken), the multiplication of copies of a work through print required the involvement of professionals in both production and distribution. It needed, too, a substantial initial investment of capital, all or part of which might be provided by the writer. This investment had to be protected against unfair competition. At the same time, print publication could bring unprecedented profits to an author. Writers were faced, then, with both new demands and new opportunities, and in this changed context they therefore became involved in two other more formal mechanisms by which they might hope to control the publication of their works and in some cases to gain direct reward from this diffusion. The first necessary step was an agreement of some sort between themselves and a printer or publisher, which would define what each party had to contribute to and could hope to gain from publication. In many cases writers would take the further step of seeking protection for the venture through the system of book privileges, which essentially allowed someone a monopoly over the production and sales of a text, and we shall go on to examine these in section 3.

Direct evidence for agreements between writers and printers or publishers is, unfortunately, scarce, and some may have been made privately, perhaps even orally, rather than being formally ratified by a notary. Paul Grendler has usefully proposed that they can be classified in four categories.[34] First, the writer, or a person or body supporting him, could agree to pay all printing costs, either by a payment in cash or by an agreement to purchase most of the copies. In other words, the printer would work on commission, would take no financial risk, and would not normally be expected to have any influence over the contents of the book. Secondly, the writer and the printer or publisher could form a joint company, sharing both printing expenses and the print run, perhaps on a fifty–fifty basis. Agreements of this sort would be very similar in nature to the publishing contracts, mentioned in chapter 2, which brought together printers, on the one hand, and on the other hand professors, lawyers, wealthy gentlemen, merchants or booksellers.

Thirdly, the printer or publisher might bring out the work at his own risk, in which case the printed copies would belong to him, and the author would receive nothing except a small number of copies, which would typically be used as gifts. Finally (and, as Grendler suggests, this arrangement was 'probably least common and a later development'), a printer or publisher who was confident that the book would be commercially successful could buy the manuscript from the author.

The first and even to some extent the second of these arrangements, involving as they did a payment on the writer's part, might nowadays look like 'vanity' publishing. And no doubt some authors were motivated simply by the desire to see their names in print and to burnish their reputations. One thinks, for instance, of the *Diaria de bello Carolino* by the doctor Alessandro Benedetti, an account of the campaign against the invading French army which was printed by Aldo Manuzio in 1496; in this case Aldo was careful not to include his own name in the volume.[35] However, the risks and pressures of self-publication would often be taken on, or at least shared, by authors for one of two other reasons: either because they wished, sensibly enough, to try to control the quality, accuracy and diffusion of the final product, or through necessity, since printers were unwilling or unable to stake a very large sum of money in an uncertain market and without secure protection against unfair competition.

One can be certain that the author footed the entire bill for publication, as in Grendler's first category, when the printed book states that it was produced at the author's expense. The annals of Antonio de Frizis, for example, show that some of the books printed by him in Naples between 1518 and 1526 were published by their authors.[36] And an author was clearly his own publisher on the rare occasions when one had a press set up in his own house. It was in this way that Alberto Acarisio published his Italian dictionary in Cento, near Bologna, in 1543, taking the additional steps of obtaining privileges from the duke of Ferrara and the pope and of dedicating the work to a bishop.[37]

Poems of chivalry were read avidly by all social classes in the Renaissance, and printers and publishers must surely have regarded them as among the safest works in which to invest, in spite of their length. It was presumably, then, by choice that authors of romances regularly arranged for the printing of their own works. The papal privilege granted to Cassio da Narni for *La morte del Danese* shows that he had his poem printed at his own expense in Ferrara in 1521.[38] Francesco Tromba's contract of 1524 for the printing of his *Dragha de Orlando innamorato* in

Perugia meant that he had to pay for the paper and would share proceeds equally with the printer-bookseller Bianchino dal Leone.[39] It is instructive, though, to compare the attitudes of epic poets to the business of printing in the fifteenth and in the sixteenth centuries. Count Matteo Maria Boiardo evidently had the question of finance in mind when he was penning the final, cliff-hanging verses for the first edition of his *Orlando innamorato* (printed before 24 February 1483), but he made no suggestion that the investment was his own. If he were to continue the story of Orlando, he wrote,

> bisognarebe agionger molte carte,
> farebe il stampitor poco guadagno!
> Ma a cui piacesse pur saper il resto
> venga a vederlo e fia stampito presto.

(it would be necessary to add many leaves, and the printer would make little profit! But, if anyone wants to know the rest, come and see him, and it will be printed soon.)

This touching concern for the printer's financial welfare might be genuine, but is much more likely to be a decorous self-distancing from the economics of publication on the part of an aristocrat who had in fact paid all the costs.[40] Certainly Boiardo's widow was the financer of the next non-Venetian edition (1495).[41] One finds a contrastingly open approach to the author's involvement in publishing in the fifth book of the Venetian citizen Nicolò Degli Agostini's continuation of Boiardo's unfinished epic, the *Orlando innamorato*, printed in Venice by Giorgio Rusconi in 1514. At the end, Nicolò inserted a plea to his readers which stresses his need to recoup his expenses through sales if the final book was to appear:

Lettori, se havete piacer di veder il sesto libro, non imprestate Questo a persona alcuna, ma chi lo vol, fatte [= fate] lo compri, acciò possi cavar li dinari ho spesi ne la Charta e ne la stampa; e non vogliate che, per darvi piacer, riceva danno, perché così facendo vi prometto dar fora il libro sesto fin un anno, più dilettevole et maggior di questo.[42]

(Readers, if you wish to see the sixth book, lend this one to nobody, but if anyone wants it, make him buy it, so that I can recover the money I spent on paper and printing. Do not desire me to suffer loss through giving you pleasure, because, if you do as I ask, I promise to bring out the sixth book within a year, more enjoyable and longer than this one.)

The second type of agreement, in which the author and a publisher or printer shared costs and profits more or less equally, lay behind the publication in 1494 of Sebastiano Manilio's translation of the letters of Seneca: these were printed in Venice in company ('per commune spesa') with the brothers Stefano and Bernardino di Nalli.[43] This was also the method chosen by Castiglione in 1527 for the printing of his *Libro del cortegiano* (see chapter 4, section 2). An example from the field of music is that of Matteo Bosca, probably a composer, and the Roman printer Niccolò de' Giudici.[44] In 1526 each agreed before a notary to meet half the costs of printing 500 copies of a book of *frottole* (light songs), a total of 27 ducats, which was made up of 10 ducats for eleven reams of paper, 1 ducat for ink and skins (to cover the ink balls), and 4 ducats each for the wages of the printer and his apprentice for two months plus 8 ducats for their living expenses for this period. The books, once printed, were to be sold jointly, and profits were to be divided equally. A similar but more detailed notarial agreement was made in Rome in February 1543 between three parties – the Spaniard Cristóbal de Morales, the bookseller-publishers Antonio Salamanca and Giovanni della Gatta, and Valerio Dorico – for the printing by Dorico of two volumes of polyphonic masses by Morales.[45] The composer was to provide the fair copy and to see to proof correction; he had to pay for paper (royal paper was to be used), for the printing of 250 of the 525 folio volumes to be produced, and for any extra illustrations; and he had to obtain, at his expense, ten-year privileges for the Papal States, Naples and Venice.[46] In return, Morales was to receive 275 copies, and he evidently expected to sell them chiefly in Spain, since in Italy he was allowed to sell only 50 copies, none of which could be sold wholesale to a bookseller or merchant. For their part, Salamanca and Della Gatta undertook to pay costs for 275 copies; in return they would receive 250 copies, none of which could be sent to Spain. Finally, Dorico was to complete printing by the end of July, and could not print any copies for himself or others without the permission of the other parties. He was to charge 14 giuli (1.4 scudi) per printed ream. Since the two volumes, which appeared in 1544, consist of 144 sheets, the printer's bill for producing 525 copies, excluding the cost of paper, would have been just over 150 scudi. The composer, then, had to make a substantial investment, probably greater than that of his publishing partners once the costs of transport and so on were included, and his potential income from the sale of copies was only slightly larger than theirs. But Morales also had his eye on other kinds of gain. He dedicated the first volume of masses to Duke Cosimo de' Medici (whose wife was Spanish), saying that others were to follow.

Cosimo's response must have been unsatisfactory, though, because the second volume was dedicated to Pope Paul III, with an explicit plea for generosity.

This contract of 1543 meant that the printer was exposed to no risks (Dorico even received an advance of 40 scudi from Morales), but on the other hand it also prevented him from making any extra profit by selling copies of his own. In a Neapolitan contract of March 1587, however, the printer Giuseppe Cacchi was allowed to earn more money by selling part of the print run of a devotional work. Cacchi agreed to produce 500 copies of seven 'psalms of mercy' composed by Gerolamo Fagiolo, with figures and red letters, together with engraved illustrations of the seven works of mercy and the coat of arms of the Carafa family, to whom the work was presumably to be dedicated. Fagiolo was to provide a ream of paper and make payments towards the printer's costs, but Cacchi was permitted to run off up to 100 further copies of the booklets at his own expense, and therefore for sale by himself.[47]

It is evident that the courtier Mario Equicola bore at least some of the expenses for the printing of his *Libro de natura de amore* in Venice in 1525. His employer, Federico Gonzaga, marquis of Mantua, facilitated preparations for publication in 1521 through his ambassador in Venice but does not seem to have contributed towards costs. In the same year Equicola wrote to Federico's mother, Isabella d'Este, asking for permission to go to Venice for ten days to have the *De natura* printed and mentioning his expenditure on the venture; by a year later he had certainly paid for the paper to be used. When printing finally got under way in 1525, in the workshop of Nicolò Zoppino, Equicola was notified of extra costs of 17 ducats incurred when certain sheets had to be reprinted. However, the volume advertises itself as printed for ('per') Lorenzo Lorio, and so it is possible that Equicola entered into a partnership of some sort with this publisher.[48]

Authors who undertook an agreement to share costs and copies would of course have subsequently faced the problem of selling off a large number of books, and for this they might have had to make further contracts with professional booksellers. Thus in 1589 a certain Ambrogio Bizzozero planned to have printed his work concerning machines newly invented by him, for which he had obtained privileges for the Papal States and elsewhere, and he decided to share profits from both the books and the inventions with a certain Polidoro Cauzio. He agreed to sell to Cauzio 500 unbound copies of the work for a deposit of 50 scudi plus 60 scudi on delivery. Bizzozero was to sell his own copies in

Rome, while his partner was to sell in Tuscany, giving half his profits to the author. Later, Bizzozero gave Cauzio the rights to sell in parts of the Papal States.[49]

Authors might find it difficult to scrape together the cash necessary for print publication. We have already seen how in the 1540s Gabriele Simeoni had to look for a patron who would undertake to pay his costs. A writer would often have had to borrow money in the expectation of repaying the loan after selling enough of the finished books. The Spaniard Juan de Ortega borrowed 20 ducats as a contribution towards the printing of his *Summa de arithmetica* by Etienne Guillery in Rome, 1515, guaranteeing the loan with the forthcoming copies of the book and taking out a privilege in order to protect himself.[50] Orazio Toscanella even had to get his maid to invest in the printing in 1578 of his translation of the exercises on rhetoric by Aphthonius Sophista, and in his will of the same year he asked his executors to ensure that her loan was repaid by buying any unsold copies from her.[51] At the same time, in his dedication he took the opportunity to try to arouse the pity of a Venetian nobleman, Luigi Foscari, reminding him of the generosity shown on an earlier occasion when Toscanella had gone eleven months without any income and with nine people to feed, all of them ill.

Other authors were fortunate enough to have the financial backing of a figure (not unlike that of the modern theatrical 'angel') whom one can term a patron-publisher. In Milan in 1473 Francesco Filelfo was expecting German printers to bring out an edition of his vast collection of letters. This very ambitious project was evidently abandoned, but a few years later it seemed that it might be revived through the mediation of Gian Giacomo Simonetta. At some time between 1475 and 1479 Gian Giacomo received a letter of advice from the publisher Pietro Antonio Castiglione, who had heard that Filelfo wanted his letters printed and that Filelfo had a printer willing to do the job for 2 soldi a quire, which the humanist considered expensive. From that comment, it seems that Filelfo was expecting to pay at least a share of the costs, and the rest of the letter suggests that he was looking to others to organize publication and perhaps also to form a partnership with him. Castiglione thought the price quoted was indeed too high, even if the retail price were 5 soldi a quire. In the light of his experience in negotiating with printers – and he claimed to have spent twice as much on publishing as anyone else in Milan – he advised Simonetta that he could undertake that costs, other than the paper, would not be over half a soldo per quire and that he would organize most of the wholesaling of the volumes.[52]

The need for the backing of someone resourceful – both wealthy and capable of resolving problems – if a fifteenth-century writer was to get into print is seen in other Milanese cases. In 1489 a certain Giovanni Antonio Corvino of Arezzo published 1,000 copies of a work by Stefano Dolcino, a former pupil of Filelfo.[53] Even if Corvino did not cover his costs, he must have seen this as a shrewd investment, for the work was an account of the marriage of the duke, Gian Galeazzo Sforza. The courtier-poet Gaspare Visconti was supported in the same way by two enterprising priests, Francesco Tanzio in 1493 and Giovanni Stefano Vimercate two years later.[54] Tanzio claimed that the author's modesty made him unwilling to be published in this way, but Visconti was probably far from opposed to ventures which could be used to strengthen his status in court circles. One of the works, the *Rithimi*, was dedicated by him to his fellow-poet Niccolò da Correggio, and we know that Niccolò received from the author some printed copies, of which he sent one to Isabella d'Este.[55] Another work, *De Paulo e Daria amanti*, was dedicated to Duke Lodovico Sforza. However, the ruling family of Milan seems to have left the subsidizing of printed literary works to private enterprise, even in the case of historical works which supported its image and status. It would be interesting to see whether it would have financed the printing of the original version of Giovanni Simonetta's *Commentaries* on the life of Francesco Sforza. Simonetta was writing this work when, in the early 1470s, he was involved in the negotiations to bring a Venetian printer to begin working in Milan, and so, it has been suggested, the *Commentaries* may have been the first work of history written especially for the press.[56] However, after a shift of power in 1479, Giovanni was exiled. Duke Lodovico then had the work revised in order to make it conform with his new regime and ordered Antonio Zarotto to print 400 copies. Printing was to be at the expense of Zarotto and others, though Sforza did at least give Zarotto the benefit of a six-year privilege.[57] As we shall see in section 3 below, the printing of Donato Bossi's chronicle in 1492 was also protected by a privilege, but Bossi had to make his own arrangements to cover expenses. Another historian who had received a court stipend, Bernardino Corio, did not complete his *Patria historia* until 1503, after Duke Lodovico's fall from power, and thus had to find support from the banker Gian Francesco Gallarate, who agreed to pay for paper and printing costs (perhaps as much as 500–600 ducats) and to try to sell the 1,200 copies within a year. After that, Corio was to reimburse him for his expenses, and any profits or losses were to be shared equally. The venture was not a success, and unsold copies were reissued nearly twenty years later.[58]

A similar situation faced authors in the early years of printing in Florence. Some found sponsorship for their editions from wealthy patrons, though not normally from the Medici family, the unofficial rulers of the city, who were certainly not hostile to printing but appear to have supported it financially only rarely.[59] Marsilio Ficino was fortunate to have had supporters willing to provide subventions for the printing of his philosophical works (see chapter 4, section 2). But some Florentine writers in this period probably financed their own editions. When Duke Ercole d'Este wanted a copy of the first edition of Luigi Pulci's chivalric romance, *Il Morgante*, in 1478, he wrote to his Florentine agent that he wanted a copy, 'and so we pray you to reach an agreement with someone called Luigi Pulci, who has a supply of copies' ('se ne trova haver').[60] It sounds very much as if the author himself was organizing sales of the poem, presumably in order to recoup publication costs. Another author who took responsibility for sales, and therefore had probably paid for printing, was Francesco Berlinghieri. His Tuscan verse adaptation of Ptolemy's *Geographia* was dogged by misfortune: printing was long drawn out and poorly executed, two dedicatees died in quick succession, and the work sold so poorly that a large stock of copies remained to be reissued after the author's death.[61] Cristoforo Landino must have underwritten an extremely costly venture, the 1481 edition of Dante's *Commedia* accompanied by his own commentary and Botticelli's engravings, to judge from his remark in a letter that 'I had published' ('edideram') 1,200 copies.[62] Only occasionally, it seems, were the financial risks of printing borne by a Florentine press or by men linked professionally with one. The commission to print a work entitled *Explanatio in Persium* was given to the Ripoli press in 1477 not by the author, Bartolomeo della Fonte, but by a stationer, Bartolo or Bartolomeo di Domenico. One wonders, though, whether the humanist would not have acted as his own publisher had this commission been given a few years later, since in 1479–80 we find him publishing two books either with others or on his own.[63] The same stationer formed a company with the Ripoli press to print a short work, the Margutte episode from Pulci's *Morgante*, in 1480; after a time he dropped out and the press continued work with its own resources. However, it was probably the same Ripoli press which, two years earlier, printed the whole *Morgante* at the expense of the author rather than at its own risk.[64]

In some cases printing costs were met by an institution. The monastic community of San Giorgio Maggiore paid the Venetian printer

Girolamo Scotto 550 lire to produce 500 copies of a music edition in 1565, and the College of Apostolic Secretaries undertook to pay the Roman printer Paolo Blado about 100 scudi in four instalments to print the same number of copies of a work in 1586.[65] The Franciscan friar Antonio Sanfelice gave 11 ducats to Mattia Cancer as a contribution towards the printing of his *Campania* in Naples in 1562, but he was reimbursed when the University of Capua gave him 30 ducats for his labours in writing the work, which was dedicated to the city of Capua.[66]

Agreements of the third kind, those where the author (or a sponsor) gave no financial subvention to printing and received no direct benefits other than a small number of copies, may well have lain behind some Venetian privilege requests which concerned works by living Italian authors but which came from printers or publishers. The publisher Luc'Antonio Giunti made an application in 1524 for the protection of a series of works which the astrologer Luca Gaurico wished to bring out ('in lucem edere'), and the bookseller Nicolò Garanta applied in 1526 for the rights to works by the poet Teofilo Folengo.[67] Significantly, in none of these cases was the author named as a beneficiary of the fines to be levied on offenders. Mattioli requested the privilege for the first (1544) version of his Dioscorides, one of the great publishing successes of the century, but privileges granted in the early 1550s to the bookseller and printer Vincenzo Valgrisi show that it was the latter who then invested in the expenses of printing and preparing the woodcut illustrations. Mattioli benefited from the work in terms of his career, as we saw earlier, while Valgrisi reaped financial rewards which were probably enormous: it was claimed that he sold over 32,000 copies of his various editions.[68] Nor would Mattioli have expected the situation to be otherwise: one of his pupils wrote to him in 1549 to wish 'great praise for you and great gain for the printer' ('a voi gran lodi e allo stampatore gran guadagno').[69]

The Florentine printer and publisher Filippo Giunti offered Scipione Ammirato an agreement of this third kind for the publication, in 1600, of his *Istorie fiorentine*.[70] As a first step in their negotiation, Giunti put proposals in writing on 3 September 1598, specifying the format, the quality of paper and the type to be used, and the rate at which printing was to proceed, and stating that the author was responsible for correcting the second proofs and for compiling the index (see chapter 1, sections 3 and 5). Ammirato was not permitted to come to an agreement with others or to add to the work until Giunti had sold all his copies, and Giunti was to have the right to address a dedicatory letter to the grand duke. The printer was to give twenty unbound copies of the work, and no more, to the author. On the following day Ammirato dictated some counter-proposals. He objected to the quality of paper suggested and to the extra chore of compiling the index himself. Nor did he want to let himself be 'pulled along by the nose' by agreeing to the unprecedented precaution of waiting until Giunti had sold all his copies. He wanted to write the dedication himself – this was the custom with a first edition printed while the author was alive – and he insisted on at least forty free copies, to be printed on royal paper. Finally, on the sixteenth of the month, Ammirato made various amendments to Giunti's original proposals, now adding the suggestions that the printer's exclusive rights to the work should last for two years and that Giunti should give him thirty copies, plus two on royal paper for which Ammirato would supply the paper and which were to be presented respectively to the grand duke and the pope. In the event, the dedicatory letter to the grand duke was signed by Ammirato.

Towards the end of the sixteenth century, as print culture achieved a more stable commercial footing, one begins to find evidence of the fourth kind of agreement, in which publishers made payments to writers in addition to underwriting the printing of their works. When Luc'Antonio Giunti the younger contracted before a notary in 1597 to have printed the second part of Prospero Farinacci's *Praxis et theorica criminalis* (Practice and theory of criminal law), he promised to pay the author the large sum of 270 scudi. Farinacci had the right to thirty-five free copies, to be delivered to him in Rome, but he chose to buy a number of further copies for the sum of 160 scudi, intending doubtless to present or sell them.[71] An author's heirs could enter into similar arrangements, as one sees from a Venetian contract of June–July 1575 between the noble Paduan Girolamo Dotto, acting on behalf of his wife, the daughter of the late Marcantonio of Genoa, and, as the second party, the printer Grazioso Percaccino (who had worked in Padua in 1566) and the bookseller Damiano Zenaro. Dotto handed over certain commentaries in his father-in-law's hand on works by Aristotle. These were to be printed and 'brought into the light of the world' ('mandati in luce al mondo'), in other words published, by Percaccino and Zenaro. These two undertook to pay Dotto 150 gold scudi unconditionally by the end of July 1576 and to complete the printing of the works within four years. If they failed to meet this deadline, Dotto could reclaim his manuscripts and have them printed at the others' expense. The original texts were in any case to be returned to him, and he was to receive six copies of each printed volume.[72]

Another way in which a writer could be recompensed by a publisher was by a payment similar to a modern royalty. This was one of the options proposed to Lionardo Salviati in 1581 when he was preparing his edition of Boccaccio's *Decameron.* According to a memorandum prepared at the time, Filippo and Iacopo Giunti offered Salviati, 'in recompense of his labour and virtue', a choice of three options: 200 scudi in cash (100 immediately, the rest in six months' time); the formation of a joint company, which would presumably have involved equal investment of capital, since Salviati would have received an equal share in profits; or 2 carlini for each copy sold. However, like Ammirato a few years later, Salviati felt that the Giunti were trying to take advantage of him. His 'royalty' would have been worth more than the cash offer only if sales passed 1,125 copies. He did not wish to be bothered with joint companies and sales, and the sum of 200 scudi seemed too small.[73] If one compares negotiations of this kind with the procedures of manuscript publication, one can see that printing had made publication much more complex for writers: more problematic in some respects, but more inviting in the opportunities which it offered to win a wider audience and even some hard cash.

A single printing house would probably have used a combination of different kinds of agreements with authors. This was the case, for example, with the press managed by Aldo Manuzio between about 1494 and 1515.[74] On occasion, Aldo might seek out material from an author: he commissioned from Urbano Valeriano the Greek grammar which he printed in 1498, and in 1502 he asked the poet Iacopo Sannazaro to send him all his works, which were much sought after.[75] But approaching an author was unusual for Aldo, as it seems to have been for other printers. More often, an author or his intermediary would make the first move, as in the cases of Lorenzo Maioli, Giorgio Interiano, and Michele Ferno acting on behalf of Cardinal Adriano Castellesi.[76] In the ensuing agreement, Aldo may sometimes have decided to bear all costs. In October 1507 Erasmus approached him with a view to republishing a translation of two plays by Euripides. Erasmus claimed that he would have preferred to undertake the venture at his own expense, in other words adopting the first type of arrangement described above, and he even offered to enter into the second type by purchasing one or two hundred copies 'at a fair price'; but he successfully proposed an agreement of the third type, under which he would make no charge for supplying a corrected copy of the original Paris edition, would pay nothing towards the costs of printing, and would receive only a few copies of the book for presentation to friends (he eventually offered to pay for twenty or thirty copies to be used as gifts).[77] Mario Equicola seems to have had a similar arrangement in mind when he wrote to Aldo in 1510 on behalf of a certain Demetrio Mosco who, he said, had written (or 'elaborated') a Greek comedy. Demetrio's friends wanted to see it printed, it seemed that Demetrio had talked to Aldo about it, and there was a proposal to dedicate it to Aldo's former pupil, Alberto Pio, prince of Carpi. If Aldo printed the comedy, Equicola was certain that it would sell like hot cakes ('so certo la spacciarete ad furia'), while Aldo would satisfy Demetrio by giving him any of his Greek books.[78] However, Aldo was probably not convinced by the proposal, for he did not print the book. He may have decided to underwrite his edition of Giorgio Interiano's description of life in the steppes of Kazakhstan, something completely out of line with his usual interests, simply because the traveller was a friend of Sannazaro; Aldo could then use the book as a means of persuading the poet to collaborate in bringing out what would undoubtedly have been a commercially successful definitive edition of his works. But Aldo was by no means always willing or able to meet all his printing costs. One of his most famous vernacular editions, the *Hypnerotomachia Poliphili* of 1499, was executed on commission. Among the financers was certainly a Veronese gentleman, Leonardo Grassi, who later lamented that the volume (so highly prized today) had sold badly; and the man who is now acknowledged as its author, Francesco Colonna, may also have paid a share, since we know that he borrowed money in order to pay the costs of printing an unspecified book.[79]

3 WRITERS AND BOOK PRIVILEGES

In chapter 2, section 3, we saw in outline how the system of book privileges operated, and in examining publishing agreements above we saw in passing several instances of writers obtaining these privileges. We can now go on to look in more detail at how they used this system. The first recorded privilege which directly benefited an author was that awarded by the Venetian state in 1486 to the humanist Marcantonio Sabellico. In recognition of the quality of his history of the city, he was granted the right to give his manuscript to a diligent printer who would print the work at his own expense; anyone else who issued it would be fined 500 ducats.[80] This arrangement would have been to the advantage both of the author – who had to meet no costs, could choose a printer whom he believed to be reliable, and had no need to fear that other editions would appear without his approval – and of the printer, protected from competition while his copies were sold. For the time, however, this was an altogether exceptional arrangement. As one can see from Fulin's collection of documents on Venetian printing from 1469 to 1526, it was not until 1492 that writers began to make applications for privileges to the Venetian state on a regular basis. Of the 254 petitions which Fulin records (not all of which led to actual publications), 79, or about 30 per cent, were made by or on behalf of writers: these include creators of original works (49 cases) and editors, commentators, translators or a combination of these (30 cases).[81] Of the 49 requests relating to authors of original works, 39 concern literary works, 8 are from artists and 2 are from musicians or composers. The surviving requests refer to only a small proportion of the books produced in the city, of course, but they were made at a fairly regular rate: 19 in the period before 1501, 27 between 1501 and 1510, only 14 in the following decade, but 19 in 1521–6.

The motivation of a publisher or printer who applied for a privilege would be the protection of his financial investment. What did a writer who made such an application want? In the first place, he would wish to protect his investment in time and creative effort, and he might also have a financial outlay to protect if he was making a contribution to printing costs or if he was an editor who had purchased the texts which were to be made public. Thus the first two documents from 1492 which Fulin summarizes concern a professor from the University of Padua, Petrus Tommai of Ravenna, who had written a work on an art of memory invented by him but did not wish others to gather 'the fruits of his labours and vigils' ('fructus laborum et vigiliarum suarum'). Three weeks later a Venetian citizen, Joannes Dominicus de Nigro, applied for a privilege as the publisher of medical works of which he had acquired the manuscripts and which had been edited by someone else. The situation was different, but very similar language was used: the publisher wanted protection lest others, having no share in the labour and expense, should gather 'the fruit of his labours and expenses' ('fructum laborum et impensarum suarum'). The repetition of the fruit-gathering metaphor, which established itself as the standard one in petitions of this sort, and the easy way in which *impensae* replaces *vigiliae*, make it clear that an author's intellectual efforts were seen as just as worthy of legal protection as a publisher's outlay of capital. While Fulin was quite right to distinguish privileges which aim to protect literary property from those which aim to protect industrial interests (p. 88), these two kinds of property were treated in exactly the same way.

Another motive which could be cited by writers in these Venetian documents was the control of textual correctness. Giovanni Aurelio Augurello, before having a Latin poem on alchemy printed in 1515, wanted to make sure 'that the printers cannot spoil it', and the doctor Alvise Cinzio de' Fabrizi requested a privilege in 1526 so that his book on the origin of proverbs should not be 'perverted, corrupted and torn to pieces' by printers, 'as such people do all day long, because no literate person can look at, let alone read, any of the works they bring out'. Andrea Manio's application of 1497, relating to grammatical works written or edited by himself, cites commercial interests (he does not want others to print and sell the works more cheaply) and the fear of textual corruption ('qualche depravatione'), and he adds a third motive, the desire to see his works printed attractively ('de bona lettera').[82] Some applications may have been made by authors because a publisher or printer had made this a precondition of his co-operation: such a situation may explain, for instance, why the Dominican friar Silvestro Mazzolini asked for protection for unspecified works of his in 1506, mentioning that Petrus Liechtenstein would publish them as long as he did not fear competition.

According to the conditions of 32 of the 79 authorial privilege requests, the petitioner would have profited directly from a successful prosecution for violation of the privilege. Usually the author would receive a share of the fine – between one-third and one-half – or at least the books which had been seized. In addition, the person bringing the accusation was often named as a beneficiary, and this meant that authors could have benefited from a prosecution even if they did not automatically receive part of the fine. But why was the author not named as a beneficiary in every case? Sometimes the reason may have been that he had made no contribution towards printing costs.[83] In other cases, though, the author may have considered that seeking any financial benefit was contrary to gentlemanly behaviour. Works composed or edited by Pietro Bembo were the subject of privilege applications, but these were always made by others: his younger brother Carlo, the printer Aldo Manuzio, his secretary and friend Cola Bruno, his nephew Giovan Matteo Bembo. Pietro was named only where strictly necessary, as author and not always as editor, and never as a beneficiary of fines.[84] An application of September 1516 relating to the *Decameron* edited by another Venetian nobleman, Nicolò Delfino, followed the pattern of the 1501 application for Bembo's Petrarch edition, since it was made by the editor's brother Lorenzo and did not name Nicolò. Antonio Pigafetta, a nobleman of Vicenza, applied in his own name in August 1524 when he wished to publish his account of his journey around the world with Magellan, but was not named as a beneficiary of the fine of 3 lire for any book printed or sold illegally.

Many different kinds of work were the subjects of Venetian privilege requests by authors. Some were intended to be of practical use: the art of memory already mentioned, a work on weights and measures 'very useful to all merchants' which was probably the first vernacular prose work to be protected in this way (1500), a treatise on palmistry, works on medicine, books which taught reading, writing and arithmetic, and works on controlling fortune.[85] In September 1521 we find a Franciscan friar applying for protection for 'fifty questions of conscience, useful for confessors and preachers'. Several historians were granted privileges: Sabellico in 1486 and again in 1497, Alessandro Benedetti in 1496 for his *Diaria*, Piero Marcello for a Venetian history in 1502, Pietro Cirneo for an account of Corsica in 1509, and Bartolomeo Cori for the only vernacular work in this group, a narration of the recent siege of Padua in 1510.[86] In the category of travel, we have Pigafetta's application, just mentioned. Several other applications concerned works relating to Latin grammar, rhetoric and philology or to grammars of the vernacular.[87] Privileges were also granted for philosophical works (1504 and 1517) and for mathematical works edited and written by fra Luca Pacioli (1508).

The final group is that of poetic works, a particularly interesting one because their value depended on the author's artistic skill as well as on the content of the work. Only two of these works were in Latin. One, of March 1509, was an elegy in praise of Venice, written at a time when the Republic was under threat from the League of Cambrai; the other, of August 1515, was Augurello's poem on making gold, which was unfortunately more of a literary exercise than a work likely to be of practical value. The first application concerning verse in the vernacular was made in March 1505 by Nicolò Degli Agostini for the fourth book which he had added to Boiardo's *Orlando innamorato*. In May 1520 Agostini made a much more ambitious application which covered his sixth book of the *Innamorato*, other original works in the chivalric tradition, translations from Ovid and Plutarch, and, for the future, 'all the new works of a similar kind to be composed and printed and caused to be printed by the said Nicolò', as long as they did not touch on sensitive topics – wars, modern politics, the Church, anything obscene or immoral.[88] Another romance, *L'Antheo gigante* (Antheus the giant), was protected by a privilege given to its author, Francesco de' Lodovici, in June 1524, though he may only have been acting on behalf of the patron to whom the poem was addressed and who financed the edition, a certain 'Lucrezia M. B.' of Bologna. Nicolò Liburnio successfully sought a privilege in March 1513 for his *Selvette*, a collection of seven short works combining prose and verse, but privilege requests were made by printers for two other works of his in 1502 and 1521. Liburnio dedicated these *Selvette* to Isabella d'Este, and it was normal for authors who had obtained privileges to use dedications as well: thus, for example, Nicolò Degli Agostini dedicated his fourth book of the *Orlando innamorato* to Isabella's husband, Francesco Gonzaga, marquis of Mantua; Alessandro Benedetti dedicated his *Diaria* to the doge and included subsidiary dedications to no fewer than eight Venetian senators.

Two applications refer explicitly to the poet's being in control of selling his work. The 1526 privilege of Alvise Cinzio, already mentioned, prevented anyone else from printing or selling his work in Venetian territory. The Florentine *cantastorie* (or improviser and reciter) Cristoforo known as 'l'Altissimo', who was a friend of Degli Agostini, planned in September 1519 to make use of the opportunities for profit afforded by the Venetian book industry: he asked for a privilege for his *Historia de Anthenore* and a collection of poems 'which, because of the love he bears towards this bountiful city and its prosperity, he wishes to have printed here and sell them'.

However, an author from outside Venice could not prevent someone else from trying to publish his works there, and in November 1526 a certain Giovanni Manenti obtained a privilege for some unpublished works of Cristoforo's which had 'come into his hands'. It was only in 1545 that the Venetian Council of Ten decided that works could not be printed without their authors' consent:

> È accresciuta in tanto l'audacia et cupidità di guadagno di alcuni stampatori in questa nostra città, che si fanno licito de imprimer quel che li pare, et nominar li compositori di quelle cose che stampano, senza alcuna loro scientia, anzi contra ogni loro voler. Essendo stà de ciò fatta querela alli capi di questo conseglio, con ricercar instantemente provisione, la qual si deve omnino far, et però:
>
> l'anderà parte, che de cetero alcun impressor in questa nostra città non habbia ardimento stampar, né stampata far vender alcuna opera in cadauna lengua, s'el non consterà per authentico documento alli Refformatori dello Studio Nostro di Padoa, a chi la cognition di tal cosa è stà deputata, l'autor di

quella, over li sui heredi più congionti, esser contenti, et ricercar, che la si stampi, et venda, sotto pena di pagar ducato uno per cadaun libro et auttor che stampassero contra il presente ordine, et di star mese uno serrato in preson, et che li sian brusati tutti li libri, che si trovessero stampati di tal sorte.

(The audacity and greed for gain of some printers in this city of ours has grown to such an extent that they permit themselves to print what they like and to name the authors of the things they print without their knowledge, indeed completely against their wishes. A complaint on this matter has been made to the heads of this council, with a very strong request for action to put a stop to this. Such action must definitely be taken, and therefore:

it is decreed that in future no printer in this city of ours shall make bold to print or to sell printed copies of any work in any language, if it is not made clear by original document to the governors of our University of Padua, to whom jurisdiction over this matter has been passed, that the author of the work, or his nearest heirs, are content and desire that it should be printed and sold. The punishment is a fine of one ducat for each book and author that are printed in contravention of this order, one month's imprisonment, and the burning of all books found to be printed in this manner.)

Even then, the impetus for this decree may have come not from a sense of the injustice being done to unprotected authors in general but from a complaint from the most highly placed Venetian author of all, Pietro Bembo. Now a cardinal, he had just had to endure the unauthorized publication in 1544 of forty-two letters, including a number of youthful love letters, and of an anthology of his verse.[89]

The scattered evidence on the granting of privileges in other cities suggests that, outside Venice too, writers wished to be able to control the diffusion of their work and that the legitimacy of this desire was widely recognized. Lodovico Sforza, duke of Milan, acknowledged in July 1490 that Donato Bossi deserved 'some honour and profit' ('aliquid honoris et commodi') for the time he had devoted to writing his Milanese chronicles, and therefore decided to protect the printing of the work with a ducal privilege. The official document of February 1492 says that, after the fifteen years of effort which Bossi put into its composition, he now wanted to have it printed, 'hoping from this printing to obtain reward [premium] for part of his labours', but that he was worried that others would copy it, so that he would unjustly 'receive little gain' ('paucum lucrum percepisset'). Later on, the document uses the metaphor of gathering the fruits of one's labours ('fructus percipere') before stating that Bossi had been awarded exclusive rights in the work, whether in Latin or in the vernacular, for ten years; any infringement would lead to a fine of 4 ducats per copy, of which 2 would go to the author.[90]

In Rome, the writers who received legal protection in the early sixteenth century included men who were editors or both editors and publishers. Thus in 1509 Tommaso Pighinucci was awarded a privilege for a medical work edited and financed by him, and in 1515 Filippo Beroaldo the younger received a privilege for his edition of Tacitus. Several other privileges were awarded to authors of original works which, as in Venice, covered a variety of genres: to Pierio Valeriano for his *Castigationes* (corrections) of the text of Virgil (1521), Zaccaria Ferreri for his *Hymni novi ecclesiastici* (1525), Iacopo Sannazaro for his *De partu Virginis* (On the childbirth of the Virgin, 1526), Girolamo Vida for his *De arte poetica* and other verse works (1527). In Sannazaro's case it was specified that the whole of the large fine for infringement of the privilege, 500 ducats, would be paid to the author. Vernacular verse could likewise be protected: Bernardo Giambullari was awarded a three-year privilege in 1514 for his continuation of the chivalric romance *Ciriffo Calvaneo*. The fine in this case was also payable to the petitioner, but at 50 ducats it was a relatively low one, and Giambullari was instructed to set a fair retail price. Roman privileges were also granted to authors of works of a more practical nature written in both Latin and the vernacular, such as Ludovico de Varthema of Bologna for his description of a journey to the Middle East (1510), and Iacobo Silvestro of Florence for a guide to the use of ciphers (1526) which described itself as 'most useful to merchants and to every other sort of person'.[91]

Authors could specify in their privilege applications that their successors should inherit their benefits. Ludovico de Varthema's ten-year privilege for his *Itinerario*, just mentioned, extended to his heirs. In Venice, Luca Pacioli's ten-year privilege of 1508 specified that one-third of the fine (of 1 ducat per volume) which would have been paid by any offenders should go to the petitioner or his successors, and the same provision was included in a privilege awarded to Bernardino Bocca of Milan in 1524. Heirs of an author could apply for legal protection when publishing his work. Soon after the deaths of Ermolao Barbaro and Giorgio Valla, relatives of theirs applied successfully to the Venetian state for protection of editions of works by the two humanists, and Pietro Giustino Filelfo obtained in 1483 sole rights in the Milanese state to publish certain works of his late great-uncle Francesco Filelfo.[92] So too the death of Ludovico Ariosto in July 1533, just after the investment of a large sum in publication of the third edition of the *Orlando furioso*, immediately led the poet's brother Galasso to try to retrieve the situation by seeking privileges in order to protect his family's interests in

Ludovico's works. In April 1535 the poet's heirs obtained a Venetian privilege for the printing of all his minor works 'so that the said heirs, rather than outsiders, should gain some profit from his honest efforts, as some recompense for the loss caused by his death'; if the ten-year copyright was infringed, they were to receive half of a fine of 1,000 ducats.[93] As has already been noted, the Venetian Council of Ten went further by decreeing in 1545 that an author's nearest heirs had to give their permission for the publication of his works. Writing, in short, could now be treated as an inheritable commodity, on a par with other kinds of property. Provided that a writer succeeded in operating the complex mechanisms at his disposal, print meant that his work acquired the potential status of an investment both for himself and for the future of his family.

CHAPTER 4

From pen to print: writers and their use of the press

In the preceding chapter we looked at the procedures which writers could use in order to control and take advantage of the publication of their works in print, in so far as it was possible to do so. We can now move on from these mechanisms to focus on the writers themselves and their use of print as opposed to the pen. After considering what attitudes, positive or negative, they showed towards the publication of their works in the new medium, we will go on to examine the ways in which print was used by a number of authors. On the basis of this evidence, we can then reach some general conclusions on the extent to which print proved important in the contexts of the aspirations and work of Italian writers in the Renaissance.

1 THE ATTITUDES OF WRITERS TOWARDS PRINT PUBLICATION

Old habits died hard. It took some time for writers to adjust their mentality to publishing their works in print and to working with the professionals who created and sold the printed text. Indeed, in certain respects manuscript publication could still seem a preferable option. There were two reasons to avoid print which may be termed practical. We have seen that writers might have to take on the burden and risk of providing an initial capital outlay if they wished to see their work through the press. Then there was the question of loss of control over the text itself. Although scribes were of course prone to alter, voluntarily or involuntarily, what they copied, transmission of a text in print was by no means more reliable. Writers could justifiably fear that a process which was overhasty, as was noted in chapter 1, and always to some extent profit-driven, would drag their texts inexorably away from their original. Editors, compositors and pressmen might all introduce deviations from the copy-text, and these would not necessarily be corrected at the proof stage. An example of the irritation which an author could express at the damage inflicted on his work by print publication is the lament which the humanist Marcantonio Sabellico addressed to Girolamo Donato about his *De Venetae urbis situ libri* (The site of Venice): 'I can scarcely say how much the carelessness, or rather the idleness of [the printers] has taken away from the true reading.'[1] Nor were scholars the only ones who saw themselves as victims, as one can see from the anger expressed by the poet Cassio da Narni in a stanza inserted at the end of his popular romance *La morte del Danese*, printed in Ferrara in 1521 by Lorenzo Rossi:

> Impressori ignoranti de più sorte
> han fatto errori, che più fiate mi hanno
> sdegnato sì che bramato ho la morte,
> per uscir for de sì strano affanno
> che mal da supportar più grave e forte
> credo non sia, né che faccia più danno,
> quanto veder lacerar gli suoi versi
> dagl'impressori in la ignorantia imersi.

(Ignorant printers of various sorts have several times made me so angry with their errors that I have longed for death, as a relief from an anxiety so strange that I believe there is no evil more heavy and hard to bear, nor one which does more harm, than to see one's verses torn to shreds by printers steeped in ignorance.)

Cassio's fury would have been all the greater because it was he who had paid for printing (see chapter 3, section 2). Even errors which he had corrected, presumably in proofs, were, he claimed, overlooked.[2] It was all too easy to use such accusations in order to counter possible criticisms of one's own shortcomings, but a cautious writer could well have considered that the risks of inaccurate diffusion in print outweighed any possible benefits. Further, at the end of chapter 2 we saw that writers in sixteenth-century Italy had increasingly to overcome problems of censorship before their works could be issued in approved form.

Writers might also be reluctant to go into print if they felt that a text was not yet in the finalized state which was required for reproduction on a wide scale. An author might judge that the matter or style of certain works made them more suitable for scribal publication. This might apply to works which commented on contemporary society and politics; examples are several texts by Niccolò Machiavelli. It might apply to some extent to the circulation of vernacular lyric poetry within a restricted circle, orally or in writing.[3] Theatrical texts, too, might be conceived solely for the audience before which they were performed.

Ariosto, for instance, wrote his comedies for the court, not for the general public, and in the prologue of the verse reworking of *La Cassaria* (1529) he complained bitterly that the earlier prose version had been stolen and given as booty to 'greedy printers' who then sold it cheap 'in the shops and the public markets'. The performed text of a drama might well have differed from the author's written text, but for several decades authors do not seem to have tried to control, or at least seem not to have been successful in controlling, the diffusion of one or the other. Only from the 1530s did publication of plays in print begin to take precedence, from the authorial viewpoint, over performance or to involve authors in preparation of a version revised for the occasion (and here it was Pietro Aretino, to whom we shall be returning in section 2, who characteristically pointed the way). Growing confidence in the medium of print among authors in general must have played its part here, though it has also been suggested that an influential factor was the cultural penetration, from the 1530s and 40s, of Aristotle's *Poetics*, which foregrounded the figure of the dramatist because of the importance given to tragedy.[4] For any type of work, a further consideration might be that, in order to be diffused in print, it needed a linguistic or stylistic revision which an author did not have the time or inclination to carry out. Thus in March 1532, during the very period when Ariosto was busily preparing for the printing of the third edition of his *Orlando furioso*, the poet took steps to prevent his four completed comedies from being printed because of 'the errors concerning language' which he recognized in them.[5]

A few writers may have been reluctant to contemplate using the press for publication because of moral or intellectual prejudice against it. Printing had been hailed by some on its arrival in Italy as a divine art, but, as can always happen with new media (one thinks of some reactions to television in the twentieth century), it was seen by others as an unwelcome intruder which could undermine the fabric of civilized society. At various moments in the Renaissance and beyond, printing was associated with a decline in standards of behaviour, of scholarship and of culture in general.[6] Some affected gentlemanly disdain for an activity which required mercantile resources and know-how and which, in an age when the term *meccanico* still had strongly negative connotations, involved a dirty and noisy manufacturing process, carried out in part by artisans with little or no education.[7] In higher social circles, the very idea of the diffusion of one's work to the masses might be looked at askance as indecorous. In Tudor England, print could be seen as having a stigma attached to it; a court poet of this period, it has been said, would have been 'embarrassed, if not insulted' if asked what he had published in print, for his purpose was 'the communication of experience within a limited group of intimate friends'.[8] The same was true of some Renaissance Italian intellectuals from similar backgrounds. The advice given in Castiglione's *Libro del cortegiano* was that the courtier should be skilled in writing both verse and prose, but that he should be circumspect about showing his work to an audience larger than just one trusted friend (I. 44).

There was also the possibility that a writer might not want his work published by any means. The Florentine historian Francesco Guicciardini ventured the opinion in the first redaction of his *Dialogo del reggimento di Firenze* (1521–5) that the time might come to publish this work before he grew old, but in the two subsequent redactions he stated simply that he was writing for 'recreation'. References to the reader in the texts of other writings of his, such as the *Ricordi* and his masterpiece, the *Storia d'Italia*, show they were not written for the author alone, but Guicciardini had no interest in their immediate diffusion, and nothing by him was printed in his lifetime.[9]

Yet from the point of view of writers, print publication had some potentially decisive advantages over scribal publication. It could establish their renown more firmly and spread it more widely and rapidly. Already in 1478 Bartolomeo della Fonte wrote that printers deserved praise because they conferred 'eternity' on writers both past and present, as well as serving scholars by providing quantities of books.[10] There was recognition, too, of the quality of permanence which printing bestowed on literary texts – it had rescued some classical works from the danger of oblivion – and of the uniformity which it could in theory bring to the circulation of a text. Another humanist, Bonaccorso, expressed in 1475 his appreciation of printed books not just for their lower price but also 'because when the impression and as it were the formation of such books is correct from the beginning, it runs through all the copies always in the same order, with scarcely the possibility of error – a thing which in manuscripts is apt to turn out very differently'.[11] Above all, as we saw in chapter 3, writers now had the possibility of profiting not only from the continuing system of patronage but also from the sale of their work to the public or even to a printer.

2 PRINT IN THE CAREERS OF WRITERS

Let us now look at some case studies of how, in practice, print was used in the context of the careers of writers. We can begin with some examples of fifteenth-century writers, most of them humanists, whose sociocultural status put them in a strong position to exploit the opportunities of the press. Of those working in Milan, the first to use print in order to enhance his own reputation was, perhaps surprisingly, the oldest of them all, Francesco Filelfo (1398–1481).[12] He did not write specifically for the new medium but exploited it to gain favour or publicity, sometimes in a rather underhand way. In 1475, it seems, he commissioned in Milan the printing of an earlier work of his but asked for the colophon to be postdated and to state that the edition had been printed in Rome, doubtless because he was due to take up a lectureship in that city and wanted some ostensibly local products to present or to sell more easily. He manipulated the evidence of a colophon again when his Latin translation of Xenophon's *Cyropaedia* (for which he had received 400 ducats in 1469, as a reward for dedicating it to Pope Paul II) was printed in Milan in 1471: some copies have a colophon which claims that they were printed in Rome, where Filelfo was planning to take up residence. Then, at the very end of Filelfo's life, both he and a former pupil, Giorgio Merula, used the press to publicize an exchange of abusive letters.[13]

In Florence, the first writer in the dominant literary circle of the Medici family to 'break the ice' (to use Ridolfi's image) by venturing into print was the philosopher Marsilio Ficino (1433–99).[14] Of the thirteen works of his which were printed during his lifetime, only two were published apparently without the author's knowledge and outside Florence or Venice. In other cases, the pattern of publication in print was very similar to that of publication in manuscript. Ficino would revise a work carefully and either prepare or arrange for the preparation of the 'archetype' – in the contemporary sense explained in chapter 3, section 1 – which was to be reproduced by scribe or printer (see fig. 11). In the case of at least two printed editions, though, it seems he did not correct proofs, since he complained about their inaccuracy. Just as rich friends of Ficino's paid the expenses of dedication manuscripts, so his supporters would act as intermediaries between him and the printing industry, footing the bill for paper and labour.[15] At least six of the early editions of his works were financed by men such as Francesco Berlinghieri, Filippo Valori, Lorenzo de' Medici (see again fig. 11), Piero del Nero and Girolamo Biondo. Biondo was very probably also the financer of the Aldine edition of Ficino's translations from Iamblichus and others (1497).[16] But Ficino was always allowed to insert his own dedications, and in at least one case (his translation of Plotinus, 1492) he was provided with a vellum copy to present to Cardinal Giovanni de' Medici.[17] It is possible that the same pattern of financing applied to most other Florentine first editions of Ficino's works between 1475 and 1496. Only one was definitely printed at the expense of a press, and that was a practical work, the *Consiglio contro la pestilenza*, probably compiled by someone else and brought out by the Ripoli press in 1481.[18]

Another member of the Medicean circle who took the opportunity to have his works published in print, both in Florence and elsewhere, was the leading scholar of the age, Angelo Poliziano (1454–94). We do not know how his scholarly works printed in Florence from 1482 onwards were financed, but his first work to be printed, an account of the unsuccessful conspiracy of the Pazzi family against the Medici in 1478, was part of a publicity campaign in print which was orchestrated by Lorenzo himself in order to counter the pope's own use of the press for propaganda.[19] No manuscript earlier than the first edition is known, and it is therefore likely that the author's 'archetype' was delivered direct to the printing house and was discarded there. Then, between 1480 and 1482, Poliziano prepared a revised edition for printing in Rome.[20] His first *Miscellanea*, a discussion of one hundred questions of classical scholarship, was most probably also conceived for the press, since no manuscript evidence earlier than the first edition of 1489 survives. At the very end of Poliziano's life, from June 1491 onwards, a number of his works were printed in Bologna with the assistance of an opportunist editorial collaborator, Alessandro Sarti. Most of these editions must have come out without Poliziano's knowledge or consent. However, he certainly authorized Sarti's edition of his Latin translation of Herodian. In the summer of 1494, he was planning the printing of his collection of Latin letters and perhaps other works, probably again through the agency of Sarti, and a book of Greek and Latin epigrams. The project for the volume of letters went ahead even after the scholar's untimely death in September of that year, but had to be abandoned when its Bolognese printer died in 1496.[21]

But the author most often printed by Florentine presses in the Quattrocento came from Ferrara: the Dominican friar and preacher Girolamo Savonarola. Over one hundred incunables, more than 14 per cent of the surviving output of Florence, contain works written by him or sermons copied down by others while he delivered them. Between 1495 and the friar's execution in 1498, editions of his works came out at the average rate of one every fortnight. The use of the press by Savonarola and his supporters was an integral part of the campaign to diffuse his message, a necessary corollary to his use of the pulpit. In a sermon of 1496 he urged the printing of an earlier sermon: 'Start to get that book on the art of a good death printed, and make sure you include those illustrations' ('Comincia a porre a stampa quello libro dell'arte del ben morire, fa' che tu ne abbi uno che vi sia di quelle figure').[22] He referred in his *Apologia dei Frati di San Marco* (printed in about 1497) to a forthcoming edition of 'our book on the Triumph of the Cross'. In at least some cases, the friar did not use the press directly: he needed the help of others who would mediate with the printers on his behalf by acting as patron-publishers. One of these was a faithful follower, the notary Lorenzo Violi, who took down some of Savonarola's sermons and paid for their printing from 1496 until well after the friar's death.[23] The printing of four of the friar's works in 1496 (one of them both in Latin and in the vernacular) was commissioned by the bookseller and publisher Piero Pacini, and, given this concentration of editions, Pacini's motives could have been religious as well as, or rather than, purely commercial.[24]

In late Quattrocento Venice, the foremost manipulator of the power of print publication among writers was Marcantonio Sabellico (c. 1436–1506). He, it has been suggested, 'probably deserves the title usually reserved for Erasmus – that of being the first writer to make a career from the new medium'.[25] When he came to have his twelve books of letters printed, he professed a lack of enthusiasm about releasing what he termed these base slaves from his house.[26] Yet the academic success which he enjoyed in Venice owed much to the ways in which he took advantage of the press.[27] Not only did he ensure publicity for his works through their circulation in print (even though he had cause to complain about printers' carelessness), but he seized the chance to improve his prospects of patronage and advancement by studding his printed texts with references to powerful families, by accompanying them with poems or letters which placed the works within an impressive network of patrician or academic contacts, and by sending gift copies of works such as the first part of his *Enneades*, a voluminous history of the world, to Italian princes and cardinals.[28] Sabellico appears to have funded the *Enneades* by himself (his privilege application of 1497 states that he 'had it printed'), but at least one recipient of a copy, Lodovico Sforza, rewarded him generously with fifty gold coins. On other occasions he may have been fortunate enough to find financial backing through the agency of middlemen such as the Brescian bookseller-publisher Antonio Moreto.[29]

The Cinquecento did not bring major changes in the underlying economic relationship between writers and printers, but it did increase the confidence with which writers used print. At the start of the century there could be a conflict between a writer's awareness of the benefits of print and an inhibiting feeling that it was somehow indecorous to demonstrate this awareness too openly. Thus Pietro Bembo, we saw in chapter 3, preferred in public to keep up the fiction that he was a gentleman amateur and that others were the publishers of his works. Yet it was he who commissioned the Aldine Petrarch of 1501, edited by himself, and he may have formed a joint company for the occasion with Aldo.[30] It was Bembo, too, who ordered his *Prose della volgar lingua* to be printed by Giovanni Tacuino in 1525, arranged for the supply of suitable paper, asked for intermediaries to obtain privileges in other states, and used all his influence to ensure that the perpetrator of a Venetian pirate edition was suitably punished. Tacuino was apparently unwilling to take on the work unless Bembo obtained privileges to prevent plagiarism in other states, and this might mean that author and printer had entered into a partnership.[31] In 1530, when he may have been in partnership with Nicolò Zoppino, Bembo took steps to ensure that copies of editions of his works were distributed to booksellers in Rome.[32] The existence of a pirated edition of the *Prose* suggests that Bembo was not acting as his own publisher out of necessity, at least on this occasion; he evidently preferred self-publication in order to retain control over the accuracy and physical appearance of the end product, as well as over profits.

Only three of the works of Niccolò Machiavelli (1469–1527) were published through the medium of print during his lifetime. The first was the *Decennale*, a historical narrative in *terza rima*, first published in manuscript in 1504 with a dedication to Alamanno Salviati and then printed, without that dedication, in 1506 at the expense of the author's colleague in the Florentine chancery, Agostino Vespucci. The second was his classicizing comedy *Mandragola*, printed in about 1518, but – typically for a theatrical work in these years – with no sign that Machiavelli was the author or in any way involved in the edition. The third, in 1521, was his dialogue *Arte della guerra* (Art of war), dedicated to Lorenzo Strozzi, a man whose generosity is praised by Machiavelli and who may well, like Vespucci earlier, have acted as his patron-publisher. Machiavelli sent gift copies of the *Decennale* and the *Arte della guerra* to at least one influential figure in each case, Ercole Bentivoglio and Cardinal Giovanni Salviati.[33] He was thus happy to use print publication on occasion. However, his other major prose works, *Il principe*, the *Discorsi su Tito Livio*, and the *Istorie fiorentine*, remained in manuscript until after his death. Machiavelli did not intend to keep them to himself or even within a closed circle of readers but can clearly be said to have 'published' them; even though he did not do so in the 'strong' sense, as defined by Harold Love, of providing large numbers of copies, he certainly did so in the 'weak' sense that he surrendered control over the future use of the manuscript supplied by him and that there was 'some practical likelihood of the text entering public channels of communication'.[34] The second and third of these works were in effect published when presented to their dedicatees, and *Il principe* was first published when the author made it available in such a way that it could reach a network of people with shared interests both within and outside the Florentine state. In the case of *Il principe*, we know that this 'author publication' was followed by the two other main modes of scribal publication defined by Love: entrepreneurial publication, or copying for sale by people other than the author (including at least the scribes Biagio Buonaccorsi, a close friend and former colleague of Machiavelli's, and Genesius de la Barrera), and user publication, or non-commercial replication for private use.[35] Why, then, did Machiavelli use print publication so selectively? The answer is probably not that the author had problems of funding (he seems to have been able to find resourceful patrons when he wished to do so) but because he, and no doubt others too, felt that, in Florence at least, circulation in manuscript was more appropriate for works of a controversial, anti-establishment nature. In the particular case of *Il principe*, it could well be that Machiavelli simply felt that the work would not achieve its purposes if he wrote it for the press. First of all, we know, from the reactions of the people who read it in the twenty years before it was printed, that its teachings could be admired and imitated in private, manuscript writings but were rejected in the more public context of print. Secondly, if the work had been printed, Machiavelli would have felt obliged to adopt a more stiffly formal style, as he did later in the *Arte della guerra*; but part of his strategy in *Il principe*, it seems, was precisely to use a deliberately informal, unadorned style, in order to shock his readers into realizing that the advice contained in *this* treatise on princes was closer to everyday reality than that of earlier treatises, whose statecraft was based on an imaginary world.[36]

While the example of Machiavelli demonstrates the continuing importance, in certain circumstances, of scribal publication, that of Ludovico Ariosto (1474–1533) and his continuation of Boiardo's chivalric epic, the *Orlando furioso*, underlines the growing importance which print publication was acquiring for writers. When he came to have the first version printed, he showed great resourcefulness in organizing the whole operation by himself from start to finish, using a decidedly hands-on approach and showing no inhibition about revealing, for example in his Venetian privilege request, his desire to receive remuneration for his efforts.[37] In 1515 he organized the importing of two hundred reams of paper from Lake Garda; he applied successfully for privileges in various Italian states and in France; and no doubt he commissioned and oversaw the printing itself, carried out in Ferrara between October 1515 and April 1516. All this was done without financial assistance from the court, even though Ariosto was at this time in the service of Cardinal Ippolito d'Este, brother of Duke Alfonso. It is significant that both the duke and the cardinal had to buy copies of the completed edition for themselves. Once printing was complete, Ariosto arranged for sales to the general public. In a letter of May 1516, Ippolito Calandra recounts how Ariosto arrived in Mantua with a chest full of copies; he presented three of them to the marquis, Francesco Gonzaga, and his family, but he wanted to arrange for the others, still unbound, to be sold ('li altri lui li vole fare vendere'). Ariosto himself pointed out to Equicola in 1520 that he had received less money than he had expected from sales in Mantua: either the bookseller acting on his behalf had not sold all his stock or – more probably, since the edition had, as far as he knew, sold out elsewhere in Italy – the bookseller was keeping the takings for himself.[38] A plausible estimate, based on the quantity of paper imported, is that 1,300 copies of the 1516 edition were printed, and we know that one copy cost 1 lira unbound (binding put the price up by 40 per cent or more). Even if only 10 per cent of the income from sales went into the poet's pocket, his profit would still have been over half of his official annual court salary of 240 lire, and close to the 150 lire which he claimed to receive in reality.[39]

Encouraged by the commercial and critical success of this first edition, Ariosto organized a second, including some linguistic revisions.[40] Needing cash to finance at least part of the operation, he borrowed 100 lire in November 1520 from a widow, Antonia del Panza. Printing was completed rapidly (and hence with more errors than usual) by the following February. Ariosto sold 100 copies for 60 lire, or 12 soldi each, to a local stationer who undertook to sell them at no more than 16 soldi each (20 per cent cheaper than the 1516 edition) and to buy any further copies from the author at the same price. We know too that Ariosto got a nobleman to oversee sales in Genoa, and he is likely to have organized sales in other cities through a combination of personal contacts and booksellers. Again, business was brisk, and he was able to pay off his loan, with 12 per cent interest, in March 1523.

Production and distribution of the third edition of the *Furioso*, now expanded from forty to forty-six canti, were organized along the same lines.[41] Ariosto protected his investment by obtaining several privileges. In early 1532 he set about purchasing a supply of paper; this time he arranged for the transport of no fewer than four hundred reams, which (if they were all used) would have led to a print run of around 2,750 copies, a bold investment on the poet's part. He met the bill of 300 lire from his paper supplier by transferring to him an advance payment of his court salary, equivalent to one and a quarter years. He was involved in correcting proofs and continued to introduce changes during this opportunity for surveillance of which his fellow-courtier and imitator Cassio da Narni had failed to take advantage.[42] Printing was completed at the beginning of October. As before, Ariosto took charge of sales. He also arranged for the printing of some copies on vellum which he sent to influential figures such as Duke Alfonso, Federico Gonzaga and Isabella d'Este.

This gift-giving to the powerful was evidently an important part of Ariosto's strategy in making use of his creation. Yet, as far as one can judge, he was also unprecedentedly determined to use publication through print in order to obtain direct pecuniary reward for his talent by circulating his work among a wider public. To what extent, then, one might ask, is this new attitude to publication reflected in his writings? In the first place, it may help to explain a feature of the narrative technique of the *Furioso* on which critics have commented: the decreased use, in comparison with other authors of romances, of the fiction that the poet is reciting his work to a specific audience.[43] Boiardo had begun his *Orlando innamorato* with an appeal for quiet addressed in the second person plural to a supposed gathering of 'lords and knights'. Ariosto, in contrast, starts by setting out his central subject matter (the war between Charlemagne and Agramante, the madness of Orlando), before turning to his master, Cardinal Ippolito, and gratefully offering as a gift his 'opera d'inchiostro' (work of ink), which will include the story of the Estense ancestor Ruggiero. One is, of course, intended to take this ink to be that used in the original act of composition, as later references to Ariosto's pen make clear (XIV. 108, XV. 9, XXIX. 2), but the author always intended the diffusion of the complete work, both to the Estensi and to the general public, to depend on printer's ink.[44] Another aspect of Ariosto's technique which shows the writer adapting to a situation in which his poem would be read by all, rather than heard by a few, is his use of canto divisions. He follows tradition in using the ending of the canto, originally representing a unit of oral performance, in order to create cliff-hanging suspense. But, as Peter Brand has pointed out, the suspension of excitement would have little significance for a reader who had only to turn the page; and so Ariosto uses the opening stanzas of the next canto to force the reader's attention away from the narrative, stepping outside the framework of the poem and commenting on its implications.[45]

In the second place, the fact that Ariosto devoted so much time and money to the publication of his poem can only have heightened his strong sense of resentment at the lack of esteem which his masters showed for his gifts as a writer. Although Ippolito is portrayed at the end of the *Furioso* as surrounded by philosophers, poets and musicians, elsewhere Ariosto puts more emphasis on the other side of the coin of patronage. Princes are seen to be courted by those who wish to win their favour, but they have neither the ability to discern true poets nor the generosity to reward them. Among the objects lost on earth which Astolfo sees stored on the moon, a pile of hooks of gold and silver represents the gifts which are given to miserly masters in the hope of reward, nooses hidden in garlands are acts of flattery, and the verses written in praise of lords are now seen to be cicadas which have swollen and burst with the sheer effort of singing too hard (XXXIV. 77). When the figure of Time empties names into the river Lethe at the start of canto XXXV, croaking crows and vultures, representing flattering courtiers, gather up some of the names but soon drop them again. Two white swans alone manage to carry some to the temple of Immortality; they are the true poets, but they are few, partly because their talent is rare, partly through the miserliness of lords (XXXV. 23). In print, but outside the text of the poem, Ariosto gave further prominence to the theme of ingratitude by using as his motto the biblical phrase 'Pro bono malum' (Evil in return for good), accompanied in the first two editions by an emblem of bees being smoked out of a log, and by including in some copies of the 1532 edition a woodcut of a ewe suckling a wolf cub.[46] In contrast with Lodovici's practice in 1535 (see fig. 4), then, Ariosto used woodcuts to refer to the frustrations rather than to the benefits of patronage. In 1517, immediately after the publication of the first edition of the *Furioso*, a crisis in Ariosto's life seemed to justify his sense of being unappreciated. When he preferred not to accompany Ippolito to Hungary, he was dismissed from the cardinal's service and lost his court salary. He gave vent in his first *Satira* (especially lines 88–108, 139–44) to his bitterness over his treatment at court: if he had received any reward, it was not because of his poetry, and Ippolito considered relatively unimportant the praise for him which it contained.

Through this satire runs the theme of the loss of liberty which a courtier's life implies (I. 115–20, 262–5), and in other satires Ariosto reveals his desire for enough wealth to flee the cage-like servitude of the court (III. 31–42, VII. 37–42). Print must have represented his main hope of escape: he was the first Italian writer openly to take advantage of the diffusion of his work through the hands of printers and booksellers to a genuinely appreciative wider public in order to achieve, if not a means of independence, then at least a source of income which would make him less dependent on the whims of his superiors. He must have placed particular hopes in the 1532 edition, because of its large print run. Unfortunately, the ill health which led to his death in July 1533 prevented him from deriving any benefits from it. As his brother Galasso wrote to Bembo soon afterwards, 'because of his illness three-quarters of the books have remained in the hands of his heirs, since they have not been sold'.[47]

In contrast with Ariosto, who had no hesitation over the publication of the *Furioso*, Baldesar Castiglione (1478–1529) claimed at first to be somewhat uncertain whether his *Libro del cortegiano* was ready to be released beyond a close circle of friends.[48] In the dedication of the first edition, completed in Venice in April 1528, he insisted that he had not had time to revise his dialogue to his satisfaction but had been practically forced into issuing it in print. He had given a manuscript to a friend, Vittoria Colonna; she, breaking a promise, had had a large part of the work copied, and this part had fallen into the hands of some people in Naples who wanted to have it printed. Castiglione preferred, he said, to revise the book hastily with the intention of publishing it ('publicarlo') himself, considering this the lesser of two evils. He had, in fact, considered 'letting it go' as early as September 1518: the question in his mind seems to have been not whether to publish the work but when it would be ready to be issued, and it is difficult to suppose that he was not contemplating having it printed. By early 1525 he had practically made up his mind. He was then in Madrid as papal nuncio, and from there he wrote in April to tell a friend in Italy that he was more eager than ever to 'let the *Cortegiano* go'. At this point he could still envisage having copies transcribed for friends, as he did when writing to a countess in June 1525. Between March and April 1527 he sent his manuscript to be printed in Venice by the Aldine press, the most prestigious in the city. Printing began in late November 1527, and privilege requests were granted in February and March 1528. The papal privilege referred to Castiglione's receiving 'the fruits of his labours' and stated that he would receive half of the 500-ducat fine to be imposed on offenders.

Castiglione's original intentions for the execution of the work, as he summarized them in a letter to his agent dated 9 April 1527, were to have 1,030 copies printed. He would pay the cost of half of the first 1,000, and also of 30 to be printed on royal paper. Of his 530 copies, 130 were to be used as gifts and 400 to be sold through a bookseller in order to cover expenses or to make a profit if possible. His agent reported on the following 21 November that the printers recommended a run of 2,000 and that they proposed to produce 130 for Castiglione at his own expense and the rest at theirs. Further, they wished the text to be revised and punctuated by Giovan Francesco Valerio, a friend of Bembo's: by now printers evidently linked the commercial success of an edition with linguistic correctness of the sort which Ariosto was soon to impose on the 1532 *Furioso*.[49] The outcome of the negotiations with the press is uncertain. An account probably written in 1528 suggests that the result may have been a compromise with the author's original proposal: Castiglione purchased the paper for 500 copies and received only 150. However, he was certainly thinking at some point about the costs and potential profits if he were to take a half share in a print run of 2,000, since he noted that paper would cost 140 ducats and printing as much again, and he estimated the amounts that could be earned from selling 1,000 copies at prices from 6 marcelli each, which would have brought in a profitable 480 ducats, down to 2 marcelli each, which would have earned a loss-making 160 ducats.[50]

It is not known whether Castiglione or his printers decided on the appearance of the work, an imposing folio with roman type, in the tradition of the Aldine editions of the 1490s rather than of the Cinquecento, but it would not be surprising if this was Castiglione's choice. Making a good first impression was, after all, one of his main recommendations to the courtier (II. 32–6). He certainly attached great importance to the production and distribution of gift copies, and on this he sent more detailed instructions to his agent in April 1528. Of the hundred copies which he now reckoned were to be his, thirty were to be on royal paper and one on vellum. This last copy was to receive the finest possible binding, Castiglione insisted, and was to be sent to Spain

– no doubt it was intended for the emperor Charles V – together with others. Of the copies remaining in Italy, he specified that some were to be bound and presented to figures such as the marquis and marchioness of Mantua and the duchess of Urbino. Castiglione thus took a very close interest in every aspect of the publication of the *Libro del Cortegiano*, even though he was in Spain. He made every effort to exploit his investment of time and money: he would have liked to cover his costs, at the very least, and he also wished to use the time-honoured strategy of presenting copies to those in power and to friends in order to further his personal relationships and his standing. The *Cortegiano* proved, like the *Orlando furioso*, to be one of the best-sellers of the century; however, Castiglione's death in February 1529 prevented him too from reaping the full rewards of his dealings with the printing industry.

The background of Pietro Aretino (1492–1556) provides a strong contrast with that of Castiglione. He was of obscure birth, the son of a cobbler, and, though he too came to converse with great figures such as Charles V, he based his career on his skill with words rather than on success in the world of courts. He achieved his early success mainly through the sharpness of his wit, in conversation as well as with his pen. Ariosto famously characterized him in the *Furioso* of 1532 through the fear which he could arouse in the great, calling him 'the scourge of princes' (XLVI. 14). But Aretino also used praise of the powerful as a means of self-advancement, and in 1524–5 the fashionable Roman press of Ludovico degli Arrighi brought out two editions of poems by him in praise of Pope Clement VII and his datary, Gian Matteo Giberti. In 1527 Aretino moved away from court circles to Venice. His first major literary project there was, ironically, in the courtly tradition, a continuation of Ariosto's *Furioso* called the *Marfisa*, begun for Federico Gonzaga. The long-suffering marquis's patronage came to an end in 1531, however, and despite Aretino's claims to be enjoying a rich style of life thanks to the generosity of rulers, he was in fact in some financial difficulties. In 1533–4 came a marked change of tactics. Previously, most of Aretino's writings had been circulated through scribal publication, but from this moment on he began to take full advantage of the resources of the Venetian presses in order to earn his living.[51]

Even for someone in his lowly social position, Aretino was daringly innovative in flaunting the income that he earned in one way or another from his publications. At the end of the dream of Parnassus which he describes in a letter of 1537, he is offered various poetic crowns but refuses them all in favour of 'a privilege by virtue of which I can sell or pawn the talent which the heavens have showered upon me'.[52] Publication was his means of survival. Francesco Marcolini brought out Aretino's first two books of letters, but because the printer was absent from Venice, Aretino had to turn elsewhere for the printing of the third book, explaining that he 'could not live without eating'.[53] Yet his pride led him to insist that his rewards were not tarnished by commerce. Earlier, on 22 June 1537, Aretino had declined to take any direct profit from Marcolini for the sales of his first book of letters. To have the books which one derives from one's imagination printed at one's own expense and to have them sold on one's behalf was, he wrote, like eating one's own limbs or prostituting one's art. His aim, rather, was to use his printed works to seek patronage. 'With God's help', he said, 'I want the courtesy of princes to pay for the labours of my writing, and not the poverty of those who buy them . . . If someone wants to make profits, let him learn to be a merchant; he can become a bookseller and give up the name of poet.'[54] In 1538 he repeated to Bembo that his method of winning 'corone d'auro e non di lauro' (crowns of gold and not of laurel) was 'to foster the pride of the great with great praise, holding them ever aloft with the wings of hyperbole'.[55]

As a man who had risen from obscurity, then, Aretino could afford to be disarmingly frank about his desire to earn gold from his writings, but he was shrewd enough to counterbalance this openness with a paradoxically conservative contempt for mercantile profits. His technique was to use and develop indirect means of benefiting from publication. Two of these devices were the traditional, respectable ones of presentation and dedication. As soon as his three *canzoni* on papal politics were printed in Rome between late 1524 and early 1525, he promised a copy to Federico Gonzaga and linked his gift with a request for shirts embroidered with gold and silk and for gold bonnets; he was greatly annoyed that the nuns who made them did not deliver them until March.[56] Like Ariosto and Castiglione, he took great care over the preparation of dedication copies: for instance, he had a copy of his *Stanze in lode de la Sirena*, for presentation to the empress Isabella, decorated by the miniaturist Iacopo del Giallo; in return he received a gift of 300 scudi.[57] Dedications could lead to gifts such as a gold chain and a silk robe.[58] Aretino liked to stress his own largesse, portraying it even as prodigality, and so he could himself show generosity by using a dedication as a thank offering for a gift, as he did with his first book of letters (1538).[59] Gaining in impudence, in 1546 he successfully asked a secretary of Cosimo de' Medici's to beg the duke not to delay in rewarding him for the dedication of his third book of letters, suggesting with tongue in cheek that he could reasonably hope for the sum of 100 scudi annually.[60] In the same year, he was guilty of some dedicatory double-dealing. He offered his tragedy *Orazia* to Pier Luigi Farnese, duke of Parma and Piacenza, in order to encourage him to send a promised gift of 150 scudi; once he had received this sum, he promptly switched the dedication to Pier Luigi's father, Pope Paul III.[61]

Aretino's other and more innovative technique, linked to that of using dedications but partly independent of it, was to insert in his printed works open references to the giving or withholding of gifts to himself. The kind of transaction which was previously carried out behind the scenes was now spotlighted for the public gaze. He inserted expressions of gratitude to his patrons in two comedies, *Il Marescalco* (v. 3) and *La Cortigiana* (prologue), when they were revised for printing in 1533–4. But the main vehicles for his manipulation of the powerful were the six books of letters printed between 1538 and 1557. Here he would give ostentatious thanks for gifts actually received, carefully specifying the sum of money or the exact nature of the gift. He boasted in 1541 that he received 600 scudi a year in pensions and another 1,000 from his writing, in January 1544 that the alchemy of his pen had extracted over 25,000 scudi from princes since his arrival in Venice, and in September 1544 that he had already received 1,700 scudi in that year alone.[62] In return, his benefactors received wide publicity for their generosity, something which had not normally happened in the previous dealings of patrons with writers. On the other hand, Aretino could also use his letters to hint at miserliness on his patrons' part. Several letters, for example, refer to difficulties in obtaining the annual pensions which he was supposed to receive from the emperor, the king of France and the prince of Salerno. To arouse fear of losing face, whether in a bullying or a wheedling manner, was thus another weapon in his armoury, and he openly acknowledged that he forced the princes of his day to treat him favourably with continual tributes of gold.[63] Ariosto, we saw, felt that rulers had too little awareness of the power of the pen to immortalize, but Aretino had the utmost confidence that his militia of inks was mightier than any sword: whether the powerful liked the fact or not, his pen paid others in the coinage of honour or shame.[64] He believed this outspokenness had wrought a transformation in the status accorded not only to himself but to all who lived by artistic skill. 'Before I began to attack the reputation [of lords]', he wrote in 1537, 'men of talent had to beg for the basic necessities of life'; now, thanks to him alone, talent wears brocade, drinks in gold cups, has necklaces and money, rides like a queen, is served as an empress and revered as a goddess.[65]

Aretino focused his readers' attention on his use of the printed word to prise open the purses of the rich; but who subsidized the printing of his works in the first place? A letter of his to an Aretine friend and possibly former teacher, Giovanni Lappoli, states as a general rule that no author's works are accepted by printers free of charge and that he will receive no satisfaction from them unless he pays what they demand.[66] Aretino was prepared to do this with his own works. He apparently expected to make a profitable investment in the printing of his epic *Marfisa*: in 1529 he asked for ten-year privileges for the work from the pope and the emperor, saying that 'I have hopes that the printing will reward me', and, when putting on a brave face after his requests were refused, he conceded that this setback might deprive him of 'the profit of some scudi'.[67] He made several Venetian privilege requests in his own name.[68] However, in writing to Lappoli he was trying to pour cold water on a mediocre poet's aspirations, and he omitted to mention the possibility, on which he seems to have been able to count at times, that printing costs might be met by others, who might or might not be professionally linked with the book trade. The letter of 22 June 1537 to Marcolini, already quoted, has to be treated with caution, because it was part of Aretino's campaign to create an image of himself as aloof from the commercial aspects of publication, and because in any case the letter was withdrawn five years later, which suggests that he may have decided to derive profits from sales after all; but his opening reference to giving Marcolini his first book of letters, as he had previously done with his other works, does suggest that Marcolini financed (and hence probably benefited from) the printing of a series of works by Aretino, some printed by Giovanni Antonio Nicolini da Sabbio at Marcolini's expense, others printed by Marcolini himself.[69] Marcolini requested Venetian privileges for various works of Aretino's in 1534 and again in 1541–2.[70] At least two other publishers commissioned editions of the first book of letters in 1539 – Federico Torresani and Venturino Ruffinelli – but they may have been acting without the author's approval. On the other hand, Aretino may have sanctioned the publishing of two of his works in 1543 by the perfumer Biagio Perugino or Biagio Paternostraio, since Biagio made privilege requests for them and Aretino addressed friendly letters to him.[71] During and after Marcolini's absence from Venice in 1545–9, Aretino looked to other professional publishers, Melchior Sessa and Andrea Arrivabene.[72] But an important part was also played by patrons who either paid printing costs or gave Aretino money in order to help him prepare works destined for the press. In the former category comes Bernardo Valdaura, dedicatee of the *Dialogo . . . nel quale la Nanna . . . insegna a la Pippa*, who evidently gave Aretino 40 scudi to pay Marcolini to print the work in 1536 and in return kept the copies in order to sell them himself.[73] When Aretino had three of his religious works reprinted in 1551, costs were paid by Guidobaldo II della Rovere, duke of Urbino. But the production of this edition and of a companion edition of 1552 was also facilitated by a gift of money from Baldovino del Monte, brother of the dedicatee, Pope Julius III. Aretino presented copies to Duke Cosimo de' Medici, predictably demanding a gift in return.[74] Similarly, the first edition of his life of Saint Catherine of Alexandria, brought out by an unknown printer in 1540, had been promoted by the commissioning of the work by Alfonso d'Avalos. To mark the fulfilment of this commission, Aretino sent to his patron a printed text, not a manuscript. However, even though the commission was apparently formalized by a contract, payment of Aretino's fee was withheld in 1542 with the excuse that he was taking too long to complete his life of Saint Thomas Aquinas.[75]

Aretino was unique in his ability to use his writings in order to exert leverage on patrons, but his literary and social success played a leading part in promoting new opportunities for other Italian writers from the 1530s onwards. In an Italy whose social foundations had been shaken by over three decades of political upheaval, he showed that a writer without advantages of birth, and working outside, though still in contact with, the social framework of the court, could make opportunistic use of the press as an instant medium of diffusion for a range of works, from ribald dialogue to biographies of saints, which were destined to satisfy the appetites of quite different publics, and he flaunted the fact that this activity could be a powerful, if indirect, means of profit. His rise to fame was an incentive to other outspoken authors such as Franco, Doni and Lando.[76] Outside Venice, too, there was a widening of the social circles from which successful authors might emerge, as in the case of the self-educated Florentine cobbler Giovan Battista Gelli.

At the same time as Aretino's career was blossoming, a younger member of his circle, Lodovico Dolce (1508–68), an ordinary citizen of Venice and not a patrician, was showing that Venetian presses now offered other means for writers to make a name and earn some income. As with Aretino, Dolce's first works to be printed (from 1532 onwards) were verse compositions, and he continued to produce works in his own name throughout his life. But from 1535 he developed a parallel career as an editor of vernacular texts by earlier or living authors, from Dante to Aretino himself, and as a translator or adapter of texts by classical authors. In 1542 he began a long collaboration with the dominant printer of mid-Cinquecento Venice, Gabriele Giolito, at whose expense Dolce was stated to be living in 1553. The example set by Dolce, in conjunction with the printers who employed him, was soon followed by others who based their careers largely on regular collaboration with the Venetian press as editors, translators and anthologizers: men such as Antonio Brucioli, Lodovico Domenichi, Girolamo Ruscelli and Francesco Sansovino. The links between the presses and these *poligrafi*, as they are generally known because of their versatility, were so strong that Doni and Sansovino came to run their own printing houses in Florence and Venice respectively. As we shall see in chapter 6, section 2, from a reader's point of view the importance of their contribution lay first in the guidance which they offered to the less experienced in understanding and imitating vernacular classics. They helped to further the transition from what Petrucci has termed the 'author's book' evolved during the late Middle Ages to the 'publisher's book' ('libro d'editore' or 'libro editoriale') typical of the sixteenth century, often containing a wealth (not to say a surfeit) of extratextual material provided by people other than the author.[77] They also made available a range of classical works in vernacular translation, though the quality of their work in this area could be compromised by their limitations as scholars or by the sheer pressure of trying to meet printers' deadlines.[78]

One of the contemporary authors edited by Dolce was Bernardo Tasso (1493–1569). In 1554–5 his first four books of *Rime* were brought out by Gabriele Giolito, apparently at the printer's expense, since all that Bernardo asked of him, through Dolce, was that the few copies due to him for presentation should be printed on paper of special quality, for which he was willing to pay himself.[79] Bernardo was disappointed with Dolce's editorial work, but the Venetian was nevertheless one of those to whom the poet turned for support when he came to publish his epic *Amadigi*.[80] This poem had been begun in 1542–3, when Bernardo was in the service of Ferrante Sanseverino, prince of Salerno, and the complex process of composition and publication was bound up with the consequences of the prince's defection from the Spanish to the French cause in 1552. Bernardo followed Sanseverino, giving up his property in Naples and his wife Porzia's as yet unpaid dowry, but in 1556–8, after Porzia's death, he joined the court of Urbino, which was allied to Spain.

He resolved to publish the *Amadigi*, its pro-French references now removed, and dedicate it to the Spanish king, Philip II, in the hope that this would be of advantage to himself and his family. In June 1557 he wrote that he was planning to have the poem produced at his own expense so as to derive profit and benefit ('utile, e beneficio') for his innocent son Torquato.[81] He was invited in the following January to have it printed at the expense of the newly formed Accademia Veneziana, but he replied that, precisely because he was poor, he preferred to publish it himself, sparing no expense on illustration, paper and so on, 'having, as a prudent father, to think of my offspring's benefit'.[82] Bernardo obtained a set of privileges himself. However, when he realized that printing costs might be as high as 275 ducats, he made a five-year agreement with Gabriele Giolito according to which printer and author were to share both the costs (Bernardo's contribution came to 150 ducats) and the profits from a print run of 1,200 copies. Bernardo was, then, planning for income from sales, but his main expectation of benefit lay in the bounty of King Philip.[83] In July 1559 his faith in the power of dedication was high: he had heard a rumour that the king was only waiting for the *Amadigi* in order to restore Porzia's dowry, probably so that he would not have to make a further gift on receiving the poem.[84] Bernardo also expected benefit from a third source, presentation copies. He had the paper for these made specially and was very upset in November 1559 when floods near Lake Garda carried it and the fulling mills away, so that printing had to be postponed until spring.[85] Of the 600 copies due to him, he had 154 bound for presentation at an extra cost of 30 ducats; no doubt many of the recipients were among the contemporaries whose names he had woven into the narrative and who included knights, rulers, cardinals, noble men and women, writers, scholars, and (perhaps with an eye on their purses) merchants and bankers.

Yet Bernardo Tasso complained that he got little tangible benefit from his investment of time and money in the *Amadigi*. He sold off some of his remaining 446 copies to Giolito at less than their price of 1 ducat each. In return for his presentation copies, he received little more than polite thanks. The copy sent to King Philip was lost on its way to Spain. In 1562 Bernardo was heavily in debt. In summary, the publication of the *Amadigi* showed that there could still be a gulf between an author's expectations of reward from printing and the reality, in which an author was not only vulnerable to acts of God but still dependent to a large extent on another uncontrollable factor, the generosity of patrons.

When Bernardo's son Torquato Tasso (1544–95) was only eighteen years old, in 1562, he obtained his father's rather reluctant permission to have his chivalric romance *Rinaldo* printed in Venice. Torquato, no doubt advised by Bernardo, put himself in a position of firm control of publication by obtaining privileges from Venice and other states.[86] He went on to become one of the most often printed authors of the second half of the Cinquecento; yet he never succeeded in exercising the same degree of control over subsequent editions of his works. In 1575 he had high hopes of earning 400 scudi from a combination of the gifts received after a recent performance of his pastoral play *Aminta* and the profits expected from the planned printing of his masterpiece, the epic *Gerusalemme liberata*. With these resources he felt he would be able to escape from the court of Ferrara and live in Rome, at least until his capital was used up.[87] He obtained a twenty-year privilege for the *Liberata* from Florence early in 1576.[88] However, Torquato was still dissatisfied with the poem, and for the time being nothing came of his plans. It was only after he had been confined in 1579 to the hospital of Sant'Anna in Ferrara, where he remained for seven years, that editions of the epic began to appear. The earliest did not have his approval, and he was to regret the association with a young Ferrarese courtier, Febo Bonnà, which led to two editions in June and July 1581. Torquato said that he had made a written agreement ('poliza') with Bonnà, but Bonnà obtained privileges in his own name, and there was always a danger of the poet losing control because of his confinement. Two years later Torquato complained that Bonnà was enjoying himself in Parisian society, having printed and sold the books as he, Torquato, had intended to do, but having failed to hand over any of the money specified in their agreement.[89] Torquato remained bitterly disappointed that he never received from the publication of the *Liberata* the profits which were certainly his due, though his fevered imagination may have led him to exaggerate his claims that he was offered 'many hundreds of scudi' to have it printed, or (in 1589) that others had milked 'over 3,000 ducats' out of it and that as many more could still be earned, while he had received nothing either in cash or in gifts.[90]

Torquato fared no better with editions of his other works. The *Aminta* was first printed in Venice by Aldo Manuzio the younger, protected by a privilege in favour of Aldo and with a dedication signed, much to Torquato's annoyance, by the printer rather than the author.[91] In 1587 he fell victim to the unscrupulous Giovan Battista Licino, who arranged for the printing of the *Discorsi dell'arte poetica* but failed to make any significant payments to him as author.[92] On the other hand, Torquato could not afford to publish his own works. In 1589 he tried to borrow 100 scudi in the hope of earning much more from a revised edition of his works. He complained in the same year that he was too short of cash to have his lyric poems printed with a commentary.[93] Duke Vincenzo Gonzaga had to finance the printing of the first part of a new Mantuan edition of the *Rime* in 1591, after inquiries had been made to see whether a Venetian printer would undertake the edition at his own expense or even give the poet some reward. A discouraging response had been received from Venice: the printers wanted first to know exactly what the contents were and whether they were saleable; in any case, Torquato's reward would have been only some fifty copies or 'a few scudi'.[94] Print thus helped to bring Torquato fame, but it also brought much frustration over the lack of tangible benefits which he felt were due to him. To some extent he may have been overoptimistic: book publishing had not even reached the point where a generous contract could be offered to the greatest living Italian poet. But he was also the victim of the lack of scruple of the cut-throat world of print. As he wrote in 1586, it was all very well for him to be known as 'good Tasso, dear Tasso', but he was also 'the Tasso who has been assassinated, especially by booksellers and printers'.[95]

3 CONCLUSIONS: PRINT PUBLICATION, WRITERS AND WRITING

A survey carried out by Christian Bec on the century from 1450 to 1550, the period during which printing was introduced, suggests that, in respect of their professional background, the condition of writers underwent only gradual and limited change.[96] He studied the careers of 210 writers with regard to their place of work and to whether they belonged to one of five categories: teachers, courtiers, lawyers, merchants (including men who had a private source of income) and clerics (including those who were also teachers or courtiers). As regards the geography of literature, a significant trend during these years is the rise of Venice, to the same levels as Florence and Rome, as a centre in which writers resided for longer periods (fifteen years on average). Among the professions, that of courtier dominates overall, rising from 23 per cent in the first third of the period to 44 per cent in the second. In the final third, though, courts provide somewhat fewer writers (39 per cent), while more writers are teachers, merchants or lawyers. An interesting novelty is the growth in the proportion of writers outside the five main categories, from about 13 per cent in the first third of the period to about 26 per cent in the last. The largest group among these writers is that of printer-publishers: their proportion rises to nearly 13 per cent by 1550. There is also a significant rise in the proportion of women writers, from about 4 per cent to about 9 per cent. A broad underlying explanation for these trends must lie in the political upheavals of the period, which undermined the traditional social order and made the court an unstable institution. But it is probable that the rise of the printing industry also played some part: the presses, and those of Venice in particular, offered alternative opportunities which enabled writers who came from a variety of social and geographical backgrounds, and who lacked the humanist training that until about 1530 was an essential passport to success in literary society, to establish a reputation outside the milieu of the court.[97] During the sixteenth century, print acted more and more as an incentive to write; without it, one can imagine, several authors would have written less or not at all.

We have seen, though, that it was not easy for writers to improve their financial status with the help of the printing press, either indirectly, in other words through patronage, or directly, from sales or other payments. Print, because of its public-relations potential, seems to have stimulated writers to exploit their work even more than previously as a means of obtaining patronage. As the case of the publication of Ammirato's *Istorie fiorentine* shows, the possibility of dedicating printed books and of using them as gifts remained crucial to writers to the very end of the sixteenth century; the negotiations between Ammirato and his printer aimed at combining the former's need for patronage with the latter's commercial interests.[98] Yet just at the moment when competition for the largesse of patrons was growing, the wellsprings of patronage were drying up as regimes tottered and resources had to be diverted away from culture. Writers have always tended to complain of penury, but there may well have been some truth in Paolo Giovio's remark of 1548 to Cosimo de' Medici that 'these most turbulent times have castrated patrons, and hence crippled the right hand of authors'.[99] Indeed, Cosimo himself acknowledged, when writing to Aretino in 1552, that princes were being forced to spend their resources on warfare, neglecting rewards to those outside the military profession.[100] On the other hand, it was too early for writers to look to contracts with printers or publishers as a significant source of income. The possibility of such income was real, but as yet it too was limited. Among those writers who worked professionally for Venetian presses in the sixteenth century, even many years of activity seem to have brought little or no improvement in financial status.[101] In Britain it was only in the eighteenth century that the levels of production and consumption of printed material became high enough for authors to become professionals. A recent study has emphasized that even in the early 1700s 'authors' primary economic relations were still typically with patrons rather than with booksellers', and that only by the middle of the eighteenth century was 'professional authorship . . . becoming both economically feasible and socially acceptable'.[102]

The introduction of printing, then, led to no dramatic, sweeping changes in the professional status of writers. However, print publication undoubtedly enhanced the general recognition of the identity of the author as the creator and owner of the text. This recognition is reflected in the practice (which has been dated from 1479) of including, on the title page or elsewhere, portraits of the author which became increasingly true to life.[103] Print empowered writers through its ability to diffuse their works and through the operation of contracts, privileges and laws which protected their interests. Once texts had entered the legal system, they became, more clearly than before, commodities which belonged to authors and their families, had a negotiable value both within and outside the network of patronage, and were subject to the same kinds of protection as other property. By the end of the sixteenth century, the idea of profiting directly from writing was widely accepted as perfectly natural and respectable, as one can see from the confident way in which writers such as Salviati and Ammirato negotiated with their printers. Thus, important though patronage, in the traditional sense, remained to writers in this century, print determined the start of an underlying shift away from it. On the one hand, authors themselves began to emerge as masters of the destiny of their works. Fratta, in his dialogue on dedications, refers to what he calls the author's *padronia* or ownership of his works, his right to correct, print or reprint them as he wishes (f. B3v). On the other hand, the growing reading public was beginning to take over the determining role of the patron. What Arthur Marotti has written of Renaissance England is also true of Renaissance Italy: 'Within the literary institution developing in the context of print culture . . . another set of social relations was emerging in which the patron was ultimately eclipsed by the increasing sociocultural authority of authors as well as by the economic and interpretive importance of the reader, the patron of the work as buyer and consumer in the modern sense of the term patronage.'[104] Even if the traditional patronage system still dominated the lives of writers to such an extent that none could afford to live outside its constraints, men such as Ariosto, Castiglione, Aretino, Bernardo and Torquato Tasso all sensed that the publishing of their works in print could make a difference to their careers and sought through the press, in different ways and with varying success, to achieve greater financial independence.

Just as the relationship between writers and the broadening reading public began to eclipse traditional patronage, so in some respects it affected the aims and practices of their writing. It has been suggested that in Renaissance England the main element which distinguished attitudes towards literature from modern ones is that it was 'aimed at a particular audience' and 'designed to achieve particular effects'. Whereas writers today do not usually direct their works principally at a constituency of people known to them, literature then had a 'public relations' function. It was a means of seeking from others what one wanted, whether this was financial support, protection, or professional or social advancement; in short, it was 'the instrument of a social transaction'.[105] The same undoubtedly holds true of much Italian Renaissance literature. The public-relations function of literature was not new, of course, but the advent of print may well help to explain its prominence in this period, particularly in dialogues, epics, lyric poetry and collections of letters, all of which genres were used to allude to contemporary figures and acquaintances of the author, and in historiography, with its obvious potential for justifying a particular regime or cause.[106] Through the press, authors could broadcast their citations of others to a readership many times greater than if they were using manuscript publication. Yet at the same time print necessarily brought about a sense of a wider audience; and here lay a source of both tension and opportunity which led to gradual changes in ways of writing. Writers became ever more conscious that they were no longer addressing only actual or potential patrons, or a small circle of like-minded readers, or even an audience within their own state, but also a greater reading and book-buying public which was largely unknown and invisible to them as they wrote and which might be spread throughout Italy or sometimes beyond. They would have been especially aware of the need to satisfy the demands of this public if, as was often the case, they themselves were funding publication in whole or in part, or if they were working on commission for a printer or publisher. Writing for a wider public meant, among other things, covering new kinds of subject matter, or approaching subjects in new ways, and we shall return to this topic in chapter 6. But the sense of public scrutiny, together with the greater sense of permanency which print bestows, also meant that writers had to give more thought to fixedness and acceptability in literary form and in matters of linguistic form – punctuation, spelling, grammar, choice of lexis. The fixity associated with print, it has been plausibly argued, foregrounds style 'by locking the exact arrangement of words permanently into place, down to the smallest detail, thus encouraging the writer to shape his sentences with extraordinary care and the reader to consider and reconsider the finer points in a way that a listener never can'.[107] That is not to say that writers before print were not attentive to details of style (one need think only of the meticulous revisions of a poet such as Petrarch), but print can only have increased this attentiveness. If Ariosto had been publishing the *Orlando furioso* in manuscript alone, he would surely not have gone to such trouble in revising its language. Even Aretino, so boastful of the power of his fluent pen, felt the need for more polish in his printed letters and asked the less talented but more assiduous Dolce to revise their presentation.

Print in the Italian Renaissance thus brought about a series of changes which affected in two principal respects the broad context in which most writers worked. First, it altered the process of publication, making it more complex but also potentially giving writers more control over the diffusion of their works. As Roger Chartier has pointed out, 'authors do not write books: they write texts that become written objects', manufactured by others.[108] The metamorphosis of text into printed object could now involve writers in dealings with a number of other people: they might have to negotiate with paper manufacturers, printers, publishers, booksellers or editors, borrow or ask for money, request privileges, meet the deadlines of press operators, look for errors in proofs, or (especially in the second half of the Cinquecento) pass the scrutiny of censors. At the same time, print publication could bring obvious advantages to writers. It gave them much greater power to diffuse their works; it could give them more control over the accuracy and the appearance of the published text, as long as they were prepared to and able to scrutinize the printing process carefully; and it could provide a new source of remuneration. Second, print affected the conditions in which writers created their works. In the woodcut of Francesco de' Lodovici presenting his poem to his patron (fig. 4), the portrayal of one of the sun's rays infusing its power into the poet refers to the inspiration of Apollo and perhaps also, since its rays resemble tresses, of the woman whom he described in his *Antheo gigante* as his

Muse; and it reminds us that the advent of print did not alter the writer's need for individual creativity. Nevertheless, writers create in what Chartier has called a 'state of dependence', even if they are thought of and think of themselves as demiurges. Among the rules on which the writer's condition depends are, Chartier observes, those of patronage, subsidy and the market.[109] Print publication tended in the long term to make writers less dependent on patronage; at the same time, the logic of the new medium gave more importance to the rules of the market, so that writers who used print publication were now more likely to pay heed to what was expected, in matters of content and style, by the wider reading public.

1 An eighteenth-century English printing press. Two ink balls are hanging on the left-hand upright of the frame, and a forme is laid on the press stone.

Typographus. Der Buchdrucker.

ARte mea reliquas illuſtro Typographus artes,
Imprimo dum varios ære micante libros.
Quæ prius aucta ſitu, quæ puluere plena iacebant,
Vidimus obſcura nocte ſepulta premi.

Hæc veterum renouo neglecta volumina Patrum
Atq; ſcolis curo publica facta legi.
Artem prima nouam reperiſſe Moguntia fertur,
Vrbs grauis, & multis ingenioſa modis.
Qua nihil vtilius videt, aut precioſius orbis,
Vix melius quicquam ſecla futura dabunt.

C 3 Char-

2 A sixteenth-century woodcut of a printing house. In the foreground, the inker is applying ink to the forme with two ink balls, while the puller is removing from the tympan a sheet just printed. On the viewer's side of the press lie a pile of blank paper and another of printed sheets. Near the window, two compositors are at work, reading the copy-text, taking types from the case and inserting them in their composing sticks. From Hartmann Schopper, *Panoplia omnium illiberalium mechanicarum aut sedentariarum artium genera continens* [Panoply containing all kinds of ignoble mechanical or sedentary trades] (Frankfurt: Georg Corvinus for Sigismund Feyerabend, 1568), octavo, f. C3r.

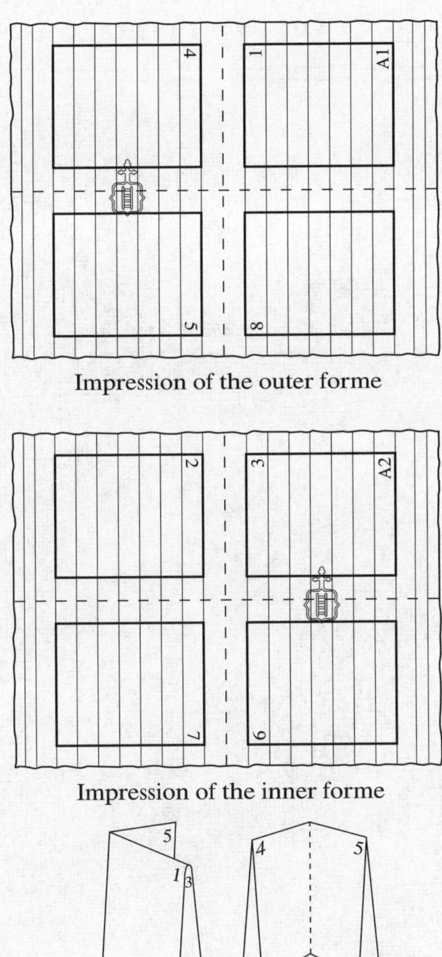

3 A printed sheet of quarto. The impression of the outer forme contains pages 1, 4, 5, 8, which in a gathering signed as A would be leaves A1 recto, A2 verso, A3 recto, A4 verso. The impression of the inner forme contains pages 2, 3, 6, 7, which in a gathering signed as A would be leaves A1 verso, A2 recto, A3 verso, A4 recto. Here page numbers are shown at the top of each page, and the signature letter and leaf number are shown at the foot of A1 recto and A2 recto, though in practice not all editions would use these markings. The vertical lines represent the chain lines in the paper, and an example of a watermark (representing a ladder, in use in 1501) is shown in the centre of one half of the sheet. Dashed lines represent folds, and beneath is shown, from two angles, the sheet after folding.

4 The title page of Francesco de' Lodovici's *Triomphi di Carlo* (Venice: Francesco Bindoni and Maffeo Pasini, 1535), quarto. In the woodcut, the author presents his work, elegantly bound, to the dedicatee, Andrea Gritti, doge of Venice. The sun probably represents the enlightening force of creative inspiration.

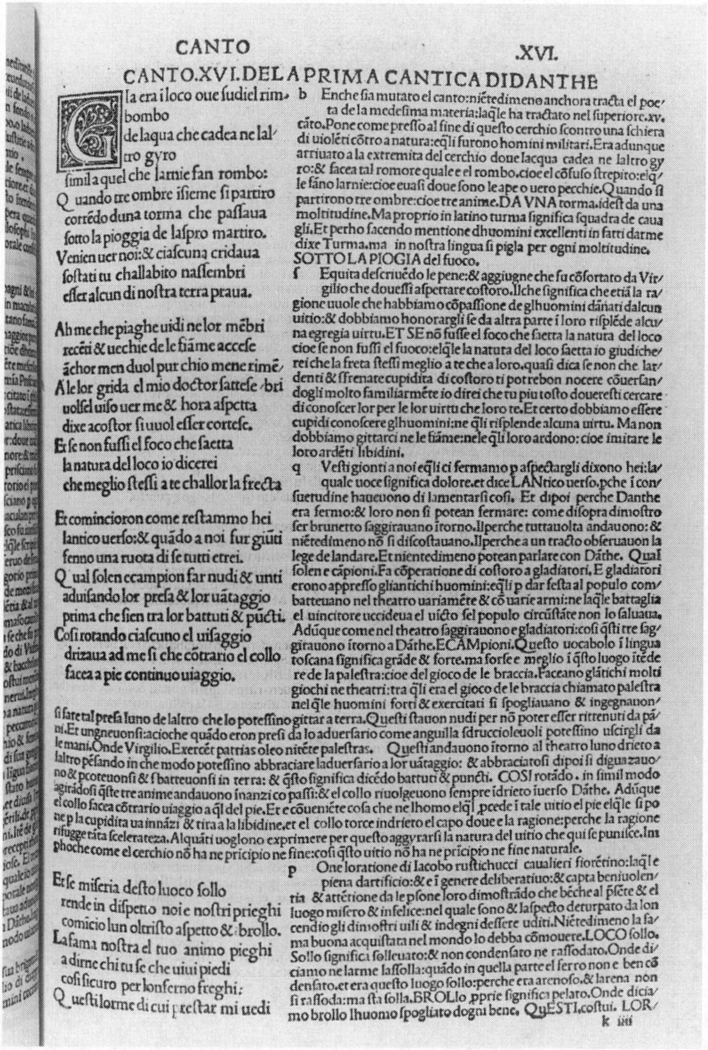

CANTO .XVI.

CANTO.XVI.DELA PRIMA CANTICA DIDANTHE

Gia era i loco oue sudiel rimbombo
de laqua che cadea ne laltro gyro
simil a quel che larnie fan rombo:
Quando tre ombre isieme si partiro
corrēdo duna torma che passaua
sotto la pioggia de laspro martiro.
Venien uer noi:& ciascuna cridaua
sostati tu challabito nassembri
esser alcun di nostra terra praua.

Ah me che piaghe uidi ne lor mēbri
recēti & uecchie de le fiāme accese
ānchor men duol pur chio mene rimēbri
A le lor grida el mio doctor sattese
uolsel uiso uer me & hora aspetta
dixe a costor si uuol esser cortese.
Et se non fussi el foco che saetta
la natura del loco io dicerei
che meglio stessi a te challor la frecta

Et comincioron come restammo hei
lantico uerso:& quādo a noi fur giūti
fenno una ruota di se tutti etrei.
Qual solen e campion far nudi & unti
aduisando lor presa & lor uātaggio
prima che sien tra lor battuti & pūcti.
Cosi rotando ciascuno el uisaggio
drizaua ad me si che cōtrario el collo
facea a pie continuo uiaggio.

b Enche sia mutato el canto:niētedimeno anchora tracta el poeta de la medesima materia:laqle ha tractato nel superiore.xv.cāto.Pone come presso al fine di questo cerchio scontro una schiera di uiolēti cōtro a natura:eqli furono homini militari.Era adunque arriuato a la extremita del cerchio doue lacqua cadea ne laltro gyro:& facea tal romore quale e el rombo.cioe el cōfuso strepito:elqle fāno larnie:cioe euasi doue sono le ape o uero pecchie.Quando si partirono tre ombre:cioe tre anime.DA VNA torma.idest da una moltitudine.Ma proprio in latino turma significa squadra de caualli.Et perho facendo mentione dhuomini excellenti in fatti darme dixe Turma.ma in nostra lingua si pigla per ogni moltitudine. SOTTO LA PIOGIA del fuoco.

s Equita descriuēdo le pene:& aggiugne che fu cōfortato da Virgilio che douessi aspettare costoro.Ilche significa che etiā la ragione uuole che habbiamo cōpassione de glhuomini dānati dalcun uitio:& dobbiamo honorargli se da altra parte i loro risplēde alcuna egregia uirtu.ET SE nō fusse el foco che saetta la natura del loco cioe se non fussi el fuoco:elqle la natura del loco saetta io giudicherei che la freta stessi meglio a te che a loro.quasi dica se non che lardenti & sfrenate cupidita di costoro ti potrebon nocere cōuersandogli molto familiarmēte io direi che tu piu tosto doueresti cercare di conoscer lor per le lor uirtu che loro te.Et certo dobbiamo essere cupidi conoscere glhuomini:ne qli risplende alcuna uirtu. Ma non dobbiamo gittarci ne le fiāme:ne le qli loro ardono: cioe imitare le loro ardēti libidini.

q Vesti gionti a noi eqli ci fermamo p aspectargli dixono hei:laquale uoce significa dolore.et dice LANtico uerso.pche i consuetudine haueuono di lamentarsi cosi. Et dipoi perche Danthe era fermo:& loro non si potean fermare: come di sopra dimostro ser brunetto saggirauano itorno.Ilperche tuttauolta andauono: & niētedimeno nō si discostauano.Ilperche a un tracto obseruauon la lege de landare.Et nientedimeno potean parlare con Dāthe. Qual solen e cāpioni.Fa cōperatione di costoro a gladiatori.E gladiatori erono appresso gliantichi huomini:eqli p dar festa al populo combatteuano nel theatro uariamēte & cō uarie armi:ne laqle battaglia el uincitore uccideua el uicto sel populo circūstāte non lo saluaua. Adūque come nel theatro saggirauono e gladiatori:cosi qsti tre saggirauono itorno a Dāthe.ECAMpioni.Questo uocabolo i lingua toscana significa grāde & forte.ma forse e meglio i qsto luogo itēdere de la palestra:cioe del gioco de le braccia.Faceano glātichi molti giochi ne theatri:tra qli era el gioco de le braccia chiamato palestra nel qle huomini forti & exercitati si spogliauano & ingegnauonsi fare tal presa luno de laltro che lo potessino gittar a terra.Questi stauon nudi per nō poter esser rittenuti da pāni.Et ungneuonsi:acioche quādo eron presi da lo aduersario come anguilla sdruccioleuoli potessino uscirgli da le mani.Onde Virgilio.Exercēt patrias oleo nitēte palestras. Questi andauono itorno al theatro luno drieto a laltro pēsando in che modo potessino abbraciare laduersario a lor uātaggio: & abbraciatosi dipoi si diguazauono & pcoteuonsi & sbatteuonsi in terra: & qsto significa dicēdo battuti & puncti. COSI rotādo. in simil modo agirādosi qste tre anime andauono inanzi co passi:& el collo riuolgeuono sempre idrieto iuerso Dāthe. Adūque el collo facea cōtrario uiaggio a ql del pie.Et e cōueniēte cosa che ne lhomo elql pcede i tale uitio el pie elqle si pone p la cupidita ua innāzi & tira a la libidine.et el collo torce indrieto el capo doue e la ragione:perche la ragione rifugge tāta scelerateza.Alquāti uoglono exprimere per questo aggyrarsi la natura del uitio che qui se punisce.Imperhoche come el cerchio nō ha ne pricipio ne fine:cosi qsto uitio nō ha ne pricipio ne fine naturale.

Et se miseria desto luoco sollo
rende in dispetto noi e nostri prieghi
comincio lun oltristo aspetto & brollo.
La fama nostra el tuo animo pieghi
a dirne chi tu se che uiui piedi
cosi sicuro per lonferno freghi:
Questi lorme di cui prestar mi uedi

p One loratione di Iacobo rustichucci caualieri fiorētino:laqle piena dartificio:& e i genere deliberatiuo:& capta beniuolentia & attētione da le psone loro dimostrādo che bēche al pſēte & el luogo misero & infelice:nel quale sono & laspecto deturpato da lo incendio gli dimostri uili & indegni dessere uditi.Niētedimeno la fama buona acquistata nel mondo lo debba cōmouere.LOCO sollo. Sollo significa solleuato:& non condensato ne rassodato.Onde diciamo ne larme lassolla:quādo in quella parte el ferro non e ben cōdensato.et era questo luogo sollo:perche era arenoso.& larena non si rassoda:ma sta solla.BROLlo pprie significa pelato.Onde diciamo brollo lhuomo spogliato dogni bene. QuESTI.costui. LOR

k iiii

5 Dante, *Commedia*, with a commentary by Cristoforo Landino (Venice: Ottaviano Scotto, 1484), folio, roman type, f. k4r. A woodcut initial marks the opening of *Inferno* XVI; each paragraph of the commentary opens with a space containing a guide letter to indicate the initial which could be added by hand. The only punctuation signs in the text are the full stop, colon and hyphen. There is a lack of word separation in 'sudiel', 'laqua' and so on. The 'titulus', a horizontal abbreviation sign above the letter, indicates a missing 'm' or 'n', as in 'i(n) loco', 'fia(m)me', and the ampersand (&) stands for 'e' or 'et'. The running title gives the canto number.

INF.

M i'nsegnauate, come l'huom s'eterna:
Et quant'io l'habbo ingrato; mentr'io uiuo,
Conuien, che ne la mia lingua si scerna.
C io che narrate di mio corso, scriuo;
Et serbolo a chiosar con altro testo
A donna, che sapra, s'allei arriuo.
T anto uogl'io che ui sia manifesto;
Pur che mia conscienza non mi garra,
Ch'a la fortuna, come uuol, son presto.
N on è nuoua a gliorecchi miei tal arra:
Pero giri fortuna la sua rota,
Come le piace; e'l uillan la sua marra.
L o mi maestro allhora in su la gota
Destra si uolse'ndietro, et riguardommi:
Poi disse; ben ascolta, chi la nota:
N e per tanto di men parlando uommi
Con ser Brunetto; et dimando, chi sono
Li suoi compagni piu noti et piu sommi.
E t egli a me; saper d'alcuno è buono:
De glialtri fia laudabile tacerci;
Che'l tempo saria corto a tanto suono.
I n somma sappi, che tutti fur cherci,
Et litterati grandi, et di gran fama
D'un medesmo peccato al mondo lerci.
P riscian sen'ua con quella turba grama,
Et Francesco d'Accorso ancho; et uederui,
S'hauess' hauuto di tal tigna brama,
C olui potei, che dal seruo de serui
Fu transmutato d'Arno in Bacchiglione,
Oue lascio li mal protesi nerui.

INF.

D i piu direi: ma'l uenir, e'l sermone
Piu lungo esser non puo; pero ch'i ueggio
La surger nouo fummo del sabbione.
G ente uien; con laquale esser non deggio:
Siati raccomandato'l mio thesoro,
Nel qual i uiuo anchora; et piu non cheggio:
P oi si parti; et parue di coloro,
Che corrono a Verona'l drappo uerde
Per la campagna; et parue di costoro
Quegli, che uince, non colui, che perde.

XVI.

G ia era in loco; oue s'udia'l rimbombo
De l'acqua, che cadea ne laltro giro,
Simil a quel, che l'arnie fanno rombo;
Quando tre ombre insieme si partiro
Correndo duna torma, che passaua,
Sotto la pioggia dell'aspro martiro.
V eniam uer noi: et ciascuna gridaua,
Sostati tu; ch'a l'habito ne sembri
Esser alcun di nostra terra praua.
A ime che piaghe uidi ne lor membri
Recenti et uecchie da le fiamme incese:
Anchor men' duol, pur ch'i me ne rimembri.
A lle lor grida il mio dottor s'attese:
Volse'l uiso uer me, et hora aspetta,
Disse: a costor si uuol esser cortese:
E t se non fosse il fuoco, che saetta
La natura del luogo; i dicerei
Che meglio stesse a te, ch'a lor la fretta.

e iiii

6 Dante, *Commedia* (Venice: Aldo Manuzio, 1502), octavo, italic type, ff. e3v–e4r. The editor, Pietro Bembo, has used several punctuation signs (full stop, colon, semicolon, comma, apostrophe) and a grave accent on the verb *è*. Words are separated by spaces or apostrophes, and there are no abbreviation signs.

7 The italic script of Bartolomeo Sanvito, a possible model for Aldo Manuzio's italic type, in a manuscript of Juvenal's *Satires*, ff. 32v–33r.

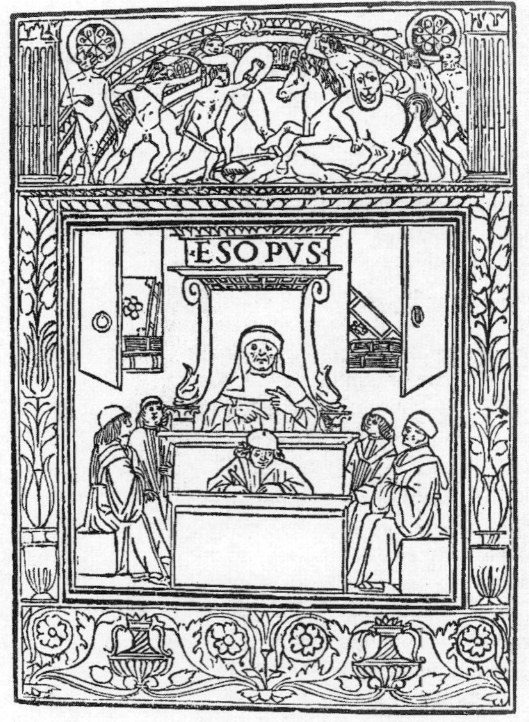

8 Two woodcuts depicting a schoolmaster and his pupils: from an *Aesopus moralisatus* (Venice: Manfredo Bonelli, 1491), left, and from an edition of the *Moretum* attributed to Virgil and the *Nux* attributed to Ovid (Venice: Maffeo Pasini, 1525), right.

¶ Incomicia el libro dele Epistole di Ouidio in rima: vulgarizate p messere Dominico da monticielli toschano. Et prima comincia il plogo: & inde segue la Epistola laqual Penolope figliola del Re Icharo mādo ad Ulixe figliolo de Laerte suo marito.

Prologo.

More e charita che in Dio san sito
E nui creo di terra tal factore
Poi che disposto e si il mio appetito
Chogni mio detto tracti pur damore
Spiri nel mio intelleto indebilito
Si chel tractato dello grande auctore
Cioe Douidio possa traslatare
De dolci versi in rima per vulgare/

Se vui comprender volete cō effecto
Cio che si siegue nel mio recitare
Sapiate che de Ouidio fu il cōcetto
Perche tal libro volse cōpillare
Che gia vedeua trāscorrer cō diffetto
Gioueni e donne nel voler amare
Unde damore scrisse molte inchieste
Honeste: savie: sciocche: e dishoneste

Lhoneste e sauie perche se seguissero
Da giouēni amāti e dale giouenette
Le dishoneste pche si fugissero
Acio che mai nō fusser cōtradette
Quelle doctrine che suo dita scrissero
Que damore doctrina ci pmette
Adonque comincia da Penolope
Laqual di castita suo specchio se

9 The opening page of a popular edition of a translation of Ovid's *Heroides*, printed in Brescia by Battista Farfengo in quarto format and using gothic type, 1491.

Pictagoras arithmetrice introductor

Philippi Calandri ad nobilem et studiosū Julianum Laurentii Medicē de arimethrica opusculū.

Considerato nobile ⁊ studioso Juliano Medice quanto sia utile: anzi necessaria lascientia arimethrica al comertio humano: et maxime a quegli che exercitano lamercatura: diche la cipta Fiorentina sanza controuersia fra laltre tiene ilprincipato: ⁊ ueduto lagrata et celebre audientia de glistudiosi adolescēti fiorētini in questa mia giouenile eta: me paruto conueniente lecose da me udite allor maggiore utilita sotto brieue cōpendio ridurre: et quelle secondo lostile fiorentino nō con picola mia fatica per le multiplice difficulta che a glipressori ocorreuano ꝑ piu comodita fare imprimere. Ilche hauēdo per diuina gratia absoluto: et uolendo digia questa mia operetta andare in luce accioche cō maggiore gratia ⁊ auctorita uada a te Juliano medice ladirizo ⁊ dedico: che se ditale scientia fra laltre studioso: ⁊ secondo loptimo costume de tua antecessori della publica utilita ⁊ honore amatore ⁊ defensore: laquale se da te come spero sara aprouata misia stimolo dimaggior cose a tentare ⁊ piu artificiose. Uale

a ii

10 Filippo Calandri's *De arithmetica*, a mathematical textbook printed in Florence in 1492 by Lorenzo Morgiani and Johann Petri, using octavo format and gothic type, ff. a1v–a2r. The woodcut on the left shows 'Pythagoras, introducer of arithmetic' in the guise of a schoolmaster with pupils. On the right is the author's dedication to the young Giuliano de' Medici.

MAGNIFICO SVMPTV LAVRENTII
MEDICIS PATRIAE SERVATORIS
IMPRESSIT EX ARCHETYPO
ANTONIVS MISCOMINVS
FLORENTIAE
ANNO.M CCCC.LXXXXII.
NONIS MAII.

REGISTRVM.

a.b.c.d.e.f.g.h.i.k.l.m.n.o.p.q.r.ſ.t.u.x.y.z.&. aa.bb.cc.dd.ee.ff.gg.hh.ii.
kk.ll.mm.nn.oo.pp.qq.rr.ſſ.tt.uu.

Omnes ſunt quinterni pręter.b.qui eſt quaternus:et.o.qui eſt ſexternus.

11 The conclusion of the main text of Ficino's translation of the works of the Neoplatonic philosopher Plotinus, in a folio edition printed in roman type. The colophon states that the edition was printed at the 'magnificent expense' of Lorenzo de' Medici, preserver of the State of Florence, from the author's archetype or master copy, by Antonio Miscomini in Florence, terminating on 7 May 1492. This is followed by the register of gatherings (identified by alphabetical symbols and with an explanation that they all have five sheets, except b, which has four, and o, which has six) and a device made up of the printer's initials, alongside which is an early handwritten ownership note.

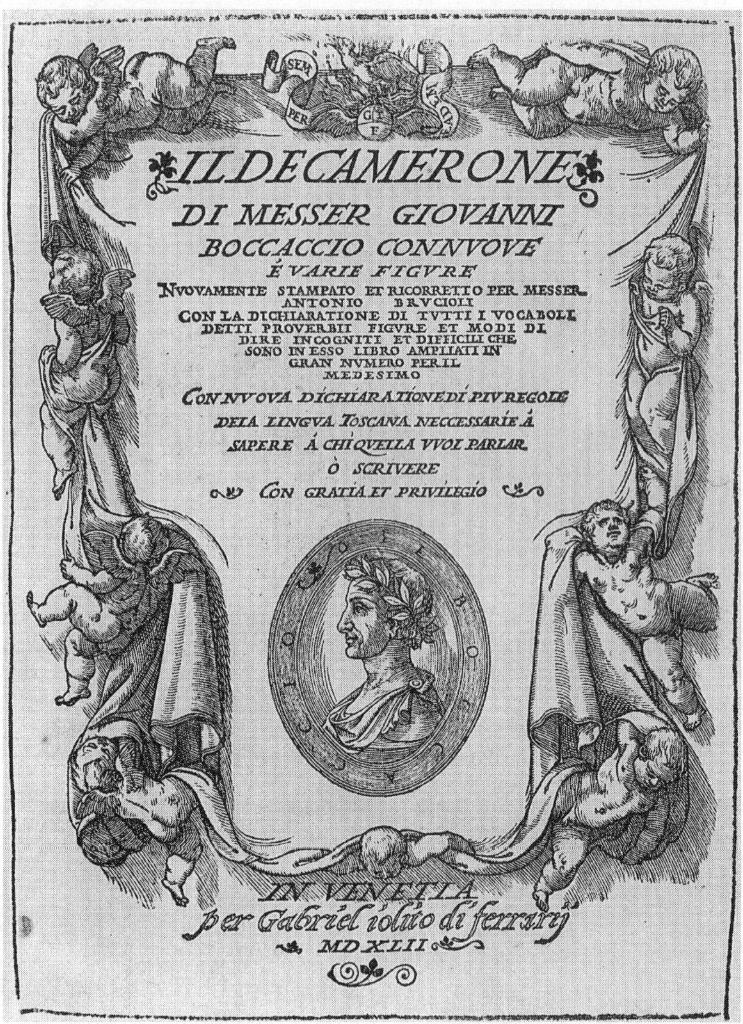

IL DECAMERONE

DI MESSER GIOVANNI

BOCCACCIO CON NVOVE

É VARIE FIGVRE

NVOVAMENTE STAMPATO ET RICORRETTO PER MESSER
ANTONIO BRVCIOLI
CON LA DICHIARATIONE DI TVTTI I VOCABOLI
DETTI PROVERBII FIGVRE ET MODI DI
DIRE INCOGNITI ET DIFFICILI CHE
SONO IN ESSO LIBRO AMPLIATI IN
GRAN NVMERO PER IL
MEDESIMO

CON NVOVA DICHIARATIONE DI PIV REGOLE
DELA LINGVA TOSCANA NECCESSARIE Á
SAPERE Á CHI QVELLA VVOL PARLAR
Ó SCRIVERE

CON GRATIA ET PRIVILEGIO

IN VENETIA
per Gabriel iolito di ferrarij
MDXLII

12 The woodcut title page of a quarto edition printed in Venice, 1542, with the phoenix device of the printer Gabriele Giolito. It identifies the work and its author, and then draws the attention of the prospective purchaser to the attractions of this edition and in particular to the contributions of the editor: 'The *Decameron* of Giovanni Boccaccio, with new and varied illustrations. Newly printed, and corrected by Antonio Brucioli. With the explanation of all obscure and difficult words, sayings, proverbs, figures and expressions in this book, greatly expanded by the same. With a new explanation of several rules of the Tuscan language necessary to those wishing to speak or write it'.

non bene intesi da alcuni, u'habbiamo anchora uoluto dar la uera & piu lucida espositione, ponendoui nel fine ordinatamente tutti gli Epitheti usati dal Bocc. & alcune altre cose necessarie & utili a tutti coloro, che desiderano di bene intendere le presenti Nouelle, ripiene di belle sentenze, di parole proprie & eleganti, d'argutie nobili, di motti festosi, & di prouerbi grati, & finalmente di tutto quel bello & leggiadro, che puo ornare le prose di chiunque con giudicioso occhio si sapra riuolgere alla imitatione di questo Autore, ilquale meritamente da dotti huomini è chiamato il Cicerone della lingua uolgare. A uoi adunque gentilissimi Lettori appartiene di non mancare a uoi stessi; poi che per me anchora non si manca ne a spesa, ne a fatica alcuna per giouarui. Habbiate queste dieci giornate di continuo alle mani: & aspettate in brieue un Petrarca correttissimo piu di quanti fino hora ne haueте ueduto.

DICHIARATIONE

DI TVTTI I VOCABOLI, DETTI, PROVERBII, e luoghi difficili, che sono sparsi nel presente Volume per ordine d'Alfabeto.

IL PRIMO NVMERO DINOTA carte, il secondo il numero delle line di quella stessa lettera, che è citata.

ABATE 50. b. 1. Voce Sira che significa padre, alcuni scriuano Abbate, ma essendo anchora tra Latini cotal differentia, ci riportaremo all'usanza de piu.

Abbaiatori 272. f. 1. per metaphora de cani, cianciatori, frappatori, quali fan poco danno, perche si suole dire, che can che abbaia non morde.

Accontatosi 95. c. 9. messosi in conto, alcuni leggano accostatosi, & l'una uoce & l'altra puo stare.

Accatauano 94. h. 3. toglieuano in presto. e accattare è hauer licentia, le Cento uecchie, che accattasse la parola del Re.

Accozzare 712. g. 2. metter insieme dodici noccioli, cioè ossi di persiche, o di ciriegia in tre mani, a quatro per mano, che è come dire, egli è da poco.

Addattare 250. e. 4. in questo luogo significa, far cadere in proposito, assettare, e a colui diciamo, che è

NN vi

13 Gabriele Giolito's duodecimo edition of Boccaccio's *Decameron*, Venice, 1552, ff. NN5v–NN6r. On the left, the last part of Giolito's letter to the readers informs them that they have been given explanations necessary to the full understanding of the stories and to the imitation of the style of Boccaccio, the 'Cicero of the vernacular'; on the right, the opening of Francesco Sansovino's glossary, with entries in approximate alphabetical order accompanied by a reference to page, section and line.

14 Niccolò Colantonio, *Saint Jerome in His Study*. Saint Jerome compiled the standard (Vulgate) translation of the Bible into Latin and, according to a legend, extracted a thorn from a lion's foot. This image shows the books and furniture of traditional scholarship in the mid fifteenth century. A manuscript volume, written in two columns per page, with rubricated initials and marginal glosses, lies open on the sloping part of the desk, above which are the implements of the writer. The other volumes piled haphazardly on their sides along the shelves are all large, with solid bindings and clasps. The chest would also have served for book storage.

15 A portrait, c. 1570, by Giovanni Battista Moroni, known as *Titian's Schoolmaster*. In the sixteenth century the smaller size of many printed books, such as the octavo being held here by the unidentified sitter, allowed reading to be carried out in a more relaxed manner than previously.

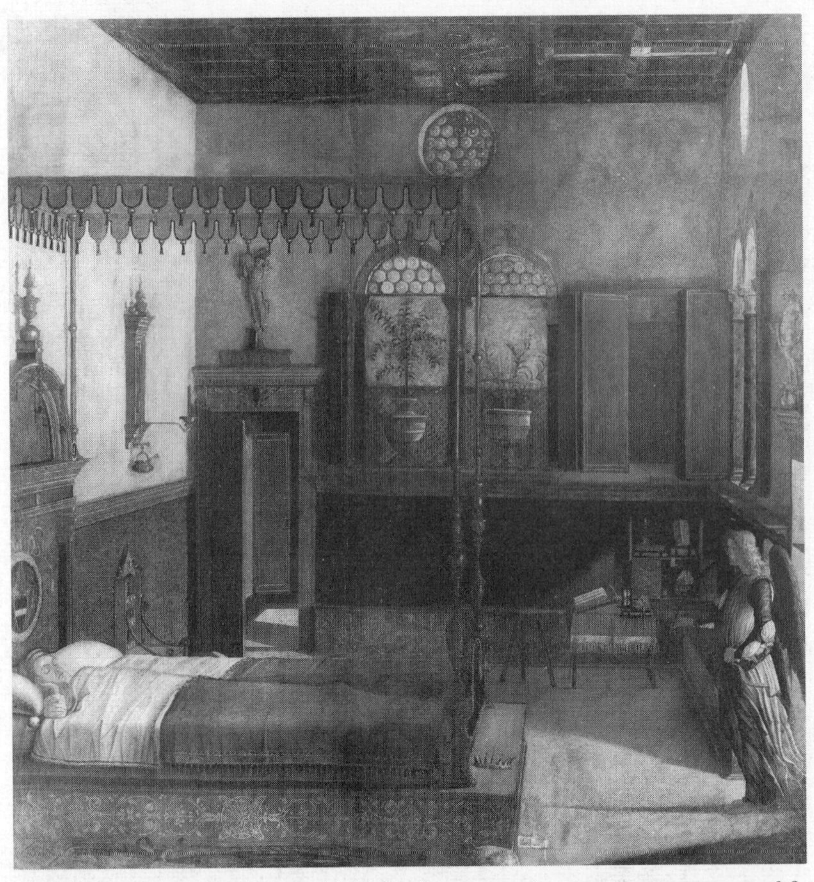

16 Vittore Carpaccio's *Dream of Saint Ursula*, c. 1495, showing the space reserved for writing and reading in a well-to-do woman's bedchamber.

17 A fragment of *The Virgin Reading*, by Vittore Carpaccio, c. 1505. In the original painting the Virgin was reading with the infant Christ, on the viewer's left.

PART III

Readers and print culture

CHAPTER 5

Reading, buying and owning printed books

The history of reading is a relatively new subject, and a complex one. As Roger Darnton has observed in a stimulating survey, it needs to answer a number of questions. Who read, and what did they read? Where and when did people read: in libraries and studies or elsewhere; alone or in the company of others? And, more problematically, why and how did they read?[1] These are useful questions to bear in mind in the final part of this book, which aims to build up a picture of just one aspect of reading in Renaissance Italy: the extent to which this activity was affected by print. First, we need to outline some evidence for the 'who' question by looking in general at literacy in Renaissance Italy, including the process of learning the basics of reading, who acquired this skill, and how well most people could read. Then, concentrating on the specific context of printing, we can consider some further aspects of the 'who' and move on to the 'what' (and 'how much') of reading by asking how far print made books more affordable by a greater number of people, and how far the increasing sizes of book collections might affect the way in which books were stored and consulted. In the next chapter, we shall analyse further what people read, as well as touching on the 'how', 'where' and 'when' of reading, by considering the changing forms of printed books and their contents, and the shifts in the nature of reading which these developments may imply. In looking at this evidence, though, one must remember that the implicit reader, the person whose ways of reading are suggested by the form and contents imposed by the producers of books, does not necessarily correspond completely with the real reader, whose response is inevitably individual and independent.

I LITERACY AND READING

Those Italian children fortunate enough to receive an education in the three R's began with reading and, as in the rest of western Europe, went on to writing and then to arithmetic or *abbaco*, which was sometimes taught at a separate school.[2] Pupils used a sheet known variously as the *tavola, carta, quaderno* or *santacroce*, 'hornbook' in English, in order to learn to recognize first the letters of the alphabet, then separate written syllables (*ba*, *be* and so forth), then whole words, and then some common Latin prayers, beginning with the Pater Noster and the Ave Maria.[3] Pupils proceeded to a booklet containing the same elementary material followed by a larger number of Latin prayers; this was known as the *saltero* (also spelled *salterio* or *psalterio*), English 'psalter', probably because it had originally contained the seven penitential psalms. The teaching of reading thus immediately introduced into education the fourth R, religion, because even these early stages were closely associated with prayers. If the education of children went any further, they would study a basic Latin grammar called the *donato*, *donatello* or *donadello*, not the *Ars minor* of Donatus but a late-medieval Italian compilation known also as the *Rudimenta grammatices* (Rudiments of grammar) or the *Ianua* (its first word, indicating that it was an 'entrance' to knowledge).

What is most striking here from a modern point of view is that children could learn to read without necessarily understanding fully what they read: because of the force of tradition and the lack of prestige of the vernacular as a written language among teachers, reading in one's native language did not play a part in the traditional curriculum. One has to distinguish, as Paul Saenger has done, between 'phonetic literacy', the ability to read aloud syllable by syllable without necessarily taking in the precise grammatical meaning, and 'comprehension literacy', the ability to decode silently, word by word, with full understanding.[4] Trissino commented in 1529 that children were taught Latin but then had to learn Italian by themselves.[5] However, some editions of the *donato* intercalated vernacular translations into the text after each Latin phrase (GW 9025–8). There is also evidence for the printing and use of a reading book which, in at least one version, included some lists of Italian proper nouns and explanations in Italian before the traditional Latin prayers, and thus did not use the classical language as its starting point, although its conclusion seemed to point forward to the rest of the traditional syllabus. The very name of this textbook, the *Babuino*, introduced a lighter touch: it literally means a baboon or a dolt, and derived perhaps from the sound of the syllables which the pupil would learn to read aloud. This work may have originated before the printing press came to Italy; but its impact in print seems to have been felt in Venice as early as the 1470s, when a fierce opponent of print, the

Dominican friar and scribe Filippo da Strada, mocked a self-taught, jumped-up ass who paraded as a university doctor, even though, the ass says, 'I had learned only the *babovino* when I set about studying from printed works' ('solo il babovino aveva io emparato | quando me posi in stampe ad studiare').[6]

Once print had arrived, some authors devised new books to help in acquiring the three R's. Among them was the schoolteacher Antonio Mancinelli: his pedagogical works included a *Donatus melior* (Improved *donatus*), first published probably in 1487, which was a version of the *Ianua* including some translations of the Latin forms into a vernacular with Roman features.[7] Children's literature did not yet exist, but by the 1580s and probably earlier, some vernacular texts were used for reading in school, in particular ones which had a simultaneous morally improving function, such as the collected Epistles and Gospels or the *Fior di virtù*, an anonymous early-fourteenth-century account of virtues and vices, and even chivalric romances including Ariosto's *Orlando furioso*, the work most widely diffused in Venetian homes.[8] Yet when Tomaso Garzoni discussed the faults of schoolboys in 1585, he gave the impression that, as far as textbooks or anything else was concerned, little had changed in the preceding century, and that the *Furioso* was not welcome in most classrooms. Along with schoolboy transgressions such as eating chestnuts on the sly, catching flies and always asking to go to the lavatory, he listed putting cakes inside psalters ('far le fugaccie dentro ai salterii'), scribbling in *donati*, drawing heads in the Latin grammar of Guarino Veronese, tearing up the *Disticha Catonis* (an elementary Latin reader) and reciting Ariosto instead of Ovid.[9]

Evidence for the extent of literacy in Renaissance Italy is rather fragmentary, and relates mainly to the north and centre of the peninsula. One source is constituted by records of schooling, and in these cases literacy would include the ability to read vernacular texts, and often Latin texts, with ease. Another source is documentary evidence of people's basic ability to write. Here literacy could well be more functional, something acquired and used in the context of one's occupation, and the standard of reading which it permitted might be quite rudimentary.

The proportion of children who were attending school outside the home in Florence in 1480 has been calculated by Grendler on the basis of the survey of households (known as the *catasto*) which was carried out in that year.[10] Only boys, never girls, are mentioned as receiving education. Of those aged between six and fourteen, some 28 per cent were at school; allowing for some pupils not recorded and for others educated informally at home, the overall male literacy rate can thus be estimated as at least 30 to 33 per cent. For the city of Venice a century later a very similar picture of male education emerges from the evidence of the professions of faith which teachers were ordered to give in 1587.[11] About 26 per cent of boys aged from six to fifteen were attending formal schools, of which the great majority (89 per cent) were independently run. But only some 0.2 per cent of girls were at school, and the combined school attendance rate for both sexes is 14 per cent. An overall estimate (allowing for children receiving education at home, in female convents and in schools which combined the teaching of religion with literacy) is 33 per cent for boys, between 12.2 and 13.2 per cent for girls and 23 per cent for both sexes.

As we have already begun to see, literacy was not spread evenly among the population. One's chances of being able to read, and especially of being able to read fluently, were strongly affected, first of all, by whether one was female or male. Girls were not normally allowed to leave the protection of the home environment in order to attend schools.[12] The best that most girls could hope for was to receive basic instruction in literacy and numeracy from their mothers at home. Few parents would incur the expense, and run the risk, of calling a male tutor into the home in order to instruct their daughters. Even those girls who learned to read were restricted to the vernacular: hardly any were given the opportunity to progress to understanding Latin and hence to much of the world of learning. Of the thirty or so female pupils mentioned in the Venetian records of 1587, some two-thirds were daughters of nobles who were educated at home by tutors, and then only at an elementary level. A few girls from wealthier families (and in Florence at least, they all seem to have been motherless daughters) might be sent as boarders to female convents, where they would learn reading and writing as well as sewing and singing.[13]

Another reason for which children might be denied formal education was the poverty of their parents. However, some free education was available, and schooling in Florence and other cities did extend to working-class children.[14] Literacy was also diffused among the less well off by the Schools of Christian Doctrine ('Scuole della dottrina cristiana') which spread widely among the cities and towns of northern and to some extent central Italy after the first had been founded in Milan in 1536. These schools, operated by lay confraternities and held on Sundays and holy days, taught reading and writing as well as catechism to both sexes (separately), and they provided reading books for those too poor to buy their own.[15]

Finally, the availability of education would have varied according to the size of the centre concerned and its professional and cultural traditions. It is likely that the proportion of children at school in Florence and Venice was matched in few if any other cities. However, communal funds were used to provide education in small towns in northern and north-central Italy.[16] In the countryside, formal education seems to have been available in a haphazard way. Classes were arranged in the small town of Cutigliano, north-west of Pistoia, in 1513–14 and 1526 by a friar who happened to be spending a period of convalescence there and who did not want to be idle; and Domenico Scandella, known as Menocchio, who spent most of his life in a small hill town in Friuli, listed teaching as one of several jobs, along with sawyer, miller, innkeeper and musician, with which he had made a living.[17]

In spite of these problems, it may well have been the case that by the sixteenth century a limited ability to read and write for practical purposes was attained, often outside school, by a majority of the urban working population, especially among males. The introduction of print may have been a crucial factor here, since school attendance rates do not appear to have risen over the period and since considerable progress seems to have been made in the last decades of the Quattrocento. In Venice, the level of male illiteracy was perhaps as high as 60 per cent in the middle of that century but seems to have gone down by 1500.[18] An important piece of evidence for Rome is the notebook used by a grocer called Maddalena to record her accounts between 1523 and 1537.[19] Of the 102 people represented in these records, only 6 used someone else to make entries on their behalf: Maddalena herself (the only woman concerned) and 5 men. This suggests that almost all those who were economically active, even manual labourers, had a functional elementary literacy. Venetian records from the second half of the Cinquecento also suggest that in this city some male artisans read for instruction and pleasure and that few were completely illiterate.[20] However, it must be stressed that this does not mean that all these people could (or would want to) read fluently, even in the vernacular. On Unification in 1861, the literacy rate in Italy was still only about 22 per cent. We must remember, then, that in the Renaissance those who were potential readers of books of any sort were a minority, almost certainly less than a quarter of the male population and an even smaller proportion of women.

We must also bear in mind that reading by oneself silently was not the only means of access to the written word. Although silent reading increased during the Middle Ages, reading aloud, alone or to a small audience, continued well after the thirteenth century.[21] In courtly society, both women and men had romances such as the *Orlando furioso* read to them – indeed, one of the objections which some Florentines made to Tasso's *Gerusalemme liberata* in the 1580s was that it was so difficult that it had to be read silently; and Dante's *Commedia* was read aloud in the Milanese court, with Lodovico Sforza listening.[22] Fathers were advised to read devotional books in the vernacular to their families.[23] One of the short stories of Matteo Bandello (I. 34) recounts how a wife, brought up in a courtly environment, retired to her room when she claimed to be unwell in order to read Petrarch, the *Decameron*, the *Orlando furioso* or Aretino, but how she got her plebeian husband to read these works aloud to her so that she should not tire herself – a situation (including the partially risqué choice of works) intended to make the husband look stupid in his overindulgence, but which is not meant to appear any more unrealistic than his other habit of serving her fine food in her room. Some texts, particularly romances, were also performed orally, and professional entertainers might then sell copies of the works which they had recited.[24]

2 BUYING PRINTED BOOKS

In order to measure the affordability of books, manuscript or printed, we need first to know what wages were earned and what degree of prosperity they represented. An annual salary of 100 or more ducats or florins was well above average and could provide a life of some ease, with basic expenditure on food, rent and clothing for a Florentine adult estimated at about 10 to 14 florins a year, and the yearly rent for a good house or shop around 15 florins.[25] A well-known professor in humanist studies, Giorgio Merula, earned 120 ducats in Venice. In Florence, professorial salaries at the Studio or university could be as high as 200–350 florins for rhetoric, 600 florins for medicine, and 1,050–1,350 for law.[26] An income of between 40 and 50 florins a year gave a reasonably comfortable existence. This, we saw in chapter 1, was what a compositor might receive, and skilled labourers in Florence and Rome earned similar sums at the start of the Cinquecento.[27] But many earned far less. An ordinary mason or smith in Florence and Rome had an optimum annual income of no more than 30 florins or so. The Florentine *catasto* of 1480 records a barber working for an annual salary of 30 florins (and only at the rate of 4 lire to the florin) and young artisans and apprentices aged from thirteen to twenty-one earning the equivalent of from 1.7 to 15 florins a year. The going rate for male and female servants in Florence around 1500 was 33.5 lire a month, about 6 florins a year (though they no doubt received free board and lodging).[28] And there is no shortage of unemployed men in the 1480 *catasto.*

The cost of manuscripts in the fifteenth century varied greatly according to the material used (vellum or paper), the length of the work, the skill of the scribe, whether the book was decorated or not, whether it was bound or unbound, whether it was new or second hand. At the top of the market, prices were very high indeed, out of reach of all but the wealthiest. It has been estimated that a commissioned vellum manuscript of 200 folio leaves, with 30 lines to the page, illuminated and bound, would have cost 25.9 ducats. Even if it had been undecorated, unbound and written on paper costing 3 bolognini for 10 leaves rather than on vellum costing 20, the bill for it would still have come to 13.9 ducats.[29] Studies of manuscripts in Florence and Naples reveal a wide range of prices. The Florentine bookseller Vespasiano da Bisticci sold manuscripts on paper for 2.5 or 3 florins, but he sent a number of books to Naples in around 1457 with values ranging from 4 ducats, for a copy of the Latin historian Sallust, to 55 ducats, for a 'large, very beautiful' missal. The secretary of King Ferdinand I of Naples paid Vespasiano up to 60 florins for a copy of Pliny's *Natural History* in 1463.[30] Ippolita Sforza, wife of King Alfonso II, had manuscripts, including the works of Virgil and a Bible, worth 70 or 100 ducats each. Even for a run-of-the-mill vellum manuscript of average size one would have to pay between 7 and 10 ducats, about a month's salary for a Neapolitan court official or scribe; a paper manuscript would have cost perhaps only a quarter or a fifth of this amount, but that still represented about a week's income for somebody relatively well-to-do.[31] The books of Francesco Sassetti, general manager of the Medici bank, were valued at between 1 and 40 florins each in 1462; their average value was 6.4 florins. He had a little ('piccholino') Dante worth 1 florin and another one, 'fine, covered in red', worth 10.[32] The inventory of a shop run by two Florentine *cartolai* which was made in 1476, when the florin was worth 5 lire 14 soldi, includes a bound copy of Petrarch's *Trionfi* on paper with the reasonable estimated value of 15s., a day's wages for a skilled labourer. However, the basic texts of schooling which the shop stocked were written on vellum for the sake of durability and were therefore quite expensive: a hornbook cost only about 1.5 soldi, but a psalter cost 1 lira unbound and 1.5 lire bound, a *donato* from 2 lire second-hand to 3.5 lire new. To buy one of the commonest devotional texts, the *Officium Beatae Virginis Mariae* or Office of Our Lady (a collection of psalms and devotional texts which was much used for prayer even though the texts were almost always given in Latin rather than the vernacular), a customer would have had to pay between 2.5 lire for a second-hand vellum manuscript and 13 lire for an illuminated copy. It is not surprising that this shop also sold blank vellum on which one could write out one's own hornbook, and indeed that in general scholars and others might well decide to write out a work for themselves rather than buy a copy.[33]

How much more affordable than these manuscripts were printed books? Here we have three sources of information: printers' catalogues, which sometimes include indicative retail prices, inventories of warehouses and bookshops, which can give estimated values, and notes of prices made by purchasers in the books themselves.[34] Giovanni Andrea Bussi, editorial assistant to Sweynheym and Pannartz in Rome, claimed as early as 1468 that printed books cost one-fifth of the price of their manuscript equivalents, so that even the poorest could afford to build a library.[35] Prices in Venice and Florence were similar to Roman ones, and an edition might even have its price lowered to speed up sales.[36] In fact, Bussi seems to have been underestimating the savings offered by the new medium. It can be calculated from the evidence of two lists of the German printers' prices that the ratio of costs between a manuscript and a printed book was more like eight to one or even higher; so for instance a work which cost 40 ducats in a good illuminated manuscript in 1461 now cost 5 ducats, including binding, in print. This sort of price was still only within the reach of the affluent. However, one ducat would now buy a respectably sized text, 100 leaves in quarto or 70–100 leaves in median folio.[37] Even for the moderately well off, that might represent a week's income, a great deal more than the same sort of book would cost today; but they could have afforded it from time to time. A case which seems to be typical is that of a Florentine law professor, Giovanni Buongirolami, whose annual teaching salary rose from 25 florins in 1492 to 120 florins in 1502. The list of his books made in 1494 contained 102 items (some entries cover more than one book or copy), mainly legal volumes, of which 62 were specified to be printed ('in forma'); he also had other books, including some kept in his wife's bedroom. Between 1499 and 1506 he records the purchase of at least one printed book about once a year, mainly ones connected with his profession, but also Petrarch and the Gospels in the vernacular.[38] As for the less well off, who previously could rarely if ever have contemplated buying a book, short texts would now have been within their reach. The account book of the Ripoli press shows that its *donatello* (1476) sold initially for 8s. and was then gradually reduced in price to 3s., between five and twenty-five times less than the value of the bound vellum manuscript copies in the 1476 inventory. The Ripoli psalter (1480) was also much cheaper than its manuscript predecessors.[39] These books printed (presumably) on paper would not have lasted long in the hands of schoolchildren, but at such low prices that did not matter.

The records of booksellers in northern Italy between 1480 and 1500 show that they could supply a wide range of printed books priced at similar levels, even if still only the cheapest books cost less than the skilled labourer's daily wage of around 15s. At the shop of a bookseller working in Padua on behalf of Antonio Moreto in 1480, one could have bought an illuminated *donato* for 16s. or, for a more advanced pupil, the grammar of Guarino for 10s.; Petrarch's vernacular verse without commentary for 2 lire; Boccaccio's *Decameron* for 4 lire; translations of the Gospels for 1.5 lire and of the Bible for 10 lire. The shop held 42 copies of the Office of Our Lady, bound and unbound, at prices from 10s. to 3.5 lire. One would have had to be well heeled to afford Dante's *Commedia* with commentary at 7 lire, but one could buy it without commentary for 2 lire. Legal tomes were expensive, around 2 ducats or more.[40] Three inventories from Parma in the 1480s and 90s show that bookshops there held large supplies of school texts, some of them quite cheap. In a list of 1484 a *donato* cost 1 soldo 4 denari, Aesop's fables 2s., Guarino's grammar 3s. 2d. An inventory of 1491 records 1,348 schoolbooks, of which 579 were psalters, 300 *donati* (their price now down to 1s.), and 82 copies of Guarino (also cheaper at 1s. unbound): an impressive indication of the resources now available in the service of literacy, even if many of these copies were destined for sale outside the city. In 1497 the psalter is listed, bound, at prices from 4s. 5d. to over 2 lire. This third inventory also includes 60 copies of the *donato*, 108 hornbooks ('tavole da leggere') unbound and 58 bound. The prices of the latter range from a mere 4d. to 8s. each, depending presumably on the materials used. There was a large supply of some devotional books – 26 copies of the *Fior di virtù*, 73 Offices of Our Lady, all bound, from 1s. 2d. to 6s. each, 96 copies of the *Pianto della Vergine* by Enselmino da Montebelluna, today a very rare text – but also various chivalric romances. The 1491 inventory contains 133 copies of eight popular narrative works costing on average only 2s. 4d.[41]

A danger with inventories such as these is that they do not necessarily reflect readers' tastes: they could include the flops which were gathering dust as well as the hits which were likely to sell. The *zornale* or ledger of the Venetian bookseller-publisher Francesco de Madiis is thus particularly valuable, because it records not only his stock of 1,337 volumes in May 1484 but also his sales of 12,934 printed books (manuscripts are never mentioned) up to January 1488.[42] It confirms that schoolbooks did sell in increasingly large quantities and at more competitive prices. Over this period Francesco disposed of 150 copies of Niccolò Perotti's Latin grammar, 248 of Guarino's (costing 6–10s. unbound and bound), 257 *donati* (at 2 lire on vellum, 6–12s. on paper), and 600 psalters (at 15–18s. on vellum, but on paper down from 3–4s. in 1484–5 to only 0.6s. in 1486, admittedly in a wholesale transaction of 100 copies). Another bestseller was the Office of Our Lady: 450 copies changed hands at 15–18s. on paper or 3 lire on vellum. For relatively inexpensive devotional reading, Francesco's customers could buy an *Arte del ben morire* at 6s. or a *Meditation de la passion* for 8s.; for recreational reading, there were many chivalric romances in prose or verse such as Andrea da Barberino's *Guerrin Meschino* at 1 lira or Pulci's *Morgante* at 1.5 lire, Poggio Bracciolini's *Facetie* at 9s. or Boccaccio's *Ninfale fiesolano* at 10s. But Francesco also had some wealthy customers willing to spend considerably more. One spent 20 ducats in a single transaction on nine legal texts. His most expensive volumes cost 5 or 6 ducats. Dante and Petrarch with commentaries were for the better off only: the former cost a ducat, the latter 3 lire. Overall, statistics derived by Lowry from Francesco's records show that, even during the few years which they cover, readers were buying more books and were able to buy them more cheaply. In 1485, the highest monthly sales figure was 409 books (and the lowest 62 books), but 534 were sold in the first three weeks of January 1488; 378 customers purchased more than one book in 1485, but 722 did the same in 1486. At the same time, the cost of the average transaction fell from 2.63 lire in February 1485 to 2.2 lire in January 1488.

By the end of the century, printed books must have outnumbered manuscripts on booksellers' shelves all over Italy, though they had not displaced them entirely. The inventory made after the death of the Florentine *cartolaio* Silvestro di Zanobi di Mariano in 1496 listed over 291 volumes, of which 141 were identified as printed and 80 as manuscript; furthermore, books identified as printed were stocked in up to thirty copies, whereas there were never more than two copies of a work in manuscript.[43] In Naples, and no doubt elsewhere, the arrival of print also gave a boost to the number of booksellers.[44]

Inventories from the sixteenth century suggest two things. First, quantities of printed books held by publishers and booksellers grew more plentiful. Among the vast stock of the Milanese bookseller-publisher Niccolò Gorgonzola in 1537 (80,450 copies of 212 works) were 215 copies of the *Babuino*, 884 *donati* with vernacular glosses, 358 copies of Mancinelli's *Donatus melior*, 1,281 Aesops with or without commentary, and 475 *abachini*.[45] Gorgonzola's warehouse also held large numbers of popular devotional works (300 copies of the *Fior di virtù*, 450 of a *Benedictione della Madonna*), of chivalric romances and of short popular poems, but high vernacular culture was also represented by works of Pietro Bembo, among them 40 copies of the *Asolani*. Booksellers, as opposed to publishers, did not always have more copies of individual editions (the average remained three or four), but more editions were now available.[46] Second, books were affordable even by the less well off. Book prices in the second half of the century would have represented even better value than before, since they did not rise in line with the upward trend in salaries and other prices.[47] In early-sixteenth-century Ferrara, an average price for a book was 12–16s.[48] In 1595 two Milanese stationers, Giovanni Battista Bosso and Giovanni Battista Sirtori, had stock including 96 hornbooks at 3.5d. each, 42 primers at 5.5d. each, at least 378 *donati* costing just 1s., and 154 copies of the catechism (*Interrogatorio*) used by the Schools of Christian Doctrine at 2.5s.[49] Sirtori's stock of devotional works included over 200 *Fior di virtù* at 1.5 or 2s. and 100 lives of the Madonna at 5s.

The prices of the books published by the Giolito company could be considerably higher but were a great deal more reasonable than those of a century earlier. A reader in 1592 would, for example, have had to pay 8 lire for a two-volume folio of 544 pages. One lira would now buy about 400 pages of duodecimo, 300 pages of octavo or 150 pages of quarto; 6 soldi would buy about 120 pages of duodecimo, 80 pages of octavo or 40 pages of quarto; and a duodecimo of 56 pages could be had for 2 soldi.[50] We saw above that the earliest Italian printers asked 1 ducat, then worth about 6 lire, for 200 pages of quarto. In 1568 Giovanni Antonio Facchinetti, papal nuncio in Venice, was asked to draw up a list of books to form the library of a monastic convent; their average price was very high, 11.5 lire, but this was because they were mainly large folio volumes, theological and philosophical texts with some Latin classics and histories, with only fifteen books, mainly in smaller formats, costing 1 lira or less.[51]

For those living in the countryside, one source of books would have been travelling salesmen. The friar who set up classes in Cutigliano (see section 1 above) bought a supply of textbooks 'in piazza'.[52] Otherwise, peasants would have to venture into bookshops in town, where Garzoni lamented that they had worthless things foisted on them.[53] In Italy as in France, the printed book probably penetrated little into the peasant world, through a combination of low literacy, low availability and lack of need.[54]

3 THE OWNERSHIP OF PRINTED BOOKS

The main source of evidence for the ownership of books is inventories, sometimes drawn up as part of the property of someone recently deceased. Like booksellers' inventories, they need to be treated with some caution. They may date from some time after the books entered a collection; owning a book is not necessarily the same as reading it; on the other hand, one can easily read more books than one owns (books can be borrowed, or read and then sold or passed on).[55] But even after one has made allowances for such factors, the many inventories which survive from the period show that the advent of print had a profound effect on the nature and size of book collections.

The rate at which printed books began to appear in public and private libraries naturally varied from case to case, and in certain libraries, such as that of the Vatican, their numbers remained small. Typically, though, while in the 1480s about 20 per cent of books in a private collection might be printed, that proportion rose to 40 or 50 per cent by the 1490s.[56] In the Cinquecento, printed books were normally dominant. For example, by 1512 some Ferrarese libraries which had been formed over several decades contained only printed books.[57] Gian Paolo Da Ponte's library of 63 volumes included in 1534 just one manuscript, a collection of verse compiled by himself, and there were only ten manuscripts (eight of them musical) among his son-in-law Adriano di Spilimbergo's 200 or so books.[58]

A few exceptional book collections dating from before print had already been of impressive size: Pope Nicholas V had in 1455 some 1,160 manuscripts, which became the core of the Vatican Library, and Cardinal Bessarion bequeathed 752 manuscripts in 1468.[59] But the high cost of manuscripts meant that even the relatively well-to-do did not normally have large numbers of books.[60] Print changed this situation: after 1465, libraries grew steadily larger, though book-owners remained a minority of the whole population. Important evidence to this effect comes from a series of Florentine inventories, covering most of the

Table 3. *Numbers and average sizes of book collections in the inventories of the Ufficiali dei Pupilli, Florence*

	1413–53	1467–1520	1531–69	1570–1608
Total no. of collections	131	75	177	199
Average no. of books per collection	6	10	13	40

Table 4. *Sizes of book collections in the inventories of the Ufficiali dei Pupilli, Florence* (percentage figures)

No. of books in collection	1413–53	1467–1520	1531–69	1570–1608
1–5	56.0	53.8	55.2	31.4
6–10	23.0	21.3	12.3	14.8
11–20	16.0	10.6	11.1	14.2
21–30	4.0	6.6	5.9	8.2
31–50	0.8	8.2	9.1	10.2
51–100			4.5	9.1
101–200			1.3	8.2
201–300			0.6	1.2
301–500				3.2
Over 500				0.5

period from 1413 to 1608, drawn up by the magistracy concerned with overseeing the possessions of minors whose care had been entrusted to the community or whose father had died intestate, the Ufficiali dei Pupilli (officials of the wards). No clergy are included, therefore, and the documents give little information on the social status of those concerned. It is clear, however, from the statistics extracted by Christian Bec that, while most Florentine book collections remained on the small side, there was a steady increase both in the numbers of libraries inventoried (see table 3) and, especially in the late Cinquecento, in the numbers of books in each household (see table 4).[61] The rising tide of books in the Cinquecento and their lower material value seem to have been the causes of the growing tendency in these inventories not to identify volumes by their titles.[62] The number of schoolbooks listed fell, most probably not because fewer were in use but partly because they were cheaper and therefore less well cared for, and partly because they were now normally produced on paper rather than on hard-wearing vellum.

From Sicilian documents of 1299–1499 studied by Henri Bresc, it emerges that the only members of the working class to have had any books were immigrants or those whose work brought them into contact with the upper classes. The average size of Sicilian libraries ranged from 3 books for merchants to about 65 for lawyers; only five people (all of them lawyers, who had a professional need for books) had over 100 volumes, but the trend was upwards, since four of these five cases date from after 1470.[63] Marino Zorzi's analysis of 937 Venetian inventories dating from 1527 to 1600 shows that books were present in only 146 of the households concerned (about 15 per cent); about 23 per cent of patricians owned books, 40 per cent of the citizen class, 64 per cent of the clergy and 5 per cent of the popular class. Some inventories list only a few books, at times only one. However, even the 'minor' private collections (that is, those outside a handful of exceptional ones) could be quite large. Four patricians had between 110 and 270 books, three had about 50. The biggest collections among the lower class, the citizens and the clergy contained respectively over 40, 240 and about 350 volumes.[64]

The largest Italian book collections of the Cinquecento reached unprecedented proportions. Cardinal Domenico Grimani is said to have had 15,000 books by 1523. The Venetian patrician Marin Sanudo owned about 500 volumes in 1502; in 1516 the total had risen to 2,800 with an average value of 1.4 ducats, still expensive but a fraction of the 6.4 florins which, as we saw above, Sassetti's manuscripts were worth. By 1530 Sanudo had 6,500 volumes. In 1604 the collection of Gian Vincenzo Pinelli included 6,428 printed books and 738 manuscripts.[65]

As collections grew bigger, so they needed to be stored and consulted differently from their predecessors. Writing desks often contained cupboards or shelves for books. Apart from that, the basic independent medieval item of furniture for storing books was the chest (also useful for security and for transport). Books could also be stored in recesses in a wall, on shelves and in presses, in other words cupboards fitted with shelves (see figs. 8 and 14).[66] Chests were still used to hold private collections even if they numbered over 100 items: Leonardo da Vinci, for example, kept 102 of his books locked in one chest and 14 in another.[67] In some institutional libraries in Italy, there had been a development from the mid fifteenth century towards a 'lectern system' to facilitate the storing and consultation of their bulky and precious manuscripts; the earliest example may be the Biblioteca Malatestiana in

Cesena, 1452. In such libraries, a room was fitted with rows of benches, each bench having before it a shelf on which books were stored on their sides, chained for security, and, above this shelf, an inclined desk on which the reader would place the book to be read.[68] But once print had arrived, further changes were needed. Space had to be found for many more books; these books were less valuable than manuscripts; they were increasingly (as we shall see in the next chapter) in a format smaller than folio; and, given the relative abundance of books, readers expected to be able to consult more than one volume at a time. The larger public and even private libraries therefore began to store books upright on shelves or in cupboards set against the wall. The inner library in the Vatican may have used this 'wall system' in addition to benches and chests in the late fifteenth century, but the first major libraries to be designed entirely in this way seem to have been Spanish.[69] In the larger private libraries, too, this system replaced the storage of books in chests and the use of lecterns for displaying as well as consulting books (a practice which one can see portrayed in, for example, Carpaccio's painting of Saint Augustine in his study).[70]

A good example of the scale and spirit of the institutional library in the age of print is the justly proud description written in 1599 of the new library built by the Augustinians of Cremona.[71] This contained 4,000–5,000 books and had space for 8,000. Around the walls ran a series of large presses ('credenzoni'), each of which could store 500 books on three levels, with two shelves at each level. An index of the contents was placed on the side of each press. The door of the middle section of the press could be lowered to form a desk at which one could sit at a bench, take the two or three books one wanted, study them and write. For the greater comfort of users, in each space between a press and a window there was a chair which one could move to the press or else sit in 'with a book in one's hand, reading for pleasure at the air of the window'. Even in a religious institution, the activity of reading had become an altogether more relaxed affair: the library was now a place which encouraged one to browse in comfort as well as a system capable of facilitating the study of a quantity of books which would have been unimaginable a century earlier.

CHAPTER 6

Printing for the reading public: form and content

We now have an idea of the size of the reading public and of the growth of its ownership of printed books. In this final chapter we can turn our attention to the provision of books for this public by producers of books in a wide sense: mainly printers and publishers, but also the writers and editors who worked for or with them. We can consider how far developments in the form, the contents and the packaging of texts suggest that printing made books more accessible than before and that it thus brought about a change in the nature of the reading public and of the activity of reading itself.

I READERS AND THE FORM OF PRINTED BOOKS

How did the printing industry go about catering for the tastes of existing readers and attracting new ones? How did it meet the challenge of the growing competition to win readers? A crucial aspect of its task was to ensure that the physical appearance of books and of the texts which they contained was suited to readers' tastes. In the first place, form conditions the initial appeal of a book, since different presentations have different statuses and different cultural connotations. Secondly, form defines the way in which the text is read. As D. F. McKenzie has observed, 'the material forms of books, the non-verbal elements of the typographic notations within them, the very disposition of space itself, have an expressive function in conveying meaning'.[1] Roger Chartier, too, has drawn attention to the ways in which technical, visual and physical devices organize the reading of writing when writing becomes a book, and has stressed that a work is not 'an abstract text whose typographic forms are without importance'.[2]

One of the key elements in the form of a Renaissance book was the typeface or typefaces used.[3] These underwent a complex set of developments. The first men to print in Italy used, as models for their typefaces, examples of the formal humanistic or 'roman' script whose letter forms are those in which the present book is printed, with the exception of a long upright minuscule (lower-case) 's' used at the beginning of, or within, words. This script had been developed in Florence around 1400 by two scholar-scribes, Poggio Bracciolini and Niccolò Niccoli, encouraged by the chancellor of the state, Coluccio Salutati. In one sense, therefore, it was an innovation, but it was known then as *litterae antiquae* (old letters) because it was a return to a script which originated in the Carolingian reform of handwriting and was used between the ninth and twelfth centuries.[4] By the time printing was introduced to Italy, this had become accepted as the norm for literary Latin texts and would therefore have been that which was most familiar and easily legible from the point of view of the sophisticated public at which the early Italian printers were aiming.[5] Two roman types in particular, both introduced in Venice, came to be seen as the best models for upper and lower case: that of Nicholas Jenson, measuring 115 mm for twenty lines of text and probably based on the formal book hands of scribes working in north-eastern Italy, such as Bartolomeo Sanvito; and the refined version of this type, measuring 114 mm for twenty lines, which was cut by Francesco Griffo for Aldo Manuzio and first used for a complete text in Bembo's *De Aetna*, 1496.[6] (For examples of roman type, see figs. 5 and 11.)

However, the association of roman script with the new learning could also be a disadvantage, making it seem inappropriate in contexts where there was a close continuity with medieval learning, notably law, religion and to some extent science. Manuscripts of texts from these fields were traditionally written in what since the thirteenth century had been called *litterae modernae* or *novae* (modern or new letters), and to which the term 'gothic' came to be extended in the sixteenth century.[7] In this script, letter forms were more angular, including a minuscule 'g' with a loop below the upper bowl (rather than two bowls joined by a stroke, as in roman); and consecutive round letters, such as in 'be' or 'do', frequently touched or overlapped. In some versions, the ascender of 'd' sloped backwards, 'r' within a word might have a form similar to the arabic numeral '2', 'z' had a curved tail, and the abbreviation for 'et' was similar to '7' rather than the ampersand '&'. The early German printers imitated an angular gothic hand known as 'textura', while the gothic hand of Italian law schools such as Bologna, the *littera Bononiensis*, had more rounded forms and is hence known as 'rotunda'. In order to cater for the tastes of those accustomed to reading certain types of text in this script, Ulrich Han, the first man to print in Rome after Sweynheym and

Pannartz, used a gothic typeface for Cardinal Torquemada's *Meditationes* (1467 and 1473), whereas he used roman for classical and humanistic texts. In Venice, Windelin of Speyer introduced gothic type in a legal text of 1472. Typically, Jenson saw the potential appeal of this initiative, followed it and improved on it, introducing his own superior gothic founts (measuring respectively 106 and 84 mm) in 1474 and using gothic thenceforward in all his legal, theological and liturgical work.[8] The rise of gothic in certain categories of Venetian printing soon had an impact elsewhere. Antonio Zarotto began his career as a Milanese printer in 1471 with roman type, but in 1474 began to use two gothic founts (both 110 mm, based on a fount used by Filippo Lavagna in the previous year) for works in the categories of liturgy, medicine, law and theology, for a school text (Aesop) and for a vernacular work which had yet to acquire its high sixteenth-century status, Boccaccio's *Decameron*. Gothic was the standard type for legal works and missals in fifteenth-century Milan.[9] In Rome, gothic took over from roman as the preferred typeface from 1477 to 1500. However, in the incunables of Rome, gothic and roman were used equally for legal texts, and gothic was used predominantly in books of octavo format and in liturgical works.[10] (For examples of gothic type, see figs. 9 and 10.)

At the start of the new century, Aldo Manuzio introduced a third and very influential type design, an italic, measuring 80 mm, which was cut for him by Griffo (see fig. 6). He applied in March 1501 for a ten-year privilege to protect this 'cursive and chancery script, of outstanding beauty, never previously made' ('lettera corsiva et cancelleresca de summa bellezza, non mai più facta').[11] As the terms 'cursive' and 'chancery' imply, the script on which this fount was based was rapidly written, rather than formal, and it had associations with administrative contexts. Although it was a modified version of gothic chancery scripts, it had been made every bit as respectable in Quattrocento humanistic circles as roman script, thanks to its adoption as a book script by Niccoli and then, in the second half of the century, by scribes from the Veneto such as Sanvito. The italic script of Sanvito and the way in which he laid out the text on the page have been identified as possible models for Aldo and Griffo (compare figs. 6 and 7).[12] Italic remained a hand associated with a relatively high social standing and a high level of learning. In the notebook of Maddalena mentioned in chapter 5, section 1, italic handwriting was used by only 39 out of the 102 writers, including 2 clergymen and a notary, with only 8 using it well, while the more traditional *mercantesca* or mercantile hand was used by 62 others, including representatives of commercial companies, suppliers and transporters of goods. But since *mercantesca* was hardly imitated in print, it had disappeared from use by about 1560.[13] In the course of the sixteenth century, roman and italic typefaces between them came to dominate Italian printing. Gothic was, however, still used in some contexts, such as liturgical works and popular books (see section 2 below).

The format of books was another aspect of presentation to which producers of books gave attention in order to make them more attractive to readers. The underlying perception was that the larger the book was, the greater its seriousness. This assumption soon came to be partly modified, as we shall see, and one must remember too that a miniature book can impress just as much as a large one.[14] But the association between physical and metaphorical weight endured long enough for Lord Chesterfield to characterize books, in a letter of 1757, as the persons to whom, because of his deafness, he now assigned his hours of audience: 'Solid *folios* are the people of business, with whom I converse in the morning. *Quartos* . . . are the easier mixed company, with whom I sit after dinner; and I pass my evenings in the light, and often frivolous, *chit-chat* of small *octavos* and *duodecimos*.'[15] Two other factors involved in choice of format were portability and price. A folio was a bulky object, to be consulted in one place, while an octavo or smaller format allowed one to slip a book in one's pocket and carry it around, consulting it where and when one wanted, for study or in moments of leisure, and it could be cheaper if a smaller typeface allowed economies in the amount of paper used.

The earliest books printed in Italy tended to be in folio or quarto formats. In Venice, folio was preferred at first; for example, of the 91 editions printed by Jenson between 1470 and 1481, 65 were in this format. But the trend over the next fifty years was for books to become smaller. In Rome, folio predominated until 1473; then quarto became more popular and was used for 70 per cent of incunables.[16] Venetian Bibles were the first to be printed in 'a handy medium folio size, not requiring the support of a lectern', and the first attempt to produce a quarto Bible was made in Piacenza in 1475.[17] The same text could be provided simultaneously in large and small formats, in order to satisfy readers who wanted to spend more or less money or who wanted to use the book in different circumstances. Thus in 1494 the printer Johannes Hamman supplied the same bookseller with a missal in folio and then a few months later in octavo.[18] Among the early Venetian privilege requests, we find the publisher Girolamo Biondo applying in 1495 to have the Gospels and Epistles of the church year (*Evangelia ac Epistolae annuales*) printed in folio, quarto and octavo, and three years later Antonio di Zanoti planning to print 'officieti' (presumably Offices of Our Lady) in octavo, sixteens, thirty-twos and sixty-fours, missals in folio, quarto and octavo, and breviaries in quarto and octavo, all illustrated.[19]

Octavo and smaller formats were chiefly associated before 1501 with texts which, by their nature, would often need to be carried from place to place: above all, devotional or liturgical texts such as missals (containing the prayers and texts recited in the mass), breviaries (containing the prayers said by the clergy at different times of day), psalters, confessionals (guides to the sacrament of penance), books of hours (containing principally the offices of the canonical hours), or the popular guide-book for pilgrims, the *Mirabilia urbis Romae* (Marvels of the city of Rome, IGI 6447–92). To some extent, octavo was used for books which would have had a primarily instructional use, but it was used only exceptionally for other classical works or even for popular works.[20]

Of the 10,251 Italian incunables listed in the ISTC in 1997, only 823, or about 8 per cent, are recorded as being in octavo. But, if we look at the pattern of the use of this format in table 5, we can see that the 1490s saw a marked rise in its popularity, especially in Venice and Rome. Printers in Venice also began tentatively to experiment with its use for academic legal texts. Two octavo editions of Justinian's *Institutiones* appeared in 1493 and 1494, and Paganino Paganini applied in the latter year for a privilege to print texts of canon and civil law 'in portable form' ('in forma portatile'), and specifically in octavo on sheets of median paper ('de octavo foglio mezano'), for the greater ease and utility of poor students.[21] Andrea Torresani followed suit with two more legal texts in octavo in 1498. By the end of the fifteenth century, then, the idea of portability in books was clearly gaining ground, but smaller formats were still largely restricted to religious texts, and printers had scarcely begun to link them with reading as a leisure activity.

It was all the more surprising, then, that from April 1501, in Venice, Torresani's partner Aldo Manuzio took the very bold step of using octavo for a whole series of literary classics in Latin, Greek and Italian. Furthermore, he linked this innovation with two others: the use of his new italic fount for the Latin and Italian texts, and the stripping of the texts of the commentaries which had conventionally come to surround them, indeed of practically any introductory, supplementary or decorative material (compare figs. 5 and 6).[22] The resulting books were

Table 5. *Octavo editions printed 1465–1500 (data from ISTC)*

	1465–1500	1465–70	1471–80	1481–90	1491–1500
Venice	297	2	38	76	181
Rome	271	6	56	42	167
Milan	99	0	39	24	36
Florence	47	0	5	11	31
Brescia	32	0	3	4	25
Naples	23	0	11	6	6
Bologna	8	0	4	1	3
Total	777	8	156	164	449

even slimmer than normal octavos, since Aldo used sheets of a new size of paper of the same height as normal median paper, about 35 cm, but slightly narrower than usual, about 42 cm.[23] The inspiration, according to Aldo in the dedication of his Virgil of 1514, came from the library of Pietro Bembo's father, Bernardo, which included slim manuscripts of verse, including at least four or five classical texts in the italic hand of Bartolomeo Sanvito.[24] Such a size was evidently fashionable in Venetian humanist circles. But the main quality to which Aldo drew attention was that of portability by those who led an active life outside the study. The dedication of the second octavo to appear, the Horace of May 1501, addressed to his patrician friend Marin Sanudo, described the volume as having been produced as an *enchiridium*, a manual or handbook, so that, thanks to its small size, he could read it in the moments of rest from his commitments in public office and as a historian. To Sigismund Thurz, secretary of the king of Hungary, Aldo dedicated Cicero's *Epistolae familiares* in 1502 as a book which Thurz could read easily outside his home and his library. The Aldine catalogue of 1503 defined these books as 'libelli portatiles in formam enchiridii', books which could be carried about in the form of a handbook.[25] They were not cheap, however. Aldo noted by hand on the only surviving copy of his catalogue of 1503 that the Latin octavos were priced at 3 marcelli each, or 1.5 lire, and Greek octavos cost 3 or 4 lire. His editions were no easier to afford than the larger books with which they were competing; indeed, they might sometimes be dearer.[26]

Aldo's innovations in format, typeface and editing in the literary classics would have been surprising, even shocking, to many, but they were immensely appealing to an elite international market of sophisticated readers, those who, as Martin Davies has put it, had 'education but little leisure, or education and too much leisure': politicians, diplomats, prelates, courtiers and the like.[27] Before 1501, octavos had been associated chiefly with religious devotion; these new Aldine octavos were 'prayer books of a lay culture'.[28] Janus Lascaris, the Greek scholar now working as a diplomat at the court of Louis XII of France, was enthusiastic about Aldo's proposal to produce an 'enchiridion' of Homer, 'especially in view of my wandering way of life' ('maxime andando vagabundo nel modo che facio').[29] The empty space surrounding verse texts would also have been welcomed by readers who were cultured amateurs, not professional academics, and had no need of the detailed and often tedious commentaries offered by other editions. Readers often took advantage of the blank margins to add their own notes or variants of the text; this space was an important feature when readers viewed books, more than they do today, as places in which to record information and opinions. The difference which this revolution made to the manner in which reading took place can be illustrated by a comparison between conventional portrayals of the scholarly reader with a book planted solidly on his desk, and sixteenth-century portraits of courtiers and churchmen casually holding an octavo-sized book in an apparent moment of leisure, and in a setting which is not necessarily one of the traditional sites of reading, the library, the private study or the lecture room (compare figs. 14 and 15).[30] The variety of manners of reading now available is well illustrated in the famous letter of 10 December 1513 in which Machiavelli described a typical day in his life in the countryside, as well as announcing the genesis of *The Prince*. In the morning, his reading is casual and mobile: he goes off to a fountain or an aviary with a poetic text under his arm. In the evening, his reading is serious and sedentary: he goes to his desk in his study and metaphorically enters the courts of the ancients, studying the past for up to four hours.

These Aldines set a fashion for the use of octavo or of even smaller formats. In Venice, Lazzaro Soardi used octavo for an edition of the plays of Terence in 1511, creating what he called a *pugillar*, a Latin term for a writing-tablet which could be held in the hand, and he followed this by using duodecimo in three editions in 1511 and 1513.[31] Alessandro Paganini experimented in 1515–16 with a series of Latin and Italian classics in twenty-fours.[32] If we trace the history of the formats in which Dante's *Commedia* was printed in Italy before 1600, we find that the fifteen incunables are exclusively in folio, but that in the sixteenth century this format is the exception rather than the norm, being used only five times, while smaller formats, from quarto down to twenty-fours, are used in the remaining twenty-six editions.[33] Of 118 titles printed between 1549 and 1591 which are listed in a catalogue of the Giolito company in Venice, only 3 are in folio, as against 38 in quarto, 49 in octavo and 28 in duodecimo.[34] As the use of smaller books spread, emphasis continued to be placed on the advantage of portability which they gave to the reader. The publisher of an octavo edition of Ptolemy's work on geography pointed out in 1548 how praiseworthy it was that everyone could comfortably carry it in the sleeve; Gabriele Giolito said in 1554 that he was printing Petrarch in duodecimo rather than octavo 'for greater convenience'; and Felice Mattioli, an heir of the Pietro Andrea Mattioli mentioned in chapter 3, decided to divide the edition of Dioscorides into two volumes because the weight of books discouraged some people from carrying them here and there around the university and elsewhere.[35]

This does not mean, of course, that larger formats did not continue to play an important role, especially for those readers who wanted imposing, formal volumes. For example, of the books chosen by Facchinetti in 1568 to form a monastic library (see chapter 5, section 2), the vast majority were in folio.[36] For older readers, the size of the typeface was an important factor, and this could require the printer to use a format larger than octavo. A Venetian privilege request of 1494 concerned a breviary which was to be printed 'in large format and in a big character for the use of the old' ('in forma magna et caractere grosso pro usu senum').[37] Gabriele Giolito's 1565 quarto edition of a popular devotional text, the *Specchio di croce* of Domenico Cavalca, was, he pointed out in his dedication, in a format larger than his two earlier editions, both in sixteens, 'for the common benefit and especially that of elderly people'.

The printed book did not bring innovations in the layout of the text, but it did make more consistent and extensive use of changes in presentation which had been introduced in certain manuscripts between the twelfth and the early fifteenth century. The radical and enduring nature of these changes meant that, as Malcolm Parkes has written in an important study, 'the late medieval book differs more from its early medieval predecessors than it does from the printed books of our own day'.[38] It was in this period that writers, scribes and rubricators packaged theological and legal texts in order to make them more easily consultable by the reader. Among the navigational devices employed were tables of contents; numbered divisions within the text; alphabetical indexes listing topics treated in the text (using references either to the numbered divisions or to the leaf and column of a particular copy); rubricated chapter headings; enlarged initials, often rubricated or decorated, which highlighted the beginning of a new stage in the text; marginal notes containing section numbers, references to sources cited or mentions of notable topics; glosses (i.e. commentaries, the ancestors of modern footnotes and endnotes) alongside or around the text in a smaller character; and headlines at the top of the page, containing running titles, often in red or blue, to inform the reader of the section of the text contained on the page, and sometimes the number of the leaf or even the page. Producers of printed books tried to reproduce these features, though before the 1470s they faced a technical problem in placing type outside the text area: Bussi claimed in 1469 that it was too difficult to print marginal notes, and a similar difficulty may partly explain the restricted use of printed signatures at the foot of the page (see chapter 1, section 3) in the 1460s.[39] A problem of a different sort was whether to rely on colouring in order to highlight important features of the text. As we saw in chapter 1, section 4, hand decoration was used for a short while only. But double printing with red as well as black ink was used for a longer period, especially in legal and liturgical texts, even though this was a time-consuming process.[40]

The most important contribution of printing to the *mise en page* of the text was the more frequent inclusion in the headline of the numbering of leaves or folios (foliation) and then of pages (pagination).[41] Both these techniques were used in Germany in the 1470s, but they spread only very slowly, probably because numbered subdivisions of texts provided an alternative means of reference, independent of the particular edition concerned, and because precise reference was in any case required only in specialized, mainly academic, contexts. Pagination was used hardly at all in the fifteenth century (the first Italian instance appears to be Aldo Manuzio's 1499 edition of Perotti's *Cornucopia*), and foliation was probably used in only about one European incunable in ten. The growth of printed numbering appears to be linked with the increasing provision of indexes and tables of contents, but at first even the presence of an index with folio references did not mean that there would be printed foliation. It was considered that numbering could be inserted by hand, and this was sometimes done professionally, by rubricators, or in plain ink in the printing house itself.[42] It could also be left to the owner of the book: in his preface to the index of Craston's Greek–Latin lexicon (1497) and in the *Metamorphoses* of Ovid (1502–3), Aldo tells readers to fill in the numbers on each leaf. The evidence of a sample of continental European books suggests, however, that, probably under the influence of Venetian presses, printed numbering spread quickly in the sixteenth century, being introduced into 50 per cent of books by about 1510 and over 90 per cent by the 1590s, and that by the end of the century the almost universally used method of numbering was pagination with arabic numerals.[43]

The spread of indexing and of foliation and pagination in the context of printing reflects the growing attention being paid to presenting texts visually in such a way as to help readers to consult and understand them more easily. This concern also showed itself in other ways. As time went on, printers used less frequently the system of abbreviations, inherited from handwriting, which saved space and time but which increased the number of sorts (pieces of type) to be used by the compositor and which hampered fluent reading. In printing, individual words were increasingly kept separate, where previously there might not have been a division between certain combinations (fig. 5 gives examples such as 'mene' and 'acostor' in an edition of Dante from 1484, while fig. 6, from an edition of 1502, has 'me ne' and 'a costor'). Editors, as we shall see later, began to add diacritic accents and punctuation in order to help comprehension. The varied resources of the compositor's case could be used in order to differentiate or highlight information: for instance, if the main text was in roman type, italics might be used for a commentary or for quotations within the text, or key points could be set in upper-case letters and indented, even in the genre of the dialogue, which purported to reproduce oral communication.[44] It is probable that at least some of the decisions about the analytical setting out of information were being made by authors, and that new habits in presenting knowledge and in acquiring it by systematic consultation were being spread to all readers. In this way, it has been suggested, in particular by two North American scholars, Walter Ong and Elizabeth Eisenstein, changes in the presentation of texts may well have led to changes of thought patterns among all users of the printed book.[45] Drawing on the same lines of argument, Alvin Kernan has suggested that systematization, the structuring of knowledge forced by the systematic production and internal ordering of the book, is one of the three basic elements of print logic, together with multiplicity and fixity.[46]

The aspects of the presentation of texts to the reader which we have been considering so far are examples of the debt of print to manuscripts; but the development of the title page (*frontespizio* in Italian) shows the printed book beginning to acquire an independent identity.[47] The text of a manuscript normally begins on the first page, either with the dedication (if there is one) or with a sentence containing the information that here begins (*incipit* in Latin, *comincia* or *incomincia* in Italian) the book entitled such-and-such by author so-and-so. The work may end brusquely with a word such as Latin *finis* (end), but the opening information is sometimes echoed in a corresponding concluding formula known as the colophon, which states that here ends (*explicit* in Latin, *finisce* in Italian) the work in question, and this concluding statement may go on to identify the scribe and the date and place of transcription. Such a brief description of the contents and such inconspicuous identification of the producer were normally sufficient, because manuscripts were often written on commission and then circulated from individual to individual, and libraries were relatively small; there was therefore little need to devote precious paper or vellum to providing more information, or more prominent information, about the manuscript and its origins. As one would expect, the first printed books followed the practices of identifying and beginning the text on the first page (see fig. 9) and of identifying the printer or publisher, if he was identified at all, in a colophon (see fig. 11). The only initial modifications were that the first page was sometimes left blank, since this was liable to be spoiled when books were transported or stored unbound, and that printers began to identify themselves at the end of a book with a woodcut mark or device (Italian *marca*), similar in purpose to a hallmark on precious metal or a designer's label on an article of clothing. This device might contain their initials (see fig. 11) or an emblem associated with them, such as the dolphin and anchor of Aldo Manuzio.[48]

Publishers of printed books soon realized, however, that the context of large-scale competitive manufacture and marketing of books called for a new approach to the packaging of their commodity. So, instead of using the first page to begin the text, or leaving it blank, from 1476 they gradually began to treat it as an independent title page, giving it the two functions of identifying the volume and of attracting potential purchasers. At first, this page might contain a line or two naming the author, the work, or both, in either order. Then other features were added in order to interest readers and to advertise to them the virtues of this particular edition. These features might include, above all, information about the printer (sometimes including his device) and the place and date of printing, previously given only in the colophon; information about contents, with perhaps a decorative border or frame, or an illustration which would be both decorative and relevant to the subject matter; and statements that the text was newly printed or newly or diligently revised, that it was illustrated or translated, that it had fuller contents than its rivals, or that the edition was protected by a privilege or printed with permission (see fig. 12). The Giolito company also used the title page from 1568 onwards in order to indicate that an edition belonged to a linked sequence of texts, thus initiating the concept of the series, for which Italian still uses one of Gabriele Giolito's terms, *collana* or 'necklace'.[49] In the course of the Cinquecento, title pages thus became more and more prolix and crowded in an effort to publicize the intellectual and legal status of the book, combining the roles which nowadays we would expect to see shared among the title page, the title verso, the cover of a paperback or the dust jacket of a hardback book, and sometimes also the contents page. A further publicity function might be carried out by a letter on the following page or pages, addressed to the reader by the editor or printer, which could often resemble a rather verbose version of a modern publisher's blurb.

Another feature which helped to attract readers to printed books was the decoration and illustration of texts by mechanical means. The development of this was gradual and led by printers of German origin, and the proportions of Italian fifteenth-century books which were illustrated are low: about 7 per cent in Bologna (nearly half of these being scientific), 12 per cent in Rome (but rising to nearly 30 per cent in the 1490s) and 17 per cent in Naples.[50] In the next century, the use of illustrations grew; for instance, they appear in fifty-seven of the ninety-one editions printed for Gorgonzola in Milan. The expectation that certain types of book had to be illustrated meant that printers might resort to inserting depictions of subjects which had little or no relation to the text. The same scene might accompany different episodes, a view of one city might be used to depict another, and in Gorgonzola's books one finds incongruities such as a depiction of Saint Paul in a story of lovers or of Saint Margaret in an edition of Ovid.[51] By the late sixteenth century, illustrations had taken on the central role in certain books, such as editions of Tasso's *Gerusalemme liberata* which Infelise describes as 'to be looked at rather than read', ancestors of the modern coffee-table book.[52]

Printers had available to them two existing techniques for creating illustrations and decorative elements such as ornamental frames or borders and initial letters (though, as we have just seen, decorated letters did not have a solely ornamental function). One method was to create images from relief woodcuts. These were relatively cheap to produce and could be printed in the forme at the same time as the type, but they could not be used for fine detail. The other way was to use intaglio engravings on metal (usually copper) plates. Here the principle is the reverse, and the ink to be absorbed by the paper fills the engraved lines rather than being applied to the relief image. Intaglio engravings could provide much finer detail and nuances of shading, but cost more (in material and labour) to produce and, most inconvenient of all, had to be printed separately from letterpress because of the different method of inking. Moreover, engravings were best printed on a cylinder press, which exerted greater pressure than the conventional screw press, though the first secure reference to a roller press, as opposed to cylinders which may have been rolled by hand, is found only in 1540. Principio Fabrizi referred, in an edition of 1588, to the difficulty of printing in two stages, 'that is, the letters and the copper plates separately, and at different times, and sometimes in different places'.[53]

Woodcuts provided what have been reckoned to be the first illustrations in an Italian printed book, the *Meditationes* of Torquemada dated 1467.[54] However, woodcut illustrations were uncommon before the 1490s, when printers began to use them more frequently. The first woodcut illustration in a Florentine book appeared in 1490.[55] In Venice, the first Italian translation of the Bible with woodcut scenes came out in 1490; the first illustrations in a *Decameron* appeared in 1492 and acted as a model for other editions for over fifty years; and editions of Dante's *Commedia* printed in 1491–2 contained designs derived from the Brescia edition of 1487, some of the illustrations for which had themselves been based on the intaglio engravings of the Florentine Dante of 1481 (see below).[56] From 1488, folio editions of Petrarch's Italian verse had a full-page woodcut illustration for each of the six *Trionfi*.[57] As for decorations, early printers regularly left blank spaces, or spaces with a small guide letter (see figs. 5 and 10), so that initials could be added by hand. A transitional compromise solution used in Venice from 1469 to around 1474 was to stamp outline woodcut border motifs and initial letters by hand, so that they could be coloured in later.[58] By the 1490s, however, decorated woodcut initials were commonplace (see figs. 5, 9 and 13) and all types of decoration by hand had become rare; a Sienese illuminator, Bernardino Cignoni, lamented in 1491 that printed books had killed off the demand for his skill.[59]

Intaglio engravings, rather than woodcuts, provided the first book illustrations in Bologna and Florence in 1477 and in Milan in 1479. They were used sporadically from then until 1514, particularly if maps were required, and once (in 1512) for a title page.[60] A particularly ambitious (indeed, as it turned out, overambitious) experiment was the attempt to adorn the edition of Dante's *Commedia* printed in 1481 in Florence, intended as a demonstration of the city's cultural and social superiority, with engravings derived from designs by Botticelli. However, only the engravings for *Inferno* I–XIX were completed, and it seems that none were ready when the book first appeared, so that some copies have no illustrations and others have an incomplete set.[61] After 1514, there was a long interval before engraved illustrations and title pages reappeared in Italian books, the first such series of illustrations being found in the maps provided with the Italian translation of Ptolemy's work on geography printed in Venice in 1548.[62]

Cartography is just one example of the important role played in printing by the use of illustrations to present technical information to readers.[63] One of the earliest and finest illustrated books, the edition of Roberto Valturio's *De re militari* printed in Verona in 1472, contains over a hundred woodcuts depicting military machines. Woodcut mathematical diagrams were used, for example, by Erhard Ratdolt and by Paganino and Alessandro Paganini for their Venetian editions of Euclid's *Elementa* (respectively 1482 and 1509) and by Filippo Calandri for his *De arithmetica* (Florence, 1492); and the diagrams in the Paganini edition of Luca Pacioli's *De divina proportione* (1509) are thought to be based on drawings by Leonardo da Vinci.[64] Some early-sixteenth-century editions of Dante's *Commedia* contained woodcut diagrams of the layout of the Inferno, Purgatory and Paradise, while Alessandro Vellutello's biography of Petrarch in his edition of 1525 was accompanied by a woodcut map of the area around Avignon where the poet had spent much of his early life.[65] And just as the genre of dialogues succumbed, as we saw, to tabular typographical presentation, so it also began to make use of diagrams and figures.[66]

2 READERS AND THE CONTENT AND PRESENTATION OF PRINTED BOOKS

How did the contents of the first Italian printed books reflect and respond to the needs of contemporary readers? One way of answering this question is to look at statistical evidence on the subject matter of editions produced. Much caution is necessary here, since surveys have necessarily been based on incomplete data: for the fifteenth century, on catalogues such as the *Indice generale degli incunaboli*, which covers only holdings in Italian libraries, or on studies of some individual cities; for the sixteenth century, on the catalogues of the British Library, or on the annals of individual printers, who can be only partly representative of general developments.[67] Many editions will have been entirely lost over the years, especially those of smaller, more popular and ephemeral works, which in the past were less likely to be cared for and collected by bibliophiles.[68] Statistics do not take account of the size of books or of print runs: a cheap quarto pamphlet is given the same weight as an expensive and bulky legal folio, and a book produced in 200 copies counts the same as one produced in 2,000. Nor can they take account of how successful and widely read an edition was. There are also problems and inevitable differences of practice in dividing books into subject categories: a classical work, for example, might be considered a literary text or a school text, depending on the context in which it was being read.

The figures, then, tell only part of the story, but as one examines their evidence certain clear trends emerge.[69] Early publishing was initially rather conservative and cautious in its choice of subject matter and language. Producers of books naturally preferred to risk their capital on what was tried and tested among established readers (just as modern film producers have a liking for remakes and sequels, not to mention prequels), and these readers naturally preferred the features to which they were accustomed. An analysis of European incunables by J. M. Lenhart suggested that some 77 per cent were written in Latin.[70] In Italy, the proportion was probably slightly higher: of the holdings listed in the IGI, 20 per cent are in the vernacular. Figures for Milan, Brescia and Bologna are similar (respectively 18 per cent, 23 per cent, 20 per cent); if Florence is an exception with 77 per cent, this is because much of its output consisted of ephemeral or popular texts for a local market. But, during this period, the overall trend of vernacular printing is markedly upwards: 21 per cent of the production comes from 1469–80, 29 per cent from 1481–90 and as much as 48 per cent from 1491–1500. Samples from the sixteenth century suggest that Rome, seat of the papal curia, and university cities such as Turin and Pavia remained strongholds of Latin printing, but that elsewhere, and especially in Venice and Florence, the vernacular came to predominate.[71] The producers of books in Italy were learning that, as well as supplying books according to the traditional habits of readers, they also needed to stimulate new demands, among both existing and new readers, by offering texts which were new or which were available in new ways.

As for the subject matter of European incunables, Lenhart suggested that about 45 per cent of them were religious in character (including theological, scriptural and devotional works), while literature and philosophy accounted for 36 per cent, law for 11 per cent and science for 9 per cent.[72] The proportion of religious printing in the vernacular was certainly high in fifteenth-century Italy – nearly 49 per cent of the vernacular holdings in the IGI are classified by Quondam as religious rather than secular – but the overall share of religious printing is probably lower if one includes Latin publications, to judge from the figures for individual centres: 34 per cent in Rome, 27 per cent in Venice to 1481, 23 per cent in Milan, 18 per cent in Bologna.[73] Of greater importance in Italy were works of classical learning (classical texts, grammars and humanist works), to which was devoted 39 per cent of the output of the Milanese presses, 21 per cent of that of the Bolognese presses, and 35 per cent of that of the Venetian presses up to 1481. Sweynheym and Pannartz in Rome overproduced classical and patristic texts, according to their appeal to Pope Sixtus of March 1472 (see chapter 2, section 1), and in this year there was a temporary slowing in the expansion of Roman printing, followed by a decline in the output of ancient works (those dating from before 476) in favour of those by medieval and contemporary authors.[74] Venetian printing too was struck by a crisis at this point: several printers ceased production and the number of editions dropped sharply in 1473, though it has been suggested that here the causes may lie in a moment of economic panic rather than in overconcentration on classical texts.[75] Whatever the causes of the crisis, it was followed by diversification. Soon afterwards, Windelin of Speyer and Jenson branched out into the printing of legal texts. These came to form a significant part of the output of Venetian presses (17 per cent up to 1481), and they were of great importance in Bologna and Milan (respectively 26 and 25 per cent of the output of these cities).

Analysis of the output of Venetian printing in the second half of the sixteenth century reflects a further major development in the subject matter of Italian books. Between about 1555 and 1565, the climate of the Counter-Reformation, the influence of which on the book trade was mentioned at the end of chapter 2, led anxious printers to turn away from secular vernacular literature to the safer and now increasingly profitable field of religious literature.[76] The development can be illustrated first of all by Grendler's analysis of the *imprimaturs* (permissions to print) issued for new titles by the Venetian government. In the 1550s the category of religion includes about 13–16 per cent of the titles and that of

Table 6. *Subject matter of editions produced by the Giolito company, 1536–1606*

	Religion	History	Literature	Treatises
1536–9	1	1	6	2
1540–4	6	3	22	12
1545–9	6	19	97	23
1550–4	13	15	104	47
1555–9	25	18	63	31
1560–4	29	14	45	38
1565–9	50	20	25	22
1570–4	42	10	10	6
1575–9	30	5	4	3
1580–4	19	4	8	6
1585–9	21	8	10	14
1590–4	9	0	4	2
1595–9	5	2	0	1
1600–6	0	1	0	1
Total	256	120	398	208

secular vernacular literature 26–31 per cent, but in the 1590s the proportion of religious titles rises to 28–36 per cent and that of secular vernacular literature falls to some 18 per cent.[77] The same pattern can be traced in Gabriele Giolito's publishing in Venice. His last *Decameron* appeared in 1552, and his last editions of Petrarch and the other most closely studied example of vernacular verse, Ariosto's *Orlando furioso*, were issued in 1560. Quondam's figures, derived from Bongi's immensely rich *Annali*, show the inexorable rise of religious books in the Giolito company's output from the 1550s, at the expense of the three other fields in which it had concentrated most of its efforts: history, literature and treatises (see table 6).[78]

One of the points to emerge from quantitative surveys such as these is the adaptability of the producers of books in Italy: they were able to adjust to the demands of readers by diversifying their output in line with shifts in the cultural and moral climate, and they were able to foster or even create demand among readers. But what we have not yet considered is how broad this readership was. The numbers of experienced readers were relatively restricted when printing arrived in Italy, as we have seen, and early printers, Martin Lowry has emphasized, 'worked for the same select clientele as their scribal predecessors'.[79] What efforts did their successors, and contemporary writers using the press, make to reach a wider audience? If we are to get a better impression of the effects of printing on reading, we now need to ask how far the contents and presentations of printed books contributed to an expansion of reading by catering for the demands and expectations of readers outside the well-educated, well-to-do, predominantly male elite.

Probably the most fundamental and certainly the most immediate way in which printing promoted reading was at the earliest stage of all, by taking over and multiplying the basic texts of education. Printed schoolbooks are among the rarest today, because they were discarded easily (and probably more than willingly) by their users and have been neglected by collectors, but they must have been very common in schoolrooms and even in homes from the 1470s onwards. Printers would have produced them in large numbers because they were certain to sell. A Donatus 'for little boys' ('pro puerulis'), presumably the *Ianua*, was the very first text printed in Subiaco, in 300 copies of which none survives.[80] The same text, in 400 copies, was probably the first venture of the Ripoli press in Florence in 1476 (GW 8990). We saw in the previous chapter that the traditional elementary texts – hornbooks, psalters, *Ianua* – were available in shops in much larger quantities than any other books. The effect of the greater availability of texts within education may well be illustrated fairly faithfully by two contemporary woodcuts showing a teacher and his pupils (see fig. 8): in that of 1491 only one pupil seems to have a textbook, while in that of 1525 at least four out of five (and the teacher) have a book. Lotte Hellinga has similarly contrasted an illustration from a fourteenth-century manuscript, in which one pupil alone has a book, with a woodcut from a text on letter-writing (the *Formulario* attributed to Landino) printed in about 1490, in which most pupils have a book and moreover practically ignore their teacher, as if their books had made them independent of him.[81]

Even if these pupils of 1490 were only seemingly indifferent to the presence of a teacher, print certainly made easier the acquisition of literacy and then the further stage of using literacy. In the first place, there began to be printed new kinds of books which could be used to teach the basic educational skills to a wider public. We saw in chapter 5 that learners in the classroom could use *donati* with translations, the *Babuino*, and Mancinelli's *Donatus melior*, as well as more traditional textbooks. From the 1520s, some authors wrote books expressly for use outside the schoolroom by all people, of whatever age, of either sex, and however poor. Giovanni Antonio Tagliente, a Venetian scribe who was nevertheless more than ready to embrace the opportunities of print, produced a *Libro maistrevole* (Venice, 1524) which claimed to allow one to teach reading 'to old and young and to women who know nothing, in two months or less, according to the intelligence of the learner'. He told users of the work that it could be used to teach one's son, daughter or friend 'and even old and young women'. A short *Dictionario* by a Florentine teacher, Giovambattista Verini, which was printed in Milan in 1532, listed the alphabet, syllables, and some nouns and verbs in Tuscan, and was intended to teach the illiterate to read anything printed in the vernacular, as well as to write and do sums, in three months. The works of another teacher, Domenico Manzoni of Oderzo, included a *Libretto molto utile per imparar a leggere, scrivere, et abaco* (Very useful booklet for learning to read, write and do arithmetic, Venice, 1546), to be used by parents in instructing their children, and *La vera et principal ricchezza de' giovani, che disiderano imparar ben legere, scrivere, et abaco* (The true and principal riches of young people who wish to learn to read, write and do arithmetic well, Venice, 1550), aimed at everyone, however uneducated ('rozzo'), especially those who could not attend school. Filippo Calandri published in 1492 his *De arithmetica*, an original mathematical text for schoolchildren, encountering various technical difficulties in the course of printing, as he mentions in his dedication, no doubt because of the combination of woodcut diagrams with letterpress (see fig. 10). Several other new texts gave instruction in handwriting or arithmetic.[82] The encouragement which print gave to the seeking out of alternative sources of teaching and learning may, one can surmise, have fostered the reaction against the dry-as-dust mentality of the pedant, whose stilted, Latinizing language was satirized on the comic stage.[83]

To someone who had acquired the ability to read, printing offered during the sixteenth century an ever wider range of material for self-instruction and self-improvement. One area in which people sought much guidance was that of writing in the Italian vernacular. This language was neglected in the schoolroom, yet it was becoming increasingly fashionable as a serious literary medium, and there were a growing number of people with literacy but who were *illetterati* (unlettered) in the contemporary sense, in other words with little or no Latin and without the training in composition which still depended on the learning of Latin. In Venice, for instance, Nicolò Liburnio aimed at the previously untapped market of young people and women who wanted instruction in correct Tuscan usage, when he compiled a work of advice on good style, *Le vulgari elegantie* (1521), for all those who have 'newly approached the purity of the vernacular', and a handbook on grammar and elegance, *Le tre fontane* (1526), for 'our well-mannered and clever youths' and 'the honest and virtuous ladies of Italy'.[84] Tagliente produced an *Opera amorosa* (1533) containing examples of exchanges of love letters (which could act as models but also as a series of epistolary *novelle*), and a manual on writing speeches and letters (*Componimento di parlamenti*, 1535) for men who 'have not attended too much the schools of Latin'.[85] These and other printed works undoubtedly contributed to the sudden expansion of vernacular writing – in manuscript as well as in print – which took place in the Cinquecento.[86]

Readers were also offered new courtesy books or manuals of polite behaviour, in the wake of the continuing success of Castiglione's *Libro del cortegiano*.[87] Historical narratives were made available for a wider readership. One of the first steps towards a 'downwards' diffusion of historiography was a digest of world history, the *Supplementum chronicarum*, which first appeared in Venice in 1483 from the press of Bernardino Benagli. Although it is in Latin, its author, the Augustinian friar Iacopo Filippo Foresti of Bergamo, wrote that he had compiled it expressly in order that young people should acquire the kind of knowledge which had hitherto been reserved for older men. This type of initiative was then extended to those who could read the vernacular but not necessarily Latin. Foresti's work was itself translated into Italian and was reprinted throughout the Cinquecento; its varied readers included Lucrezia Borgia, Leonardo da Vinci (who described himself as an 'omo sanza lettere' or unlettered man), a Florentine law professor, the miller Menocchio and the self-educated nun Prospera Corona Bascapè.[88] In the second half of the Cinquecento, men such as Francesco Sansovino and Tommaso Porcacchi, working for the Venetian presses, continued the process of making history easier to read and digest by translating, rearranging and summarizing the work of classical and modern historians or by providing their own compilations.[89] The same tendency to recycle and stitch together information for a general readership is found in contemporary works on technical, practical and social topics such as the *Specchio di scientia universale* (1564) by the Bolognese doctor Leonardo Fioravanti, a survey of knowledge which rambles from crafts and trades to moral and social issues, useful inventions and advice for women on makeup, or the *Piazza universale* (1585), an encyclopedia of trades and professions by the cleric Tommaso Garzoni, or the various collections of medical, cosmetic and other recipes ('libri di segreti'). It is no coincidence that both Fioravanti and Garzoni felt it appropriate to praise the enlightenment which printing had brought to many who previously simply could not afford knowledge.[90]

Readers also had available to them many books which can be described as 'popular', though they were not necessarily written by those of lower social status and would be read by the well educated and those of limited culture alike.[91] Popular editions typically had a content, religious or secular, with a traditional, unchanging appeal to a wide audience; the author and the printer or publisher were often anonymous; the text was in gothic or else in roman type, rather than the more sophisticated italic, and the title page often had a combination of gothic and roman; a format smaller than folio was used, and costs could be kept down by setting the text in two columns with small margins on low-grade paper. The Venetian state protected this market in 1537 when a law spared books costing 10 soldi or less, described as 'cose minute' (small things), from quality control over paper.[92] A strict definition of popular editions might insist that they were short works, consisting of just one or two folded sheets or even a half-sheet, which could be carried around by the itinerant salesmen mentioned in chapter 2 in order to reach readers who did not habitually frequent bookshops and bookstalls.[93] Grendler has taken a much broader view of popular printing, identifying certain common physical features from a selection of longer works of edification and entertainment: the *Fior di virtù*, Thomas à Kempis's *Imitation of Christ*, the Office of Our Lady and a number of chivalric romances. Editions containing these works were typically of quarto or smaller format; they were no longer than about two hundred pages; they had many small illustrations (these would have had the functions of dividing up the text into sections and of providing landmarks, thus helping readers to find their way around and to remember the topic); and they were printed in a gothic typeface or in a roman which was old-fashioned rather than one of the new designs of Jenson or Aldo. In chivalric romances, gothic persisted alongside roman until at least 1583; italic was very rare until Gabriele Giolito began to use it as an alternative to roman for the *Orlando furioso* in 1542, and thereafter it was associated particularly with modern epics aiming to imitate Ariosto's sophisticated model.[94] 'Cose minute' some popular books may have been, but the market for them was evidently strong enough to allow a number of printers and publishers – examples are the Ripoli press in Florence, the priest Battista Farfengo in Brescia (see fig. 9), Giovanni Battista Sessa and the partnership of Francesco Bindoni and Maffeo Pasini in Venice – to specialize in them, without necessarily restricting themselves to this type of output.

An important function which popular printing took over from handwritten letters or oral diffusion was to provide the latest information and comment on current affairs. Many of the resulting editions were in verse. A popular genre was that of the *lamento*: for example, the catastrophic invasion of King Charles VIII of France and its aftermath in 1494–5 inspired some twenty surviving poems.[95] Giuliano Dati's 'Letter on the newly found islands', a poem on Columbus's discovery of the new world, was printed at least five times (GW 7999–8003). Prose reports were often based on a letter from an observer in the field to a senior figure at home. There was a particular liking for reports of disasters or prodigies, and title pages could anticipate modern tabloid headlines or news vendors' placards by stressing the 'shock-horror' aspect of the event through the use of woodcut illustrations and through their wording: for instance, the 'stupendous and horrible things' seen in woods near Bergamo in 1517, where mysterious battalions of soldiers did battle but then turned into pigs; the three suns which appeared in France in 1536, 'a most stupendous thing'; the 'tearful and pitiful case' of the Roman flood on Christmas Eve 1598 and the miracles which had occurred.[96] Printed news reports were a key element in the propaganda of the Church, and a favourite subject was the conflict between Christian and Turk in the Mediterranean.[97] The style of reporting could vary from the calm to the dramatic, as one can see by comparing two editions, of 1536 and 1538. The former, printed in Bologna by Giambattista Faelli, has a sober title (*Copia di una lettera da Constantinopoli della vittoria del Sophì contra il gran Turcho*) and a woodcut coat of arms. The other, printed in Venice by Giovanni Andrea Valvassori, has a title which sensationalizes the event with its inflated adjectives and references to astrology (*Avisi da Constantinopoli di cose stupende, et maravigliose apparse in quelle parti, con la interpretatione c'hanno fatto gli Astrologi, et Indovini del gran Turcho circa la ruina sua*) and is accompanied by a woodcut of a gory battle scene; the account itself is not in the form of a letter to an individual but is addressed to all those interested in hearing the latest news and uses direct speech to enliven the account. The distribution of smaller items such as these would have depended to a large extent on itinerant sellers, since the texts would go rapidly out of date. Aretino introduces in his comedy *La Cortigiana*, I. 4, just such a salesman, a certain Furfante who attracts customers with his cries of 'istorie, istorie'. Weekly printed news reports, ancestors of the modern newspaper, began to appear in Venice in mid century and were given the name *gazzetta*, perhaps from a coin worth 2 soldi which would buy one of them.[98] Print also provided a medium for the satire of the 'pasquinades', originally poems which were affixed to the statue of Pasquino in Rome.[99] Printed almanacs gave information on the year to come, and readers' curiosity or fears about the future were catered for through prognostications, which, Garzoni complained, had an all too ready sale.[100]

Women's access to the skill of reading was, as we saw in chapter 5, seriously limited in the patriarchal society of Renaissance Italy. Nevertheless, some printed books were aimed above all at women readers, or at least at women as well as men. Certain types of religious books in particular were traditionally considered important for a female readership. Anne Jacobson Schutte's survey of vernacular religious bestsellers (titles issued five times or more) in the period from 1465 to 1494 suggests that these editions were intended for both sexes. They include moral treatises such as the *Fior di virtù* (which leads the bestseller list by some way) and fra Cherubino da Spoleto's works of advice (*Regole*) on the spiritual life and on the married life; confessional manuals, including one addressed by Sant'Antonino of Florence to all people, from the learned to those lay persons who spend too much time reading short stories and chivalric romances; and works on the life and passion of Christ (such as fra Domenico Cavalca's *Specchio di croce*) and the life of the Virgin, all of which tended to stress the plight of Mary as mother.[101] One of Rome's early publishers, Giovanni Filippo De Lignamine, explicitly addressed two works by Dominican friars (Cavalca's *Pungilingua*, a treatise on sins of the tongue, and Iacopo Campora's *Dell'immortalità dell'anima*) to unlearned men 'and even to uneducated women' ('mulierculis quoque ipsis'); but the editions were not intended for a popular audience, since both were in folio format and roman type.[102] In 1490, the printer Battista Farfengo indicated that his edition of the story of two martyrs was to be read by the whole class of men and women ('marium et feminarum omnis ordo').[103]

A way of assessing which religious books were intended primarily for female readers is to see which were dedicated to women. One must remember that dedications tended to be addressed to people in the upper ranks of society and do not necessarily reflect what was actually read by women in general; but a dedication to a woman would at least have encouraged other women to read a work. An analysis carried out by Gabriella Zarri of the dedications of some sixty spiritual works printed between 1475 and 1520 shows that lay people and especially lay women were the main audience for the devotional books promoted by orders such as the Franciscans and Dominicans. Only one of the works in Zarri's sample was addressed to a male dedicatee, and even works without a dedication, such as most of those by Savonarola, have woodcuts indicating their main destination in veiled women, either nuns or widows. Such books, together with preaching, were, she concludes, the main vehicle for the diffusion of the friars' teaching on religion and moral behaviour.[104] Similarly, printed handbooks for confession were often addressed to devout women.[105]

We saw earlier (table 6) that religious books came to dominate the output of the Giolito company in Venice from the mid 1560s. From 1538 to 1564, authors, editors, translators or the printers themselves dedicated to women only seven religious works produced by the firm, most of them works of moral edification: a treatise on prayer, Cavalca's *Specchio di croce*, sermons of Cornelio Musso, the *Imitation of Christ* (dedicated to Lucrezia Giolito, Gabriele's wife, so that her daughters could learn to read and at the same time acquire devotion, since it was better for girls to be able to recite a prayer than a love sonnet), a saint's life, a work on acquiring divine grace (dedicated to Gabriele's daughter Fenice), and the rule of Saint Augustine (dedicated to a community of nuns). From 1565 to 1589, though, women were the dedicatees of nineteen Giolito editions of works of prayer and devotion, including a verse translation of the Office of Our Lady (so that women could understand as well as recite these prayers), an anthology of prayers (dedicated to Fenice, who by now had become a nun), works on the Virgin Mary and on other saints, spiritual exercises and meditations, and instructions for nuns.

Early examples of religious books written and printed for a specifically female readership are two of the four treatises composed by a Venetian Carthusian monk and brought out by Jenson in 1471.[106] One, the *Decor puellarum* (Adornment of young women), was addressed to unmarried women and included advice on their acquisition and use of literacy. Girls could be taught to read, as long as it was for a good purpose, by a sister, their mother or another honourable female relative, but not by a male. They should never read or write 'vain or carnal things' or anything they could not understand. The books proposed for reading included stories of virgin saints or the Church Fathers, the *Fior di virtù*, the *Specchio di croce*, the Carthusian's other spiritual works and the New Testament. Only some books of the Old Testament were to be read, however, because girls were ignorant and 'unlettered' ('senza littere') and could fall into heresy (v. 9). (The recommended reading in the equivalent tract for males, the *Palma virtutum* (Triumph of virtues, II. 5), included some of the same texts but permitted the Bible without restriction and was much more ambitious, adding Boethius, Lactantius and Dante.) Girls should avoid hearing stories or books (presumably read aloud to a gathering) if these concerned sexual desire, gluttony or other sensuality (IV. 6). The author distinguished clearly between praying aloud ('oratione vocale') and mental or meditational prayer.[107] Prayers to be said aloud included the Pater Noster and Ave Maria, which would have been learned by heart; both the *Decor* (III. 2–3) and the treatise destined for married women, *Gloria mulierum* (Glory of wives, I. 2) instructed the illiterate to recite these, while the literate were to read aloud from the Office of Our Lady and the Psalms. The *Decor* includes a long vernacular prayer to the Virgin to be read or copied out (ff. 10v–13r), but most 'vocal' prayers were in Latin.

The Office of Our Lady, recommended by the anonymous Carthusian, was not read exclusively by women but was a book of great importance to them. About half of the Florentine book inventories of the period record one or more copies of it, and sometimes it is the only book in the household. The work is sometimes described as a 'libriccino di Nostra Donna' (little book of Our Lady), but this could be shortened to just 'libriccino di donna' (woman's little book) or could even become 'libriccino da donna' (little book for women), showing its particular association with females. A copy could be produced with expensive materials: Florentine copies, doubtless manuscripts in many cases, might have clasps of silver or brass and be covered in blue damask or leather.[108] For a woman, then, the Office could form a precious part of her personal possessions. It could also serve her as a text for learning to read, even though the fact that it was almost always in Latin would have made it difficult to understand.[109] But its main value was of course as a prayer book. It played a part, for instance, in the devotions of a Bolognese widow praised by Sabadino degli Arienti: he tells us that she 'reads, hears and understands with pleasure and attentively pleasant things, and especially the glory of those women who have lived and live in the world with honour, fame and religion', and she 'says the office of the glorious Queen of Heaven'.[110] It is interesting that this widow had texts read to her, as well as reading them herself, and one might also conclude that she recited the Office without necessarily understanding it as well as she did the saints' lives. A visual affirmation of women's devotional reading can be seen in the spread of images of the Virgin and of female saints with a book: portrayals of the Annunciation or of the Virgin Annunciate, of the Virgin with Christ or with Christ and the young Saint John (also significant for women's role in educating their children), of the penitent Mary Magdalene and so on (see for example fig. 17).[111]

Images which associate women with devotional books might, on the other hand, also suggest that men wanted to steer women towards this kind of reading and away from other kinds, including certain recreational works. Some men did indeed think in this way. Boccaccio himself had criticized Mainardo Cavalcanti in 1373 for allowing women in his household to read 'my trifles'.[112] Vespasiano da Bisticci gave as a shining example to mothers the young Alessandra de' Bardi, who learned to read with the Office of Our Lady and would recite it daily. Girls should not, he said, be given works such as the 'hundred tales' (presumably the *Decameron*) or the sonnets of Petrarch; although these are morally decent ('costumati'), women must learn to love only God and their husbands, and, in order to temper their natural frivolity, they should read holy books such as the lives of saints.[113] The first book of Dolce's dialogue on the upbringing of women (*Dialogo della institution delle donne*, 1545) recommended the Old and New testaments, some classical literature, Dante and Petrarch, Bembo and Sannazaro, Speroni's dialogues and Castiglione's *Cortegiano*, but he wanted girls to avoid Latin poets (except some of Virgil and the chastest parts of Horace) and 'all lascivious books', especially the *Decameron*; in any case, study should not lead a woman to neglect her duties in the household. In the same period, two of Sabba da Castiglione's *Ricordi* (113, 121) reveal similar prejudices.

In spite of such repressive tendencies, a significant number of non-religious works in the vernacular were produced for women by contemporary authors and printers. Women of all classes were keen readers of chivalric romances, and Ariosto's privilege application for the *Orlando furioso* in 1515 stated that his audience included ladies ('madone').[114] But women also read to inform themselves on matters ranging from domestic skills to literature and science. Several pattern-books for lace-making and embroidery were addressed to them, including the ever enterprising Tagliente's *Esemplario nuovo* of 1531.[115] Some women were intent on 'reading for writing', in other words on reading as part of the process of acquiring skills as authors, especially as lyric and even epic poets.

The evidence of dedications suggests that printers and their associates were well aware of the interest, or at least the potential interest, of some women in reading as a leisure or instructional activity. Four editions of Petrarch and eight of Boccaccio were offered to a woman or to a group of women.[116] (Only one edition of Dante's *Commedia*, the 1515 Aldine, had a female dedicatee, and she was an exceptional one, the poetess Vittoria Colonna; but that is not surprising in view of its difficult content.) The printer Giovanni Francesco Torresani dedicated his octavo edition of Castiglione's *Libro del cortegiano* 'to gentlewomen' in 1533, so that they could carry it comfortably in every place and at all times. Between 1538 and 1564, the Giolito press offered to women many and varied non-religious editions: works of Boccaccio (but only in the early years, up to 1546), verse written by contemporaries (Sannazaro, Parabosco, Tullia d'Aragona, Muzio, Bernardo Tasso, an anonymous account of Romeo and Juliet, even Latin verse by Pierio Valeriano), verse edited by Domenichi and Dolce, letters by Tasso and Parabosco, two books of the history of the Byzantine monk John Zonares (it was very unusual for a historical work to have a female recipient), and some treatises and dialogues in the vernacular: Heinrich Cornelius Agrippa on the nobility of women, Dolce on their upbringing, Erasmus on the upbringing of children, Castiglione on the courtier, and Seneca on conferring and receiving benefits (*De beneficiis*). The mid 1560s saw a marked change of policy in dedications, and from then until 1589 only one non-religious work printed by the Giolito company (a comedy by Paolo Bartolucci) was offered to a woman. However, the earlier Giolito dedications, taken with those of works from other presses such as Piccolomini's astronomical treatises *La sfera del mondo* and *Le stelle fisse* (1540) and the first version of his *Institutione di tutta la vita de l'homo* (a treatise on the upbringing of children and the conduct of lay adult life, 1542), suggest that women were increasingly keen to read about social, moral and other topics. These dedications seem not merely to represent an attempt by printers and authors to find a new market but to reflect contemporary confidence in women's ability to enter the world of vernacular learning and literature, since, as Piccolomini wrote in *La sfera*, access to Latin was denied to them. Indeed, the dedications can be seen to reflect the achievements and aspirations of women themselves as they became accomplished users of the vernacular and even expressed resentment at men's domination of the instruments of literary production.[117]

The ownership of printed editions by laywomen is difficult to gauge, because books were usually registered in inventories as the property of a man. Those belonging to some female members of the ruling family of Ferrara are, however, listed separately from the main ducal library. There were as many as seventy-four books in the collection of Eleonora d'Aragona, wife of Duke Ercole I d'Este, in 1493; those specified as printed were almost all vernacular religious texts. The first wife of Alfonso I, Anna Sforza, had a small collection of exclusively religious books, at least one of them printed. Lucrezia Borgia, his second wife, had fifteen books in 1502–3, of which two were specified as manuscript and six as printed; these latter included the letters of Saint Catherine of Siena and the vernacular Epistles and Gospels alongside at least two non-devotional texts, the translation of Foresti's chronicle and Dante's *Commedia* with commentary.[118] A woman from a patrician Venetian family is recorded as owning two cupboardfuls of printed and manuscript books in 1583.[119] But most women would have had only a very small number of books of their own. The collection of a widowed Sicilian noblewoman, recorded in 1495, included just seven books, all printed: in town, she had the Bible, a book on Saint Jerome and three small unnamed volumes, while in her residence outside town she had a volume in which were bound together, in a curious combination, the sermons of fra Roberto Caracciolo and the *Guerrin Meschino*.[120] At the lower end of the social scale, even those women who could read would have had still fewer personal books, perhaps none at all. Some women in sixteenth-century Venice are recorded as having just one book. This was the case with the illiterate prostitute Isabella Bellocchio, who in 1589 had Ariosto's *Orlando furioso* on display on her mantelpiece, presumably as a sort of status symbol.[121] To judge from portrayals of a woman's bedroom, books were not numerous but clearly played an important role. Carpaccio's *Dream of Saint Ursula* shows a book open on a table, with half a dozen others on shelves (see fig. 16). In Lotto's *Annunciation* (from the late 1520s), the Virgin turns from a book which is open for prayer, and two other books are perched on a shelf set high on the wall. Sixteenth-century artists also showed laywomen holding a book: for example, women reading Petrarch were portrayed by Bronzino (his subject is the poet Laura Battiferri) and Andrea del Sarto, while Savoldo's *Lady with a Dragon Fur* is pausing from reading, her finger marking her place in a closed book.

Some of the works dedicated by the Giolito to women were, we saw, translations into the vernacular. These could open doors to a culture denied to any reader who lacked a good knowledge of classical or modern languages, and for this reason they would have been an especially useful resource for women. The first major translation commissioned for print, Landino's version of Pliny's *Natural History*, which came out in 1476 (see chapter 2, section 1), was in the library of Eleonora d'Aragona, and Sabadino degli Arienti tells us that his wife Francesca liked to read it in addition to holy books.[122] In the mid sixteenth century, Sperone Speroni and Alessandro Piccolomini called for more works to be made accessible through translation, taking up an idea of Pietro Pomponazzi's, and the same period saw a marked increase in the number of translations in print.[123] Gabriele Giolito issued very few works in Latin, and nearly one-third of his output of historical texts was in translation.[124] The printing business of Michele Tramezzino in Venice from 1539 to 1579 relied almost entirely on translations.[125] Francesca degli Arienti had had to content herself with hearing Virgil read aloud, presumably in Latin, but in 1540 printed translations of the first six books of Virgil's *Aeneid* were dedicated to Sienese women by Alessandro Piccolomini and others. The advantages which translation brought to women can be judged from a description of the education of two young noblewomen, Emilia and Irene di Spilimbergo, written in 1559 (in a rather contorted Italian) by the grandfather who had brought them up:

datagli comodità de tutti libri, che nella lingua nostra materna sono fora de boni scrittori, che per gratia de Dio in questa nostra età molti valorosi et dotti spiriti ha scritti et translati da la grecha et latina lingua, in questi degni et honorati libri i quali veduti et studiati da esse così diligentemente, che non solo ne ha tratto el beneffitio delle Instorie over scientie et arte, ma tutto quel frutto et sugo che ogni pratico et dotto studente ne avesse potuto cavare, et così arichitesi delle Istorie antiche et moderne et delle fabole poetiche, che con qualunque persona parlavano credevano che le fosse instruitissime della greca et latina lingua.

(they were given access to all books by good writers which have been published in our mother tongue, books which by God's grace in this age of ours many valiant and learned spirits have copied and translated from Greek and Latin; and they examined and studied these worthy and honoured books so diligently that not only did they derive the benefit of histories or sciences and arts, but all those essential fruits which any experienced and learned student could have drawn from them. They were thus so enriched with ancient and modern history and poetic stories that anyone who talked to them thought they had had a very good classical education).[126]

Many religious works became available in translation, most notably the Bible in the version of Nicolò Malerbi (or Malermi), first printed in 1471, and in that of Antonio Brucioli, whose New and Old testaments appeared in 1530 and 1532 respectively. Brucioli explained in his dedication of the New Testament that he wanted people of all social backgrounds to receive the word of God and that he felt it wrong that women and most men should repeat prayers in Latin and Greek parrot-fashion, without understanding them.[127] However, the very idea of a vernacular Bible was controversial. Fra Filippo da Strada, a fierce opponent of print, disapproved in the 1470s of the way the press had widened access to the Scriptures, and nearly a century later regret was expressed at the Council of Trent that now the Bible in translation was addressed even 'to uneducated women' ('ad mulierculas').[128] In spite of these complaints, it has been suggested that the transition to print culture, in place of a mainly oral culture in which doctrine was diffused mainly through the preaching of the clergy, encouraged the rereading of texts and the comparison of different interpretations, privileging individual reflection and meditation.[129]

If the producers of printed books, in a climate of growing competition, were to attract as many readers as possible – from the less well educated, for whom buying a book was an exceptional event, to more scholarly readers, who might want reassurance about the quality of the edition in question – there were several key matters for which they would often need to seek out the help of men of letters acting as editors. Editors may have had an advisory role, helping with decisions about which works to print, but their two main functions were to provide a correct copy of the text to be printed and to assist readers in understanding and consulting the text by providing indexes, commentaries and other supplementary material.[130]

Given the susceptibility to error of the printing process, correctness was not only desirable in itself but also a strong selling point. Claims of a 'recent' or 'new' correction would make an edition seem especially desirable, and the title page was used to advertise ever more inflated claims to editorial care. Revising a text for printing was, however, likely to be far from straightforward. Unless the editor had access to an exemplar approved by the author, there was the initial problem of locating and obtaining one or more reliable copies of the work. Then he might be faced with difficult choices between variant readings, or decisions on whether an obscure word was authentic or the result of an earlier error of transmission. He would be working without any accepted methodology of textual criticism, and with the study of earlier phases of the vernacular still in its infancy. In the second half of the Cinquecento, editors might have to work as censors, sometimes 'correcting' a text under the scrutiny of the Holy Office; a notorious example is the preparation of the Florentine *Decameron* of 1573. Consciously or not, the editor might also be subject to commercial pressures. The great majority of manuscripts were produced on commission for an individual or at least with a specific readership in mind. In contrast, those employing editors to prepare texts for print had to sell a relatively large stock of books as quickly as possible, and were thus normally aiming at a readership whose background was much less clearly defined and which was often interregional.

The need for the language of a text to be widely acceptable – easily understood, but also close to what was generally regarded as 'correct' – could therefore become crucial to the editing process. This factor was liable to conflict with editorial respect for types of language which most customers would find difficult to read or lacking in cultural prestige: in particular the language of older texts, containing some forms no longer in use, and that of texts from regions other than Tuscany. Prose writing was particularly vulnerable to intervention, because changes could be made without heed to metre and rhyme. In Venice, the standard towards which editors gravitated was at first Tuscan with an admixture of forms from the Veneto. But by around 1500 literary fashion was moving towards a stricter imitation of the Tuscan of the fourteenth century. That was the period of Dante's *Commedia*, but more especially of Petrarch's verse and Boccaccio's prose, which came to be seen as the high points of vernacular literature so far. The trend towards studying and emulating the past was confirmed by the appearance of printed grammars of the vernacular – the first was Gian Francesco Fortunio's *Regole grammaticali della volgar lingua* in 1516 – and above all by Bembo's justification and analysis of the imitation of Trecento Tuscan in his *Prose della volgar lingua* of 1525. Already from about 1515 editors were becoming more assiduous in eliminating non-Tuscan usage and traces of the Latinizing influence (spellings such as *nocte* rather than *notte*, lexical borrowings such as *puerculo* in the sense of 'young boy') which had infiltrated the vernacular in the previous century under the influence of humanism. One must remember, too, that the growing ranks of new users of the written vernacular were avid for texts to which they could turn as models for their own writing. In view of these tendencies towards the normalization of the vernacular, it is not surprising that editors often put uniform linguistic 'rules' before the varied evidence of their sources (indeed, some of them also compiled grammatical treatises).

'Correction' therefore often meant the imposition of a spurious 'correctness', on the assumption that texts could be improved only by making them conform with the editor's ideals of perfection, just as some Victorian architects sought to preserve medieval English churches by means of a restoration which was well-intentioned but alien to the spirit of the original. Editors could be quite open about the motives behind their interventions if the text in question did not originate in a period or place regarded as authoritative. Lodovico Domenichi, for example, made it abundantly clear in his 1545 edition of Boiardo's *Orlando innamorato* that he had polished up an original which he saw as marred by the rough-hewn language typical of the late fifteenth century. In most cases, though, and especially if the author was Tuscan, editors claimed (not always, one suspects, with hand on heart) that the corruption which they were curing had been introduced by copyists or by previous printers, or by both.[131]

The practice of most editors, then, tended to distort the original, but it did have the important side-effect of helping to consolidate and diffuse among readers a standard for literary Italian, based on Trecento Tuscan models but without some of the archaic forms which grated in the ears of many Italians of the Cinquecento. At the same time, as the status of the vernacular rose, a minority of more scrupulous editors of older texts, including Pietro Bembo in Venice and Vincenzio Borghini in Florence, were prepared to learn from the standards of the best classical textual critics of the day.[132] These men set limits on their modernization of early authors, were cautious about using correction by conjecture, attempted to recover the earliest available manuscript evidence for their texts, and studied and respected earlier varieties of the vernacular.

The editor's work in 'correcting' a text might be motivated in part, we have seen, by the desire to make its language more accessible to readers, and this desire was closely related to the second main editorial function, that of making texts easier to use. One of the tasks which this function might lead editors to undertake was the addition of two features which modern readers take for granted: punctuation and diacritic accents. Fifteenth-century printed texts used, and sometimes used only sparingly, a limited repertory of punctuation signs: mainly the full stop, the colon and the oblique *virgula* (/) equivalent to the modern comma, in order to indicate pauses, and the question mark; and the paragraph (¶ or similar) to indicate the start of a new section. Accentuation was used only exceptionally.[133] The turning-point in the use of these two resources in vernacular texts, in order to help interpretation and resolve ambiguities of sense and sound, is found in the 1501–2 octavo editions of Petrarch and Dante in which Bembo, as editor, and Aldo Manuzio, as printer, introduced the apostrophe to indicate elision (fig. 6 gives examples such as 's'udia'l' and 'ch'a l'habito' versus 'sudiel' and 'challabito' in the 1484 text shown in fig. 5), the semicolon to indicate a slight pause, and the grave accent to distinguish *è* (meaning 'is') from *e* (meaning 'and') or very occasionally to indicate some stressed syllables where more than one pronunciation was possible (as in *empiè*, *pièta*). The comma (in its modern semicircular form) and the full stop were also used more regularly than they had been previously (see figs. 5 and 6). In the course of the first half of the sixteenth century, the modern distinctions between, for instance, *parlo* ('I speak') and *parlò* ('he/she spoke'), or *che* ('that', 'which') and *ch'è* ('which is') were generally adopted. The opportunities presented by print led to the development of some overcomplex and hence unsuccessful accentuation systems and spelling reforms for the vernacular. Print also provided authors with the stimulus to add punctuation: it seems that Ariosto wrote his first drafts of the *Orlando furioso* with hardly any punctuation marks and added them only when his manuscript was to be given to the printers.[134]

Editors could also provide a number of other resources for the reader outside the text itself. They might compile indexes, summaries of sections of a work, marginal notes or, from the 1540s onwards, 'allegories' or glosses which suggested a moral or spiritual interpretation of works such as the *Decameron* or the *Orlando furioso*.[135] Such paratexts (to adopt the convenient term coined by Genette) would almost inevitably lead the reader to approach the main text in a way not intended by the author.[136] This was most obviously the case with 'allegories'; but even the other devices could lead to a tendentious reading, because the editor was focusing on topics which were particularly important to *him*. For instance, Dolce's index to Castiglione's *Cortegiano*, printed from 1552 onwards, was compiled with a moralizing purpose and a pro-aristocratic bias.[137] Occasionally, if the work was important enough, editors were called upon to compose a commentary or to write a biography of the author. From the 1530s, as interest grew in the imitation of the language of the classic vernacular authors – especially Petrarch and Boccaccio, but now also Ariosto – editors devoted particular effort to promoting the understanding and the active use of their texts. In a peninsula still divided linguistically even more than it was politically, Tuscan, and especially fourteenth-century Tuscan, would have been a tongue remote from that of many readers. Editors therefore provided guidance for readers and would-be writers in the form of notes on meaning and usage (placed at the end of sections of the text or in the margins), glossaries explaining difficult words (see fig. 13), lists of the epithets used with certain nouns, or (for Petrarch and Ariosto) rhyming dictionaries. Printers would make a point of listing these devices on their title pages; for example, the quarto edition of the *Decameron* which Gabriele Giolito printed in 1552 boasted to readers that it was 'newly brought back to its true reading with all those allegories, annotations and indexes which are contained in our other printings, and moreover adorned with many illustrations; with a separate index of words and subjects composed by Lodovico Dolce' (see also fig. 12). Filippo and Iacopo Giunti complained in 1563 that one of the risks of publishing was that someone else would bring out a book 'with new additions, notes, indexes and other suchlike things, which one sees done every day to the great loss of whoever has previously printed the book plainly'; these additions could also be a way of getting round a privilege restriction.[138] By having a paratext added or revised, then, a printer could steal a march on his rivals in the campaign to win readers.

Texts might also be presented afresh after treatment far more drastic than the provision of supplementary matter. Readers were coming to expect to find texts ordered in such a way that they could find their way around them easily, and book producers were always in search of new readers; so texts could be recast, simplified or summarized, sometimes together with new visual aids to their use. Among works liable to be treated in this way were those used by people coming to grips with the literary vernacular or with Latin.[139] In the second half of the century, the teacher and writer Orazio Toscanella specialized in this kind of appropriation of texts. He aimed to help readers to visualize ideas, to make them more easily memorable and usable, reducing works on rhetoric, or texts which were used to teach good writing, to tables, trees and diagrams; he even devised a 'rhetorical machine' in the form of a diagram which would allow one to find the argument to prove a particular thesis.[140] This kind of reworking was parallel to the way in which writers were searching for 'universal keys' in other fields: in the art of memory, for example, and in the study of history, the popularizers of which were rearranging historical texts and breaking them down into easily assimilable units that could then be used to 'unlock the doors of politics'.[141]

3 CONCLUSIONS

Some twenty years after the introduction of printing to Italy, a minor Lombard writer, Bettino da Trezzo, noted with admiration the effect which the new art had had upon readers. Through the new method of making books in abundance, he wrote, 'all those who have intelligence, and their minds inclined to study, can make themselves well educated and learned' ('se pon fare | letrate et docte tutte le persone | ch'àn intellecto, cum le mente prone | al studio').[142] This 'abundance' was, of course, only relative. By modern standards, print runs were small, book prices were still high in relation to wages, and in any case most people were still denied the very opportunity to learn to read. Remarks such as Bettino's do not mean that printing had a widespread or sudden impact on reading among all Italians. Nevertheless, it is clear that the increased availability of printed books, and then their greater accessibility in terms of contents and presentation, did open up many new opportunities both for the privileged minority of the well educated and for those who had 'minds inclined to study' but who might otherwise have had limited access to the written word.

At the end of Part II of this book, it was suggested that the coming of printing in the Renaissance began a gradual process of change for authors which would culminate only in the eighteenth century. One can suggest that something similar happened for readers too. The late eighteenth century seems to have seen a dual shift in patterns of reading: first, a change in method, from an 'intensive' reading and rereading of a small corpus of books to an 'extensive' style of reading as more, and more varied, material became available; and secondly, the emergence of a wider readership that would grow to mass proportions in the nineteenth century.[143] In the fifteenth and sixteenth centuries, reading was of course still restricted to a minority and was essentially 'intensive' in nature. Yet one can detect in this period an anticipation of the later broadening of reading, the first intimations of change. To return to the questions mentioned at the start of chapter 5, we can see that the spectrums of the 'who' and 'what' of reading were both extended as more material was made available to those who did not have a Latin-based education, including women. As for the 'when' and 'where' of reading, the advent of smaller and more easily portable printed books freed reading from the desktop. We have seen, too, that the 'how' changed as printed books gradually made reading easier in various ways. The spread of punctuation helped readers to interpret the text fluently and correctly; the greater use of indexation and other kinds of signposting allowed readers to traverse the terrain of the text and locate information in it more rapidly; and editors made efforts to act as guides to the understanding and use of the most important works, even if they sometimes led readers in the wrong direction.

So far we have not considered whether print affected the 'why' of reading. As Darnton writes, men and women have always read for diverse reasons: 'in order to save their souls, to improve their manners, to repair their machinery, to seduce their sweethearts, to learn about current events, and simply to have fun'.[144] If we look at changes in the motivation for reading which took place during the Renaissance in Italy, we can see shifts of emphasis which were due not to print but to the social and moral climate of the time: people came to read less in order to seduce sweethearts and have fun, more to save their souls and improve their manners. However, the greater availability and accessibility of the printed book did have the important effect of multiplying choice and thus allowing individuals to read for a greater diversity of motives. The achievement of all those involved in print production – the makers, financers and sellers of books as well as those who wrote or edited the texts to be printed – was to provide a better opportunity for more people, from a wider spectrum of society, to enjoy the benefits of reading, by deriving from the written word their own personal usefulness and pleasure.

Notes

1 THE ARRIVAL OF PRINTING AND ITS TECHNIQUES

1 *De cifris*, p. 310.
2 2 Vespasiano da Bisticci, *Le vite*, II, 183–9.
3 Scholderer, 'The invention of printing'; Febvre and Martin, *L'apparition*, pp. 69–80.
4 There are excellent surveys of fifteenth-century printing in the introductions (written mainly by Victor Scholderer) to BMC, IV–VII (with a map in vol. VII, p. viii, showing the earliest dates of printing in Italian towns), and in Scholderer, 'Printers and readers'. On Rome and Subiaco, see too Balsamo, 'I primordi', pp. 233–42; Bussi, *Prefazioni*; Carosi, *Da Magonza a Subiaco*; Modigliani, *Tipografi* (on the pre–1467 company).
5 The Latin word means 'swaddling clothes' or 'cradle', and hence metaphorically 'childhood', 'origin'. Sandal's figures (which I have modified slightly) are in 'Dal libro antico', pp. 251–2.
6 Quondam, 'La letteratura in tipografia', pp. 578–87.
7 On the development of new mass media, see e.g. McQuail, *Mass Communication Theory*, pp. 12–21. On the factors behind the advent and success of print, see Hirsch, *Printing, Selling and Reading*, pp. 14–16; Febvre and Martin, *L'apparition*, pp. 38–9, 243–58; Balsamo, 'Tecnologia', especially pp. 81–4.
8 Petrucci, *Writers and Readers*, p. 174. See too Febvre and Martin, *L'apparition*, pp. 21–37.
9 Folena, 'La tradizione', pp. 54–5.
10 The classic study is Destrez, *La pecia*; see too Steele, 'The pecia'; Febvre and Martin, *L'apparition*, pp. 24–6; Pollard, 'The *pecia* system'; Vezin, 'La fabrication', pp. 35–8; Bataillon and others, *La production.*
11 For the composition of printer's ink, see Bloy, *A History of Printing Ink*, and Fahy, 'Descrizioni', pp. 56, 58, 59 n. 17.
12 On the arrival, manufacture and commerce of paper, see Febvre and Martin, *L'apparition*, pp. 39–60; Gaskell, *A New Introduction*, pp. 57–77; various authors in Cavaciocchi (ed.), *Produzione*, pp. 49–327. For its comparative cheapness, see e.g. Martini, 'La bottega', pp. 45–7, and Cherubini and others, 'Il costo', pp. 342–53.
13 Febvre and Martin, *L'apparition*, pp. 70–2. Examples of the involvement of

goldsmiths are Bernardo Cennini in Florence (BMC, VI, xii) and the early Roman company studied by Modigliani, *Tipografi*, pp. 57–77.

14 Rouse and Rouse, *Cartolai*, pp. 22–34; Nuovo, *Il commercio librario nell'Italia del Rinascimento*, pp. 33–7.

15 Rouse and Rouse, 'Nicolaus Gupalatinus', pp. 228–9.

16 For Belfort and del Tuppo, see BMC, VI, x, xl–xlii; for Zanetti, see most recently G. Castellani, 'Da Tolomeo Ianiculo' and 'Da Bartolomeo Zanetti'; for Arrighi's printing, see Casamassima, 'Ancora su Ludovico degli Arrighi', and Menato and others (eds.), *Dizionario*, under Arrighi.

17 De la Mare, 'New research', pp. 412–15, 466–76; see too de la Mare, 'Script and manuscripts', and Bühler, *The Fifteenth-Century Book*, pp. 25–39.

18 Bertoni, *La Biblioteca Estense*, pp. 35–40; M. Fava and Bresciano, 'I librai' (1918), p. 94.

19 For examples, see Reeve, 'Manuscripts'; Bussi, *Prefazioni*, p. lxxi (a list of manuscript copies of Bussi's Roman editions) and plate XXXII (a richly decorated 1507 manuscript copy of a Bible printed in 1471); Bruni and Zancani, *Antonio Cornazzano*, pp. 111–13 (nos. 61 and 62), 120–1 (no. 68).

20 M. Fava and Bresciano, 'I librai' (1918), p. 94.

21 The following description is based principally on Febvre and Martin, *L'apparition*, pp. 80–102; Gaskell, *A New Introduction*, pp. 5–170 (with many useful illustrations); Fahy, 'Introduzione', especially pp. 40–50, and 'Descrizioni'; Veyrin-Forrer, 'Fabriquer un livre' (also usefully illustrated).

22 Mardersteig, 'Aldo Manuzio'.

23 H. Carter, *A View of Early Typography*, pp. 21–2.

24 Tinto, *Il corsivo*, pp. 14–19.

25 Only exceptionally, as in the case of the nuns of the Ripoli press in Florence, was the compositor female; in what follows I assume a male compositor. On the female presence in the printing industry, see Parker, 'Women in the book trade'.

26 For examples of printer's copy, see Trovato, 'Per un censimento'; Spotti, 'Il manoscritto'; Richardson, *Print Culture*, p. 191 n. 44 and p. 194 n. 27.

27 For different interpretations of the purpose of vellum in this context, see D. Fava, 'Libri membranacei', p. 55, and Lowry, *Nicholas Jenson*, pp. 86, 188–9.

28 The marble stone inscribed in Bologna with the minimum dimensions for each size is reproduced in Briquet, *Les filigranes*, I, 2–4, and Montecchi, *Il libro nel Rinascimento*, pp. 115–16. On paper sizes and bibliography, see too Needham, 'ISTC as a tool', pp. 41–7, and 'Aldus Manutius's paper stocks' (including discussion of sizes other than the four described in the Bolognese 'standard'); Fahy, 'La carta nell'analisi' and 'La carta nel libro quattrocentesco'.

29 Vezin, 'La fabrication', p. 39, and 'Manuscrits "imposés"'; Farquhar, in Hindman and Farquhar, *Pen to Press*, pp. 21–5; Hellinga, 'The codex', pp. 67–70.

30 Identification of format is treated in detail in Gaskell, *A New Introduction*, pp. 84–107.

31 Smith, 'Printed foliation', p. 58. In general, see Haebler, *Handbuch*, pp. 50–6; Sayce, 'Compositorial practices', pp. 3–30.
32 Sayce, 'Compositorial practices', pp. 30–4.
33 Haebler, *Handbuch*, pp. 43–50.
34 Motta, 'Demetrio Calcondila', p. 164.
35 Letter from the printer, 'Barbagrigia', pseudonym of Blado, to the authors Molza and Caro, in Caro, *Commento di ser Agresto*, p. 11.
36 Pettas, *The Giunti*, p. 129.
37 Barberi, *Paolo Manuzio*, p. 43.
38 P. O. Kristeller, *Supplementum ficinianum*, II, 108–9.
39 Fahy, *L'"Orlando furioso'*, pp. 129–38; Bertoli, 'Organizzazione', p. 183.
40 This is the conclusion of Bertoli, 'Organizzazione'.
41 An example of such a proof, on water-stained paper, is studied in Bertoli, 'Una bozza di stampa'. The work concerned was an official document, in which accuracy was essential. For French examples, see Veyrin-Forrer, 'Fabriquer un livre', pp. 289–92.
42 Masetti Zannini, *Stampatori e librai*, pp. 203, 280–2.
43 H. Brown, *The Venetian Printing Press*, pp. 175–6, 218–21.
44 Ruscelli, *I fiori delle rime de' poeti illustri* (Venice: G. B. and M. Sessa, 1558), f. PP7r–v, quoted in Fahy, *Saggi*, pp. 167–8. On haste in proof correction, see too Richardson, *Print Culture*, pp. 24–5.
45 Trovato, *Con ogni diligenza corretto*, pp. 86–9. For examples of the various types of correction, see the index of subjects in Mortimer, *Italian 16th Century Books*; for examples of pen correction, see Bühler, 'Manuscript corrections'.
46 Nolhac, 'Les correspondants', no. 2; in the event, there were three leaves of emendations.
47 Fahy, 'La carta nell'analisi', p. 7.
48 See most recently Harris, 'Una pagina capovolta', and Hellinga, 'Press and text'.
49 Fahy, *Saggi*, pp. 161, 163–5. Scholderer, 'The shape of early type', and Veyrin-Forrer, 'Fabriquer un livre', p. 290, give examples of types lying on the forme.
50 Pettas, 'The cost', pp. 70–1 (inker and puller were paid respectively 1 florin and 1 florin 3 lire per month; 1 florin was worth 6 lire 3 soldi in 1484); Barberi, *Paolo Manuzio*, p. 43 n. 3 (5.6 scudi for the *battitore* and 6.62 scudi for the *tiratore*).
51 Sartori, 'Documenti', no. VII, p. 126.
52 Santoro, 'Due contratti', pp. 188–90.
53 Pettas, 'The cost', pp. 70–1. In this case the low figure for the printers suggests that they may have received board and lodging as well. A nun was paid only 2 florins at the Ripoli press for working as a compositor during February 1481 (Wilkins, 'On the earliest editions', p. 6), but her religious duties cannot have allowed her to work full time.
54 Balsamo, 'Una iniziativa', p. 13.
55 Barberi, *Paolo Manuzio*, p. 43 n. 3.

56 See for example Santoro, 'Due contratti', pp. 191–2; Masetti Zannini, *Stampatori e librai*, pp. 148–9; Dondi, 'Apprendisti'; Vaglia, 'I Da Sabbio', p. 78.
57 For the concepts of edition, state, cancel and issue, see Gaskell, *A New Introduction*, pp. 313–16, and Fahy, *Saggi*, pp. 65–88.
58 There is one case in which copies which are not typographically different are classified as being of a variant state: when they are printed not on ordinary paper but on large paper or on vellum, usually for presentation (see chapters 3 and 4).
59 For examples, see Costabile, 'Forme di collaborazione'.
60 See the example of Valdezocco, chapter 2, section 1.
61 See for example Tinto, *Annali*, p. 118: the partners in a contract of 1581 wanted the printed books to be baled and taken to a warehouse rented by them. On warehousing, see Nuovo, *Il commercio librario nell'Italia del Rinascimento*, pp. 46–65.
62 Bühler, *The Fifteenth-Century Book*, pp. 79–80, 84–8; L. Armstrong, 'The hand-illumination' and catalogue nos. 78–104 in Alexander (ed.), *The Painted Page*; Marcon, 'Una aldina miniata'.
63 Armstrong's entry for catalogue no. 89 in Alexander (ed.), *The Painted Page*; Rouse and Rouse, *Cartolai*, pp. 48–56. For the similar practice of Schoeffer in Mainz, see Hellinga, 'Peter Schoeffer'.
64 Bussi, *Prefazioni*, pp. 83–4 (Sweynheym and Pannartz; in this list the print run is multiplied by the number of editions of a work or, in the case of multivolume works, by the number of volumes); Farenga, 'Le prefazioni', p. 139 and n. 11 (De Lignamine).
65 Trovato, 'Il libro toscano', pp. 548–53.
66 Fulin, 'Documenti', doc. 2 (1478); BMC, v, 326 (Justinian and Gregory IX, 1490–1); *Aldo Manuzio editore*, p. 57; Lowry, *The World of Aldus Manutius*, p. 174 n. 96; Fletcher, *New Aldine Studies*, pp. 100–2.
67 Grendler, *The Roman Inquisition*, pp. 9–12 (Venice); Villari, *La storia*, II, XXX (1,100 copies, Florence, 1505); Biagiarelli, 'Il privilegio', p. 348: in mid-sixteenth-century Florence, 'l'ordinario è stampar d'ogni libro mille'. For further evidence and discussion, see Mortimer, *Italian 16th Century Books*, index of subjects under 'edition, size'; Lowry, *Nicholas Jenson*, pp. 182–3; Nuovo, *Il commercio librario nell'Italia del Rinascimento*, pp. 38–45.
68 Ganda, *Niccolò Gorgonzola*, pp. 71–2.
69 Frova and Miglio, 'Dal ms. Sublacense', pp. 254–5, 272; Hellinga, 'Three notes', pp. 199–202, and 'The codex', pp. 71–3.
70 Villari, *La storia*, II, XXX.
71 Fahy, *Saggi*, p. 160 n. 6.
72 Masetti Zannini, *Stampatori e librai*, p. 201.
73 Fahy, *L'"Orlando furioso"*, p. 101.
74 Kolsky, *Mario Equicola*, p. 225. Here the gathering is loosely termed a *quinterno*.
75 Frey (ed.), *Der literarische Nachlass*, I, 247.

76 Sartori, 'Documenti', no. VII, p. 126 (one man to compose the equivalent of two pages a day, Padua, 1475); Santoro, 'Due contratti', pp. 188–90 (two men to compose and correct four folio pages a day, Milan, 1477); Pettas, 'The cost', p. 71 (Florence). See too Pollak, 'Production costs', p. 321.

77 St Gregory, *Moralia in Job*: BMC, IV, 64.

78 The first two are reproduced respectively in Febvre and Martin, *L'apparition*, p. 89, and Fahy, *Saggi*, plate III.

79 Mardersteig, 'La singolare cronaca', p. 266; Masetti Zannini, *Stampatori e librai*, p. 140; Venier, 'Immagini', pp. 27–8. For other examples, see Trovato, 'Il libro toscano', p. 554 n. 96.

80 Hellinga, 'Press and text', pp. 3–4.

81 Modigliani, *Tipografi*, p. 11.

82 Cittadella, *La stampa in Ferrara*, pp. 13–15. The stationer (*cartularius*) Bernardo Carnerio was to provide the printer André Belfort with at least four reams of paper every fifteen days; there were about 450 usable sheets out of the 500 in each ream (see chapter 2), and I have assumed twelve working days in the fortnight.

83 Mardersteig, 'La singolare cronaca', pp. 258–9; Pollak, 'The daily performance'.

84 See for example Fulin, 'Documenti', no. 2, pp. 100–1 (payment per gathering, 1478); Pettas, *The Giunti*, p. 126, and Ganda, *Niccolò Gorgonzola*, pp. 17–18, 27 (payment per ream, 1482 and early 1500s); Fulin, 'Nuovi documenti', pp. 403–4, and Masetti Zannini, *Stampatori e librai*, pp. 200–3 (payment per bale, 1507 and 1583).

85 Masetti Zannini, *Stampatori e librai*, pp. 200–3 (Blado); Mortimer, *Italian 16th Century Books*, no. 64 (1593). See too Gaskell, *A New Introduction*, p. 140; Veyrin-Forrer, 'Fabriquer un livre', pp. 294–8.

2 PUBLISHING, BOOKSELLING AND THE CONTROL OF BOOKS

1 Bussi, *Prefazioni*, p. 73.

2 Balsamo, *Produzione*, p. 33 (Modena); Fulin, 'Documenti', docs. 2 and 9 (Venice, 1478, Leonard Wild working for Nicholas of Frankfurt, and 1492, Paganino Paganini); Febvre and Martin, *L'apparition*, pp. 169–70 (Venice, 1478, and Florence, 1483); Pettas, 'The cost' (Florence, 1484). On costs and the need for financial support, see in general Febvre and Martin, *L'apparition*, pp. 165–89, and Colla, 'Tipografi', pp. 40–7.

3 The evidence, first interpreted by Grendler, *The Roman Inquisition*, pp. 14–15, comes from Tinto, *Annali*. The company was formed in January 1581 by Michele (the younger) and Venturino Tramezzino with Luc'Antonio Giunti the younger and Giovanni Varisco (Tinto, *Annali*, pp. 117–19); a one-eighth share of costs was 240 ducats (p. xxxv n. 2); the work was Giovanni Tarcagnota's *Historie del mondo* (no. 248, which had been printed in 1580) with a supplement (no. 251, printed later in 1581).

4 Pettas, *The Giunti*, pp. 129–30 (Florence, 1497); Montecchi, *Aziende tipo-*

grafiche, p. 11 (Modena); Cherubini and others, 'Il costo', pp. 422–3 (Rome); Rouse and Rouse, *Cartolai*, pp. 38–40 (Ripoli press).

5 See for example H. Brown, *The Venetian Printing Press*, pp. 24–5; Dorez, 'Le cardinal Marcello Cervini', p. 309; Sartori, 'Documenti', p. 133; Martini, 'La bottega', pp. 45–6; Pettas, *The Giunti*, pp. 124–5; Ganda, *I primordi*, pp. 38, 89; Stevens and Gehl, 'Giovanni Battista Bosso', p. 45.

6 Blackburn, 'The printing contract'.

7 Febvre and Martin, *L'apparition*, pp. 169–70; Pettas, *The Giunti*, pp. 127–8. One can contrast the estimate in Cherubini and others, 'Il costo', pp. 399–401, of the cost of producing an illuminated vellum manuscript: here the vellum counts for about 22 per cent and copying for 50 per cent.

8 Richardson, *Print Culture*, pp. 15–18.

9 Pettas, 'The cost', p. 73, and *The Giunti*, pp. 147–9; Balsamo, 'Una iniziativa', p. 11; Martin, 'Comment mesurer un succès littéraire: le problème des tirages', in *Le livre français*, pp. 209–23.

10 Bussi, *Prefazioni*, pp. lviii–lix, 82–4; Scholderer, 'The petition', pp. 72–3, and 'Printing at Venice', pp. 75–8.

11 Fulin, 'Documenti', doc. 58.

12 Biagiarelli, 'Il privilegio', p. 348.

13 Roover, 'Per la storia', p. 116.

14 Cittadella, *La stampa in Ferrara*, p. 7; Scholderer, 'Printing at Ferrara', p. 91; Modigliani, *Tipografi*, pp. 21–2.

15 H. Brown, *The Venetian Printing Press*, p. 13; Lowry, *Nicholas Jenson*, pp. 115–16.

16 Ascarelli and Menato, *La tipografia*, pp. 100–1, 103–4, 114, 118–19, 128, 129 (Rome), 220–2 (Turin); Menato and others (eds.), *Dizionario*, under N. Bevilacqua, A. Blado, F. Calvo; Biagiarelli, 'Il privilegio' (Florence); Bellettini, 'La stamperia camerale di Bologna'.

17 Ceccarelli, 'Il "Zornale"', p. 101, and Lowry, *Nicholas Jenson*, p. 178 (de Madiis); Camerini, *Annali dei Giunti*, vol. 1, part 1, and Pettas, *The Giunti*, pp. 104–23; Harris, 'Nicolò Garanta'; Fahy, 'The Venetian Ptolemy', pp. 93–7, 108–9 (Pederzano).

18 Rouse and Rouse, *Cartolai*, pp. 41–2.

19 Ganda, *I primordi*, pp. 54–7 (Giovanni da Legnano); Mardersteig, 'La singolare cronaca', p. 258, and Varanini, 'Per la storia' (Corner); Fattori, 'Per la storia' (Giovanni da Verona); Contò, 'Notes', pp. 24–5 (Manzolo).

20 Lowry, *Nicholas Jenson*, pp. 18–21 (Venice); Sighinolfi, 'Francesco Puteolano', pp. 331–5, 455–6 (Bologna).

21 Modigliani, *Tipografi*, pp. 7–56, 81–91; BMC, IV, vii–xiii, including reference to the patronage of the Maffei family of Volterra and of the Milanese lawyer Giovanni Alvise Toscani in the 1470s; Farenga, 'Le prefazioni' (De Lignamine) and 'Il sistema delle dediche'; Alhaique Pettinelli, 'Elementi culturali'.

22 Lowry, *Nicholas Jenson*, especially chapters 1, 3–5.

23 Tenenti, 'Luc'Antonio Giunti'; see too for example Dondi, 'Giovanni

Giolito', and Marciani, 'Editori', p. 522, on the younger Melchior Sessa's partnership in cloth.

24 For example, two of the books published by Francesco de Madiis (see note 17 above) use Latin *per* before both his name and that of the printer Battista Torti; five of the sixteen books known to have been published by Lorio in Venice between 1514 and 1527 use *per* (Rhodes, 'Lorenzo Lorio'); and the Roman bookseller Vincenzo Luchino used terminology which suggested that books published by him were printed by him (Barberi, *Tipografi romani*, pp. 111–13).

25 For Venetian examples, see Rhodes, *Silent Printers*; see too Harris, 'Nicolò Garanta', pp. 105–6.

26 Biagiarelli, 'Incunabuli fiorentini'; Infelise, 'Gli editori veneziani', p. 28.

27 Scholderer, 'Printing at Venice', pp. 74–86; Lowry, *Nicholas Jenson*, pp. 113–15, 163–5.

28 Roover, 'Per la storia' and 'New facets'; Lowry, *Nicholas Jenson*, pp. 130–2.

29 Lowry, *Nicholas Jenson*, pp. 116, 124–31.

30 Fulin, 'Documenti', doc. 2; Sartori, 'Documenti', nos. XXIV (1477), pp. 148–9, XXXIII (1478), p. 157, and XLVI (1479), p. 170.

31 Scholderer, 'Printing at Milan', pp. 97–8; Ganda, *I primordi*, pp. 10–25. Merli's role as financer was taken over in 1472 jointly by a nobleman, Biagio Terzago, and Castaldi himself.

32 Motta, 'Di Filippo di Lavagna', pp. 35, 38–9, 57–8.

33 Rouse and Rouse, *Cartolai* (the examples are nos. XCII and LXVIII); Lowry, 'La produzione', pp. 370–1; Trovato, 'Il libro toscano', pp. 549–51.

34 Villari, *La storia*, II, xxix–xxxi.

35 Balsamo and Tinto, *Origini del corsivo*, pp. 67–74; Nuovo, *Il commercio librario a Ferrara*, pp. 93–100.

36 Bonifacio, *Gli annali*, pp. 13, 21.

37 Valenti, 'Per la storia'.

38 Sighinolfi, 'Francesco Puteolano', pp. 331–5, 455–6.

39 BMC, VI, xlv (Perugia); Scholderer, 'Printing at Milan', p. 99, and Ganda, *I primordi*, pp. 34–40 (Zarotto); Motta, 'Di Filippo di Lavagna'; Balsamo, *Produzione*, pp. 30–1 (Vurster).

40 Motta, 'Demetrio Calcondila', pp. 157–8, 163–6; Bühler, *The University and the Press*, p. 39, and Balsamo, *Produzione*, pp. 26–7 (Beroaldo).

41 Di Filippo Bareggi, *Il mestiere*, pp. 249–51; Bonora, *Ricerche*, pp. 63–72.

42 Pastorello, 'Di Aldo Pio Manuzio', p. 189; Lowry, *The World of Aldus Manutius*, pp. 83–6, 119–26.

43 Fulin, 'Nuovi documenti', pp. 401–5. For later examples, see Costabile, 'Forme di collaborazione', pp. 139–40; Bellingeri, 'Editoria e mercato', pp. 168–73; Wickham Legg, 'An agreement in 1536'.

44 A more detailed classification is proposed in Veneziani, 'Introduzione', pp. 17–19, and 'La marca tipografica', pp. 164–5.

45 BMC, V, xii, xxvii–xxviii (Nicholas of Frankfurt), xxii–xxiii (Scotti), xxv–xxvi (Torresani); Fulin, 'Documenti', doc. 2 (Nicholas of Frankfurt); Sartori,

'Documenti', p. 198 (Torresani); Volpati, 'Gli Scotti', pp. 366–9.

46 Rogledi Manni, *La tipografia a Milano*, pp. 36–8.

47 Barberi, *Tipografi romani*, pp. 147–63.

48 Veneziani, 'La marca tipografica'; Rhodes, *Silent Printers*.

49 On these topics, see in general Febvre and Martin, *L'apparition*, pp. 307–47; Hirsch, *Printing, Selling and Reading*, pp. 61–77; and the richly informative Nuovo, *Il commercio librario nell'Italia del Rinascimento*.

50 Modigliani, *Tipografi*, pp. 41–2 (Han); Lowry, *Nicholas Jenson*, pp. 167, 230; Manzi, *Annali di Mattia Cancer*, pp. 13–14. On distribution, retailing and bookshops, see Nuovo, *Il commercio librario nell'Italia del Rinascimento*, especially pp. 59, 66–90, 105–28, 160–98.

51 Rhodes, *Annali tipografici di Lazzaro de' Soardi*, p. 84; Tenenti, 'Luc'Antonio Giunti'.

52 Mazzoldi, 'I primi librai', pp. 41–2 (Amadeo Scotti, 1517), 42 (Curzio Troiano Navò, 1553).

53 Dorez, 'Le cardinal Marcello Cervini', p. 303.

54 Mazzoldi, 'I primi librai', pp. 31–2 (John of Cologne); Lowry, *Nicholas Jenson*, pp. 161, 173–4; Trovato, 'Il libro toscano', p. 553 (the German–French company); Bongi, *Annali*, I, ciii, and Cittadella, *La stampa in Ferrara*, p. 28 (Giolito); Nuovo, *Il commercio librario nell'Italia del Rinascimento*, pp. 188–9 (Varisco), 186–8 (Sessa); Grendler, *The Roman Inquisition*, p. 16, and Pesenti, 'Il "Dioscoride"', pp. 71–6 (Valgrisi).

55 Lowry, *Nicholas Jenson*, pp. 183–4; Ganda, *Niccolò Gorgonzola*, p. 22.

56 Grendler, *The Roman Inquisition*, pp. 169–81; Masetti Zannini, *Stampatori e librai*, pp. 171–3, 237–42. For Neapolitan examples, see Bongi, *Annali*, I, cviii.

57 *Histoire de l'édition française*, I, 170. See too de la Mare, 'The shop', p. 239.

58 'Et non si mete fora robe in la balcone': H. Brown, *The Venetian Printing Press*, p. 39.

59 Ganda, *Niccolò Gorgonzola*, p. 7. For Venice and Rome, see Moro, 'Insegne librarie'; Veneziani, 'Introduzione', pp. 21–3; Masetti Zannini, *Stampatori e librai*, p. 136.

60 Various *scancie* (shelves or bookcases) and *tavole* are included in a Veronese inventory of 1586: Carpanè, 'Libri', pp. 213–16, 229.

61 On the links between bookselling and bookbinding, see Hobson, 'Booksellers and bookbinders'. Examples of evidence for the presence of binders are found in Masetti Zannini, *Stampatori e librai*, p. 49; Ganda, *Niccolò Gorgonzola*, pp. 22–3; Venier, 'Immagini', p. 57, no. 23; Lowry, *Nicholas Jenson*, p. 193; Carpanè, 'Libri', pp. 216, 219; Martani, 'Librerie', pp. 214, 242. For the price of bound versus unbound copies, see Lowry, *Nicholas Jenson*, pp. 189–90.

62 See, for example, Carpanè, 'Libri', pp. 208–9. Nuovo (*Il commercio librario nell'Italia del Rinascimento*, pp. 168–74) suggests that some bound books offered for sale would have been second hand.

63 Masetti Zannini, *Stampatori e librai*, pp. 13, 311.

64 Letter from the printer in Caro, *Commento di ser Agresto*, pp. 9–10.

65 Bertoli, 'Librai'. On the role of these pedlars, see Noakes, 'The development', pp. 43–8; Bertoli, 'Nuovi documenti'; Nuovo, *Il commercio librario nell'Italia del Rinascimento*, pp. 105–10.

66 Bongi, *Annali*, II, 26–37; Casadei, 'Sulle prime edizioni'.

67 Marciani, 'Editori', pp. 518–19, and 'Il commercio librario'; Urban, 'La festa della Sensa', pp. 330–4; Nuovo, *Il commercio librario nell'Italia del Rinascimento*, pp. 91–104.

68 The standard study is Pollard and Ehrman, *The Distribution of Books by Catalogue*. See also Ganda, *I primordi*, pp. 52–3; Venier, 'Immagini', pp. 36–44 and 57–61, nos. 24–37; Breitenbruch, 'Ein Fragment'; Nuovo, *Il commercio librario nell'Italia del Rinascimento*, pp. 25–31, 230–45.

69 Balsamo, 'Commercio librario'; Biagiarelli, 'Il privilegio', pp. 349–50.

70 Dorez, 'Le cardinal Marcello Cervini', p. 297. See too Pettas, *The Giunti*, pp. 143–5; for maritime mishaps befalling books exported by Luc'Antonio Giunti the younger, Tenenti, 'Luc'Antonio Giunti', pp. 1029–31, 1037–8; for examples of books damaged en route from Germany to Italy, Marciani, 'Editori', pp. 545–6, and Mazzoldi, 'I primi librai', p. 42.

71 H. Brown, *The Venetian Printing Press*, p. 37 (de Madiis); Noakes, 'The development', pp. 47–8 (Ripoli press); Hirsch, *Printing, Selling and Reading*, pp. 75–7, and Pettas, *The Giunti*, p. 140 (exchanges between Francesco Calvo in Milan and Johann Froben in Basel, between the Giunti in Venice and Christophe Plantin in Antwerp); Dondi, 'Giovanni Giolito', pp. 152, 175–7 (exchange of books), 153, 188–9 (use of warehouses).

72 For instance, Marciani, 'Il commercio librario' and 'Editori', *passim*; Bernstein, 'Financial arrangements', p. 45 n. 37.

73 Lowry, *The World of Aldus Manutius*, p. 97.

74 Bongi, *Annali*, I, civ, cvii–cix.

75 Zanelli, 'Debiti e crediti'.

76 What follows is based chiefly on E. Armstrong, *Before Copyright*, pp. 3–7; Trovato, *Con ogni diligenza corretto*, pp. 33–7; Nuovo, *Il commercio librario nell'Italia del Rinascimento*, pp. 208–29; for Venice, Fulin, 'Documenti', H. Brown, *The Venetian Printing Press*, and Agee, 'The Venetian privilege'; for fifteenth-century Milan, Motta, 'Di Filippo di Lavagna', and Rogledi Manni, *La tipografia a Milano*, pp. 74–81; for Florence, Biagiarelli, 'Il privilegio', and Pettas, *The Giunti*, pp. 153–84; for Rome, Blasio, *Cum gratia et privilegio*. On control in general, see Hirsch, *Printing, Selling and Reading*, pp. 78–103. Horatio Brown transcribed Venetian privileges and related material from 1527 to 1597 in the MSS It. VII 2500–2 (= 12077–9) of the Biblioteca Nazionale Marciana, Venice. A valuable project to build up a database of these and other Venetian documents is described in Infelise, 'L'editoria veneta'. On the records of the Auditore delle Riformagioni in the Florentine Archivio di Stato, see T. Carter, 'Another promoter', p. 895.

77 For the texts of Aldo's privileges, see Fletcher, *New Aldine Studies*, pp. 139–40, 142–56. Garanta applied to protect a new design of italic in 1527: see Harris, 'Nicolò Garanta', p. 110. On music printing, see Duggan, *Italian Music*

Incunabula; T. Carter, 'Music-printing'; Fenlon, *Music, Print and Culture*.

78 Agee, 'The Venetian privilege', p. 18.

79 For example, Solerti, *Vita*, I, 761–2.

80 Text from C. Castellani, *La stampa*, pp. 80–1, and Fletcher, *New Aldine Studies*, p. 148, with accents and some punctuation added. On the *De corruptis poetarum locis*, which Aldo never printed, see Dionisotti in Bembo, *Prose e rime*, p. 30.

81 Ganda, *Niccolò Gorgonzola*, pp. 35–8, 103–9.

82 Rogledi Manni, *La tipografia a Milano*, pp. 47–9.

83 Renouard, *Annales*, pp. 301–20; Lowry, *The World of Aldus Manutius*, pp. 154–8; Fletcher, *New Aldine Studies*, pp. 52, 92–4, 144–7; Shaw, 'The Lyons counterfeit'; BMC, VII, lv (Brescia).

84 Agee, 'The Venetian privilege', p. 7.

85 What follows is based on H. Brown, *The Venetian Printing Press*, chapters VIII–XVIII; Fulin, 'Documenti'; Sorrentino, *La letteratura italiana*; Lopez, *Sul libro a stampa*, pp. 59–118; Rotondò, 'La censura ecclesiastica'; Grendler, *The Roman Inquisition*; De Frede, *Ricerche*; Frajese, 'Regolamentazione e controllo'; Rozzo, *Linee*, pp. 21–119.

86 Niero, 'Decreti'.

87 Bongi, *Annali*, I, xxxiv.

88 On the Fabrizi case, see the entry by F. Piovan in the *Dizionario biografico degli Italiani*, XLIII (1993), 794–6. See also chapter 3, section 3.

89 Grendler, *The Roman Inquisition*, pp. 57–9, 103, 186–9, 120–1.

90 Ibid. pp. 148–61.

91 Frajese, 'Regolamentazione e controllo', p. 691.

92 Lopez, *Sul libro a stampa*, p. 115.

93 Biagiarelli, 'Il privilegio', pp. 344–6.

94 Frajese, 'Regolamentazione e controllo', p. 691.

95 Mackenney, *Tradesmen*, p. 182; see too Braida, 'Quelques considérations'.

3 PUBLICATION IN PRINT: PATRONAGE, CONTRACTS AND PRIVILEGES

1 *Trattatello in laude di Dante*, in *Tutte le opere*, III, 484 (first redaction), 527 (second redaction). Studies of scribal publication from the fourteenth to the seventeenth century include Root, 'Publication before printing'; Rizzo, *Il lessico filologico*, pp. 301–23; Febvre and Martin, *L'apparition*, pp. 28–32; Bourgain, 'L'édition des manuscrits'; Love, *Scribal Publication* (particularly useful for questions of definition); Marotti, *Manuscript, Print*.

2 *Letters on Familiar Matters ... XVII–XXIV*, letter XXIII, 6, p. 271.

3 Ibid., letter XXII, 3, p. 216.

4 Rizzo, *Il lessico filologico*, pp. 308–19; P. O. Kristeller, *Supplementum ficinianum*, I, clxviii–clxxi; Grafton, 'The Vatican', pp. 34–5.

5 Petrucci, *Writers and Readers*, pp. 145–68; see too pp. 193–4.

6 *Letters of Old Age ... I–IX*, letters V, 1, and VI, 5, pp. 152–6, 197–200.

7 *Letters on Familiar Matters ... XVII–XXIV*, letter XVIII, 5, pp. 50–1.

8 *Comedia delle ninfe fiorentine*, in *Tutte le opere*, II, 834–5; *De casibus*, in *Tutte le opere*, IX, 6; *De mulieribus*, in *Tutte le opere*, X, 22.

9 Useful starting points for the analysis of patronage are the chapter 'Patrons and clients' in Burke, *Tradition and Innovation*, pp. 97–139, and the essays in Kent and Simons (eds.), *Patronage, Art, and Society*.

10 Santoro, 'Contributi', p. 35; Ganda, 'Vicende', pp. 218–19 (Corio). It has been suggested that the relationship between a patron and a writer employed by the state was characteristic of the social system of clientage (*clientelismo*), i.e. service given to a patron in exchange for protection: Ianziti, 'Patronage'.

11 Bruni and Zancani, *Antonio Cornazzano*, pp. 16, 81.

12 Ibid. pp. 81–7.

13 On Cosimo's literary patronage, see Hankins, 'Cosimo de' Medici'; on his reputation, see A. Brown, 'The humanist portrait'.

14 Bentley, *Politics and Culture*, pp. 59, 67.

15 Santoro, 'Contributi', p. 37; Ganda, 'Vicende', p. 219 (Corio).

16 Robin, *Filelfo*, pp. 6, 59–60; Lubkin, *A Renaissance Court*, pp. 111–12; Welch, *Art and Authority*, p. 146.

17 Robin, *Filelfo*, pp. 13–17; Kettering, *Patrons*, pp. 3–4, 12–39.

18 Martines, 'Love and hate'.

19 A useful scheme of the stages in the life of a book, defined as publishing, manufacturing, distribution, reception and survival, is offered in Adams and Barker, 'A new model'. On the slow establishment of authors' rights in the context of printing, see in general Febvre and Martin, *L'apparition*, pp. 233–42. For the situation in sixteenth-century Paris, see Charon-Parent, 'Le monde de l'imprimerie humaniste'.

20 On these presentation portraits, see Mortimer, 'The author's image', pp. 63–70.

21 For an example, see Biagiarelli, 'Editori', pp. 214–15 (Bartolomeo della Fonte and Lorenzo de' Medici).

22 P. O. Kristeller, *Supplementum ficinianum*, I, clxxiv (Ficino); Fulin, 'Documenti', doc. 132 (1503 privilege); Erasmus, *Opus epistolarum*, III, 424 (quoted in Hoyoux, 'Les moyens', p. 33). On the use of author's copies for presentation, see too Kallendorf, 'In search of a patron'; Nuovo, *Il commercio librario nell'Italia del Rinascimento*, p. 181 and n. 17. For the similar French situation, see Davis, 'Beyond the market'.

23 Fahy, 'Per la vita', pp. 255–8. Lando had dedicated his *Paradossi* to Cardinal Cristoforo in 1543. On dedications to the Madruzzo family, see Borrelli and others, *Edizioni per i Madruzzo*.

24 For the example of Aldine editions on vellum, see Lowry, 'Aldus Manutius and Benedetto Bordon', and Frasso, 'Appunti'.

25 Bongi, *Annali*, I, 109. On dedications in early Roman printing, see Farenga, 'Il sistema'.

26 Mortimer, *Italian 16th Century Books*, no. 195.

27 Marotti, *Manuscript, Print*, p. 292. See too Laufer, 'L'espace visuel', p. 584;

Davis, 'Beyond the market', pp. 78–9. Another sign of the continuing importance attached to the art of dedication was the appearance in 1601 of a six-volume anthology of *Lettere dedicatorie di diversi* (Bergamo: Comin Ventura), mentioned in Corinne Lucas, 'Vers une nouvelle image', p. 91 and n. 42.

28 Di Filippo Bareggi, *Il mestiere*, p. 265; see pp. 265–71 on the use of dedications for profit.

29 Plaisance, 'Les dédicaces', pp. 173–4. For similar payments to composers, see Bernstein, 'Financial arrangements', pp. 49–50.

30 On the success of Mattioli's work, see Accademico Rozzo, 'Vita di Pietro Andrea Mattioli'; Stannard, 'P. A. Mattioli', pp. 68–73; and Pesenti, 'Il "Dioscoride"' (see pp. 77–8 for Giacomo Ruffinelli's rival involvement in Mantua). On Mattioli and Madruzzo, see Fabrizio Leonardinelli's preface in Borrelli and others, *Edizioni per i Madruzzo*, p. 11 n. 8.

31 For examples, see Richardson (ed.), *Trattati sull'ortografia*, pp. 154–8, and Bongi, *Annali*, I, 288; for editions not printed under the author's control, see Ianziti, *Humanistic Historiography*, pp. 216–17, and Bruni and Zancani, *Antonio Cornazzano*, pp. 175–6. An author might also dedicate different parts of a work to different people.

32 Corinne Lucas, 'Vers une nouvelle image'.

33 The mention of merchants may have been an allusion to Bernardo Tasso's *Amadigi*; see chapter 4, section 2. See also chapter 4 n. 7 on the contemporary connotations of *meccanico*.

34 Grendler, 'Printing and censorship', pp. 31–2.

35 On Benedetti, see the modern edition by Dorothy M. Schullian, and Lowry, *The World of Aldus Manutius*, pp. 116–17.

36 Manzi, *Annali di ... Antonio de Frizis*, nos. 3 (Scipione De Gennaro), 8 and 9 (Luca Prassicio), 28 (Bartolomeo Donato).

37 Trovato, *Con ogni diligenza corretto*, p. 35.

38 Beer, *Romanzi di cavalleria*, p. 190 n. 25.

39 Ibid. pp. 176–7.

40 Harris, *Bibliografia*, I, 15–17, 21; II, 20–31.

41 Ibid. I, 26–8; II, 44–55. No copies survive of either edition.

42 Ibid. I, 53. I thank Giulio Lepschy for elucidating this passage.

43 Fulin, 'Documenti', doc. 17.

44 Blackburn, 'The printing contract'. Many sixteenth-century music editions were probably paid for by composers or their patrons: T. Carter, 'Music-printing', p. 62.

45 Barberi, *Tipografi romani*, pp. 108–9, 129–32; Fenlon, *Music, Print and Culture*, pp. 54–5; Morales, *Missarum liber primus (–secundus)*.

46 This suggests that, as one would expect, applicants had to pay an administration fee, but I do not know of evidence for its size.

47 Archivio di Stato, Naples, Notai del Cinquecento, vol. 2, ff. 51v–52; Manzi, *Annali di Giuseppe Cacchi*, p. 17; Menato and others (eds.), *Dizionario*, under Cacchi.

48 Kolsky, *Mario Equicola*, pp. 196 n. 67, 208, 219 n. 148, 225–6; Rhodes, 'Lorenzo Lorio', p. 281.
49 Masetti Zannini, *Stampatori e librai*, pp. 206, 288–9.
50 Barberi, *Tipografi romani*, p. 24; Blasio, *Cum gratia et privilegio*, p. 85.
51 Di Filippo Bareggi, *Il mestiere*, p. 265.
52 Adda, *Indagini storiche*, Appendix, pp. 8–9.
53 Ganda, *I primordi*, pp. 58–9, 174.
54 Renier, 'Gaspare Visconti', pp. 524–6; BMC, VI, 723, 787; Ganda, *I primordi*, pp. 185–6. On Tanzio, see Renier, p. 817 n. 1, and Trovato, *Con ogni diligenza corretto*, p. 139 n. 33.
55 Renier, 'Gaspare Visconti', p. 793 n. 1.
56 Ianziti, *Humanistic Historiography*, pp. 210–31 (p. 210).
57 Motta, 'Di Filippo di Lavagna', pp. 48–9, 67–8. One of the partners may have been the diplomat Pietro Gallarate: Ianziti, *Humanistic Historiography*, pp. 216–17.
58 Ganda, 'Vicende'.
59 Ridolfi, *La stampa in Firenze*, pp. 13–28; Trovato, 'Il libro toscano', especially pp. 540–3, 557–8.
60 Wilkins, 'On the earliest editions', pp. 3–4.
61 Veneziani, 'Vicende'.
62 Ledos, 'Lettre inédite', p. 723.
63 Biagiarelli, 'Editori', pp. 214–17; Rouse and Rouse, *Cartolai*, pp. 77, 81; Trovato, 'Il libro toscano', p. 550. On della Fonte's earlier contacts with the press in Padua, see Ridolfi, *La stampa in Firenze*, pp. 42–4.
64 Wilkins, 'On the earliest editions', pp. 4, 17.
65 Agee, 'The Venetian privilege', p. 8 (Scotto); Masetti Zannini, *Stampatori e librai*, pp. 203, 280–2 (Blado; see also chapter 1, section 3).
66 Manzi, *Annali di Mattia Cancer*, pp. 12–13, 150–1.
67 Fulin, 'Documenti', docs. 245, 254; on the latter application, see too Harris, 'Nicolò Garanta', pp. 108–9, 128–9, 134–6.
68 Accademico Rozzo, 'Vita di Pietro Andrea Mattioli', p. 201.
69 Pesenti, 'Il Dioscoride', p. 79. Mattioli's request is in ASV, ST, reg. 33, f. 117r.
70 Bertoli, 'Organizzazione'. In this category of publications undertaken at the risk of printers one can include volumes II–IV (1546–50) of the edition of Eustathius' commentary on Homer, printed at the expense of Antonio Blado and others, but only after they had received an interest-free loan of 600 scudi from Marcello Cervini. The latter had paid for the paper and proof correction of volume I (1542). See Dorez, 'Le cardinal Marcello Cervini', and Mortimer, *Italian 16th Century Books*, no. 176.
71 Tenenti, 'Luc'Antonio Giunti', p. 1059; Del Re, 'Prospero Farinacci', pp. 183–4, 201–4.
72 Marciani, 'Editori', pp. 538–9. I have not been able to identify this Marcantonio, clearly distinct from the commentator Marcantonio Zimara.
73 T. Carter, 'Another promoter'. The silver carlino (or giulio) was worth

two-thirds of a lira, and the gold scudo was worth 7.5 lire: Cipolla, *La moneta*, pp. 13–14, 33.

74 On Aldo and contemporary writers, see Lowry, *The World of Aldus Manutius*, pp. 218–29.

75 *Aldo Manuzio editore*, nos. XII, XLI.

76 Ibid. nos. X, XLI, LIX.

77 Allen, 'Erasmus' relations', pp. 305–6; see Erasmus, *Opus epistolarum*, I, nos. 207, 209.

78 Nolhac, 'Les correspondants', no. 82.

79 Casella and Pozzi, *Francesco Colonna*, I, 44–6, 88–9, 124, 153.

80 Fulin, 'Documenti', doc. 3; Chavasse, 'The first known author's copyright'.

81 Fulin, 'Documenti'. Of the 95 privilege requests made in Venice in 1550, 69 came from printers and booksellers (almost all major entrepreneurs), 13 from authors, 2 from translators and editors, 11 from unidentified persons: Infelise, 'L'editoria veneta', p. 6.

82 Similarly, Cosimo Bartoli requested a privilege in 1567 because he wanted his *Discorsi historici* printed 'di bel carattere': Masetti Zannini, *Stampatori e librai*, p. 141.

83 Thus Lionardo Salviati may have waived his right to a share of any fines arising from the privilege for the *Decameron* edited by him in Florence and printed in 1582 because he did not want to pay a share of the costs ('partecipare'): T. Carter, 'Another promoter', p. 897 n. 8.

84 Fulin, 'Documenti', docs. 115, 148 (and see chapter 2, section 3), 248, 250; Cian, *Un decennio*, pp. 224–5; Frasso, 'Appunti'.

85 Fulin, 'Documenti', docs. 4, 103, 121, 109, 178, 240, 246, 256.

86 Ibid. docs. 227, 3, 70, 50, 122, 176, 180.

87 Ibid. docs. 63, 150, 252, 177, 248, 250.

88 Ibid. docs. 149, 223; Harris, *Bibliografia*, I, 33, 75; II, 62–7, 86–7.

89 The text of the decree is in H. Brown, *The Venetian Printing Press*, p. 211; see too Trovato, *Con ogni diligenza corretto*, pp. 36–7, who quotes Giacomo Moro's suggestion about the intervention of Bembo.

90 Motta, 'Di Filippo di Lavagna', pp. 49, 68–70.

91 Blasio, *Cum gratia et privilegio*, pp. 80–98.

92 Fulin, 'Documenti', docs. 171 (Pacioli), 240 (Bocca), 18 (Barbaro), 117 (Valla), and see also doc. 206 for another application relating to Barbaro in 1516; Motta, 'Di Filippo di Lavagna', pp. 51–2, and Ganda, *I primordi*, pp. 66–7 (Filelfo).

93 For the 1532 *Furioso*, see chapter 4, section 2. For the 1535 privilege, see Bongi, *Annali*, I, 281.

4 FROM PEN TO PRINT: WRITERS AND THEIR USE OF THE PRESS

1 Sabellico, *Opera*, f. b4r. The work had appeared in an edition dedicated to Donato.

2 Beer, *Romanzi di cavalleria*, pp. 159–60 (I have slightly modified punctuation in the quotation), 167.
3 See for instance Bullock, 'Some notes', and Balduino, 'Petrarchismo veneto'.
4 Andrews, 'Written texts' (p. 85 for the evidence on publication preceding performance, pp. 86–7 for Aretino); Riccò, 'Testo per la scena', pp. 210–26 (pp. 221–2 for the comment on Aristotle).
5 Ariosto, *Lettere*, nos. 198–9.
6 Richardson, 'The debates'.
7 On *meccanico*, see Altieri Biagi, '"Vile meccanico"', and Cox, *The Renaissance Dialogue*, p. 39.
8 Saunders, 'The stigma of print', pp. 139, 154. For English hostility to print up to the eighteenth century, see Kernan, *Printing Technology*, especially pp. 1–23, 41–4.
9 Fiorato, 'François Guichardin'.
10 Biagiarelli, 'Editori', p. 215 and n. 11.
11 From the preface to Ovid, *Metamorphoses* (Milan: Filippo Lavagna, 1475), quoted in Scholderer, 'Printers and readers', p. 210 n. 2.
12 Sheppard, 'A fifteenth-century humanist'.
13 Ibid. 17–18; BMC, VII, 1136–7. For the scholarly use made of the press by Bonaccorso of Pisa, a pupil of Filelfo's, and Alessandro Minuziano, a pupil of Merula's, see Rogledi Manni, *La tipografia a Milano*, pp. 39–40, 42–3, 55–6.
14 Ridolfi, *La stampa in Firenze*, p. 21; P. O. Kristeller, *Supplementum ficinianum*, I, lvii–clxxxi.
15 P. O. Kristeller, *Supplementum ficinianum*, I, clxviii–clxxxi; see too I, clxxv, for the financing of the printing of Pico della Mirandola's *Heptaplus* by Roberto Salviati in 1489.
16 Fulin, 'Documenti', pp. 113–14 (doc. 28) and 123 (doc. 48); P. O. Kristeller, *Supplementum ficinianum*, I, cvi–cvii. Biondo obtained other Venetian privileges in 1495 and 1498, published a work by F. M. Grapaldi in 1517, and was a commercial partner of the sons of Luc'Antonio Giunti (Pettas, *The Giunti*, p. 109).
17 D. Fava, 'Libri membranacei', pp. 58–60.
18 P. O. Kristeller, *Supplementum ficinianum*, I, clxxvi; BMC, VI, 623.
19 A. Brown, *Bartolomeo Scala*, p. 159 and n. 68; Trovato, 'Il libro toscano', p. 543.
20 Perosa in Poliziano, *Della congiura*, pp. v–xvii.
21 Perosa, 'Contributi', pp. 92–3; Hill Cotton, 'Alessandro Sarti'; Veneziani, 'Platone Benedetti'.
22 Ridolfi, *La stampa in Firenze*, p. 24.
23 Romano, 'Predicazioni'; Villari, *La storia*, II, xxix–xxxi.
24 Rhodes, *Gli annali*, nos. 608, 644, 654, 683, 684. On Pacini, see Biagiarelli, 'Editori', pp. 217–19.
25 Lowry, *The World of Aldus Manutius*, p. 28.

26 Sabellico, *Opera*, ff. a1v, K8v.
27 Chavasse, 'The first known author's copyright'.
28 For examples, see Sabellico, *Opera*, ff. g2v–g6v, i1v; Chavasse, 'The first known author's copyright', p. 34.
29 Sabellico, *Opera*, ff. f5v–f6r; for another possible case, see f. K8v. On Moreto, see Monfasani, 'The first call', pp. 14–22, 28–31.
30 Trovato, *Con ogni diligenza corretto*, pp. 159–60 nn. 7–12.
31 Fulin, 'Documenti', docs. 248, 250; Bembo, *Lettere*, II, nos. 543, 555, 571, 579, 637, 644; Cian, *Un decennio*, pp. 54–7; Tavoni, 'Scrivere la grammatica', pp. 784–90; Nuovo, *Il commercio librario nell'Italia del Rinascimento*, pp. 214–17.
32 Bembo, *Lettere*, III, no. 1095; Trovato, 'Per la storia', p. 466.
33 Ridolfi, *Vita*, I, 131, 142–4; II, 461–2 (*Decennale*); II, 507 (*Mandragola*); I, 309; II, 522–3 (*Arte della guerra*). On the *Decennale*, see also Trovato, *Con ogni diligenza corretto*, pp. 35–6, and Scarpa, 'L'autografo'.
34 Love, *Scribal Publication*, pp. 35–46 (p. 40).
35 Ibid. pp. 46–54, 73–83. For the early manuscripts of *Il principe* (*De principatibus*), see Giorgio Inglese's introduction to his critical edition, especially pp. 10–18, 37–56, 155–6. One can perhaps distinguish between a 'strong' and 'weak' use of entrepreneurial publication by Buonaccorsi, who copied the work both for sale and for presentation to a friend and patron, Pandolfo Bellacci.
36 Richardson, '*The Prince* and its early Italian readers', pp. 22–3.
37 Ariosto, *Lettere*, no. 16; Catalano, *Vita*, I, 428–39, 530; Fahy, *L''Orlando furioso'*, pp. 97–101.
38 Ariosto, *Lettere*, no. 29.
39 Catalano, *Vita*, I, 206–7; II, 136.
40 Ibid. I, 530–2; Fahy, *L''Orlando furioso'*, pp. 101–2.
41 Catalano, *Vita*, I, 595–604; Fahy, *L''Orlando furioso'*, especially pp. 93–175.
42 Ariosto's concern with accuracy is also reflected in the creation of a group of copies, on better and slightly larger paper, intended to contain the fully corrected text: Fahy, *L''Orlando furioso'*, pp. 167–75. On Cassio, see section I above.
43 See for instance Durling, *The Figure of the Poet*, pp. 112–14; Larivaille, 'Poeta, principe, pubblico'.
44 In a letter of 14 July 1512, Ariosto offered to have a transcription made for Francesco Gonzaga, but he is referring only to a sample section of a work in progress.
45 Brand, *Ludovico Ariosto*, pp. 135–7.
46 Fahy, *L''Orlando furioso'*, pp. 112–18.
47 Catalano, *Vita*, II, 344–5.
48 The fullest account is Bertolo, 'Nuovi documenti'.
49 The process of correction is studied in Ghinassi, 'L'ultimo revisore'.
50 In his note he made the error of writing 'duc.' for 'marzelli' in some cases.
51 On this change, see Larivaille, *Pietro Aretino*, pp. 87–104. On Aretino's works in print, see Quondam, 'Aretino e il libro'.

52 Aretino, *Lettere* (1960), p. 353.
53 Aretino, *Lettere* (1609), III, f. 194r–v.
54 Aretino, *Lettere* (1960), p. 429.
55 Ibid. p. 504.
56 Baschet, 'Documents inédits', pp. 119–25.
57 Aretino, *Lettere* (1960), pp. 163, 1019 (letter 91 n. 1); see too pp. 139–40, 398–9. See Bongi, *Annali*, I, 109, for a possible identification of the dedication copy of the third book of letters.
58 Aretino, *Lettere* (1960), p. 600; see too pp. 542–3, 582–4.
59 Ibid. pp. 194–5.
60 Bongi, *Annali*, I, 109–11.
61 Ibid. pp. 131–2.
62 Aretino, *Lettere* (1960), p. 768; *Lettere* (1609), III, ff. 61r, 70v.
63 Aretino, *Lettere* (1609), III, f. 19v.
64 Aretino, *Lettere* (1960), p. 178.
65 Ibid. p. 135.
66 Ibid. p. 203. On Lappoli (known as Pollio or Pollastra) and Aretino, and on the printing of Lappoli's play *Parthenio* in 1520 at the expense of the Sienese bookseller Giovanni Landi, see Clubb and Black, *Romance*, pp. 23–6, 29–31.
67 Luzio, *Pietro Aretino*, pp. 29–32, 85–7.
68 The records in the ASV, ST up to 1550 concern the *Stanze* to the empress Isabella, 1536 (reg. 29, f. 109r); the life of Our Lady, 1539 (reg. 30, f. 130r); the third book of letters, 1545 (reg. 34, f. 120v); the *Orazia*, 1546 (reg. 34, f. 186v); the fourth book of letters, 1549 (reg. 36, f. 139v).
69 Aquilecchia, 'Pietro Aretino', pp. 73, 80–5. Giovanni Giustiniani thought it possible in 1540 that Marcolini or another of what he termed 'Aretino's printers' would agree to pay the costs of printing Giustiniani's comedies (i.e. his translations of Terence?), 12,000 lines long, in quarto, and that he himself might also receive some payment: Landoni (ed.), *Lettere scritte a Pietro Aretino*, vol. I, part I, 253–4.
70 For the *Cortegiana*, *Parafrasi dei Sette Salmi* and *La passione di Giesù* in 1534 (ASV, ST, reg. 28, ff. 78r, 101r); for the life of Saint Catherine, the second book of letters, *La Talanta*, the *Ipocrito* and the second edition of the first book of letters in 1541–2 (ASV, ST, reg. 31, f. 144r; reg. 32, ff. 40v, 90r).
71 EDIT16, A2177 (Torresani), A2178 (Ruffinelli), A2216, A2219 (Biagio; the request concerning the life of Saint Thomas Aquinas is in ASV, ST, reg. 33, f. 46r). Biagio also requested a privilege for the *Dialogo del gioco*: ASV, ST, reg. 32, f. 185r.
72 EDIT16, A2219, A2222.
73 Aretino, *Lettere* (1960), p. 220.
74 Aretino, *Lettere* (1609), III, ff. 36v–37v, 68r–v, 80v.
75 Aretino, *Lettere* (1960), pp. 632–3, 688–9, 698–9, 836–7. Here too gift copies were distributed: see pp. 715, 716–17, 861.
76 Grendler, *Critics*, pp. 7–10.

77 Petrucci, 'La scrittura del testo' and 'Storia e geografia', pp. 1264–75; see also *Writers and Readers*, pp. 145–68.
78 For an example of this pressure – Dolce hastening to complete a translation for Gabriele Giolito – see Bongi, *Annali*, I, 252–3. Accounts of the work of these men can be found in Di Filippo Bareggi, *Il mestiere*; Trovato, *Con ogni diligenza corretto*; Richardson, *Print Culture*; Bonora, *Ricerche*.
79 B. Tasso, *Lettere*, II, 145.
80 Foffano, 'L'"Amadigi"', pp. 266–70; Bongi, *Annali*, II, 97–109; Dionisotti, 'Amadigi'.
81 B. Tasso, *Lettere*, II, 275.
82 Ibid. pp. 358–61, 362–5.
83 For example, ibid. pp. 477–9, 491–3.
84 Ibid. III, 138.
85 Ibid. II, 477–9.
86 Solerti, *Vita*, I, 58–60; II, 3–4, 94–5.
87 T. Tasso, *Le lettere*, I, no. 22; Solerti, *Vita*, I, 204–5.
88 Solerti, *Vita*, I, 219–20; II, 108–10.
89 Ibid. I, 333–4, 339–40; II, 156–7, 162, 452; T. Tasso, *Le lettere*, II, no. 258.
90 T. Tasso, *Le lettere*, II, no. 151; IV, no. 1131.
91 Solerti, *Vita*, I, 343–4; II, 22–3; III, 48.
92 Ibid. I, 518–21.
93 T. Tasso, *Le lettere*, IV, nos. 1079, 1084, 1094.
94 Solerti, *Vita*, I, 677–8; II, 336–7.
95 T. Tasso, *Le lettere*, III, no. 633; for similar complaints, see II, no. 205; III, nos. 640, 707; V, no. 1280.
96 Bec, 'Lo statuto'.
97 See especially the portrait of mid-Cinquecento literature offered in 'La letteratura italiana nell'età del concilio di Trento', in Dionisotti's *Geografia e storia*, pp. 183–204.
98 See chapter 3, section 2, and compare Chartier, *The Order of Books*, pp. 47–8, on the French situation.
99 Giovio, *Lettere*, II, 122.
100 Larivaille (ed.), *Lettere di ... Aretino*, p. 77.
101 Di Filippo Bareggi, *Il mestiere*, pp. 242–81. But Doni enjoyed at least temporary prosperity: Grendler, *Critics*, pp. 61–2.
102 Rose, *Authors and Owners*, pp. 3–4. On this period, see too Kernan, *Printing Technology*.
103 Barberi, *Il frontespizio*, I, 117–20; Mortimer, 'The author's image'.
104 Marotti, *Manuscript, Print*, p. 292.
105 Tompkins, 'The reader in history', pp. 206–11.
106 For the dialogue, see Cox, *The Renaissance Dialogue*, pp. 34–46.
107 Kernan, *Printing Technology*, pp. 172–81 (pp. 173–4).
108 Chartier, *The Order of Books*, pp. 9–10.
109 Ibid. p. x.

5 READING, BUYING AND OWNING PRINTED BOOKS

1 Darnton, 'History of reading'.
2 Lucchi, 'La Santacroce'; Grendler, *Schooling*, pp. 142–61, 174–88, 306–29; Plebani, 'Omaggio', pp. 74–82; Trovato, *Storia . . . il primo Cinquecento*, pp. 24–32.
3 For a woodcut of school scenes including a hornbook, see Essling, *Les livres à figures*, I, I, 287–8.
4 Saenger, 'Books of Hours', p. 142.
5 *Scritti linguistici*, p. 91.
6 Lucchi, 'La Santacroce', pp. 608–12.
7 E.g. '*edo*: io magno'; '*ivi*: io annai'. See Grendler, *Schooling*, pp. 183–4, 417–18.
8 Grendler, *Schooling*, pp. 275–305; Palumbo-Fossati, 'Livres et lecteurs', pp. 483–4.
9 *La piazza*, p. 741.
10 Grendler, *Schooling*, pp. 74–8.
11 Ibid. pp. 42–7.
12 On the education of females, see especially Klapisch-Zuber, 'Le chiavi', and Grendler, *Schooling*, pp. 93–102.
13 Klapisch-Zuber, 'Le chiavi', pp. 777–8; Grendler, *Schooling*, p. 96–100. On the educational role of convents, see too Weaver in Del Sera, *Amor di virtù*, p. 10 n. 2.
14 Grendler, *Schooling*, pp. 102–8; Clubb and Black, *Romance*, p. 69 (Arezzo).
15 Grendler, *Schooling*, pp. 333–62.
16 Ibid. p. 15.
17 Lucchi, 'La Santacroce', pp. 596–8; Ginzburg, *Il formaggio*, p. 120.
18 Cipolla, *Literacy*, pp. 22–3, 57–9.
19 Petrucci, 'Scrittura', especially pp. 183–5.
20 Mackenney, *Tradesmen*, pp. 182 4, 193–4; Grendler, *Schooling*, p. 47.
21 Saenger, 'Silent reading' and 'Manières de lire'; see too Petrucci, *Writers and Readers*, pp. 132–44; Nelson, 'From 'Listen, lordings''; Martin, 'Pour une histoire de la lecture', in *Le Livre français*, pp. 227–46; and chapter 6, section 2 on the *Decor puellarum* and *Gloria mulierum*.
22 Beer, *Romanzi di cavalleria*, pp. 208, 240; Marazzini, *Il secondo Cinquecento*, p. 121 (Tasso); Calmeta, *Prose e lettere*, p. 71 (Dante).
23 Cherubino da Siena, *Regole*, p. 9; Burke, 'The uses of literacy', pp. 122–3.
24 See chapter 2, p. 00. Calmeta referred at the start of the Cinquecento to professional 'citaredi' (singers who accompanied themselves) who performed works of others and then left manuscript copies behind (*Prose e lettere*, p. 4).
25 Goldthwaite, *The Building*, pp. 347–8; for the rents, see De la Mare, 'New research', p. 411.
26 Lowry, *Nicholas Jenson*, p. 187 (Merula); Verde, *Lo studio*, II, nos. 4, 27, 37, 40, 74 (Florentine professors).
27 Goldthwaite, *The Building*, pp. 317–42, 435–4 (Florence); Martani, 'Librerie', p. 236 n. 26 (Rome).

28 Verde, *Lo studio*, III, 1018 (barber); III, 131, 1030, 1047, 1048, 1050 etc. (young men); II, 323–4, III, 1201 (servants).
29 Cherubini and others, 'Il costo', pp. 359–401 (pp. 399–401 for the estimate on vellum; the price of paper is taken from p. 352). There were 74 bolognini to the papal ducat .
30 De la Mare, 'New research', p. 411.
31 M. Fava and Bresciano, 'I librai' (1918), pp. 95–6, 99; see too Tristano, 'Economia'.
32 De la Mare, 'The library', pp. 172–4.
33 Martini, 'La bottega'. The shop stocked 29 written hornbooks plus 75 blank sheets for hornbooks, 6 psalters and 18 *donadelli.*
34 On catalogues, inventories and prices (which could vary from place to place and from day to day), see Nuovo, *Il commercio librario nell''Italia del Rinascimento*, pp. 25–31, 118–24, 129–59, 230–45.
35 *Prefazioni*, p. 4; see too pp. lv-lxiii, by Miglio, on the cost of books.
36 BMC, V, ix and 156 (Cicero, 1470); Roover, 'Per la storia', pp. 111–15 (1472–6).
37 Cherubini and others, 'Il costo', pp. 401–21; M. Davies, 'Two book-lists'. The median folio price varied according to whether the work was in prose or in verse, since the latter gave less work to the compositors.
38 Verde, *Lo studio*, II, 328–35.
39 Martini, 'La bottega', p. 76 n. 18; Noakes, 'The development', pp. 46–7.
40 Fulin, 'Nuovi documenti', pp. 395–401.
41 Martani, 'Librerie'.
42 Brown, *The Venetian Printing Press*, pp. 36–9, 429–52; Ceccarelli, 'Il 'Zornale''; Lowry, *Nicholas Jenson*, pp. 178–202; Nuovo, *Il commercio librario*, especially pp. 39–42, 115–17, 133–5, 162–5.
43 Bec, *Les livres*, pp. 325–37; Verde, 'Libri', pp. 151–70; Trovato, 'Il libro toscano', pp. 546–7. Silvestro's stock included 8 printed *donadelli*, fewer than the 15 manuscript copies recorded in a *cartolaio*'s inventory of 1426 (De la Mare, 'The shop') and the 18 recorded in the 1476 inventory (n. 33 above).
44 M. Fava and Bresciano, 'Librai' (1918), p. 93.
45 Ganda, *Niccolò Gorgonzola*, pp. 55–9, 126–38.
46 Nuovo, *Il commercio librario nell'Italia del Rinascimento*, pp. 147–59. Domenico Sivieri's shop in Ferrara, c. 1503, offered 426 titles: Nuovo, *Il commercio librario a Ferrara*, pp. 139–273.
47 Pullan, 'Wage earners', and Mackenney, *Tradesmen*, pp. 97–101 (Venice); Parenti, 'Prezzi', and Goldthwaite, *The Building*, pp. 333–4, 435–9 (Florence).
48 Nuovo, *Il commercio librario a Ferrara*, pp. 74–81.
49 Stevens and Gehl, 'Giovanni Battista Bosso'; on the *Interrogatorio*, see Grendler, *Schooling*, pp. 345–52.
50 Grendler, *The Roman Inquisition*, pp. 12–14. The prices of Hebrew books printed by Daniel Bomberg were similar: Baruchson-Arbib, 'The prices'.
51 Rozzo, *Biblioteche*, pp. 223, 226–34.
52 Lucchi, 'La Santacroce', pp. 597–8.

53 *La piazza*, pp. 846–7.
54 Davis, 'Printing and the people', pp. 194–209 (on France); Burke, *Popular Culture*, pp. 250–4.
55 The miller Menocchio, for instance, definitely bought only one of the eleven books which he says he read; of the others, we know that one was given to him and six were lent: Ginzburg, *Il formaggio*, pp. 34–9.
56 Information based on Bertola, 'Incunaboli' (Vatican); Sartori, 'Documenti', docs. 67 and 90 (Padua); Connell, 'Books' (Venice); Franceschini, 'Codici', Bertoni, *La Biblioteca Estense*, pp. 235–52, and Quondam, 'Le biblioteche', pp. 22–3 (Ferrara); Verde, *Lo studio*, II, 256–8, 328–35 (Florence); Omont, 'Inventaire' (Naples); Bresc, *Livre et société* (Sicily). The story that a famous collector of fine manuscripts, Federico da Montefeltro, Duke of Urbino, refused to have printed books in his library has been shown to be false: Michelini Tocci, 'La formazione', pp. 16–18.
57 Franceschini, 'Codici', p. 335.
58 Rozzo, *Biblioteche*, pp. 65, 90.
59 Grafton, 'The Vatican', p. 34; Lowry, 'Two great Venetian libraries', p. 130.
60 For instance, the Florentine merchant Bardo de' Bardi, who died in 1441, owned just twelve books, valued between one lira and 5 ducats: Sambin, 'Libri in volgare'. Even the wealthy Francesco Sassetti possessed in 1462 no more than 61 works: De la Mare, 'The library', pp. 172–4.
61 Bec, *Les livres*; see too Verde, 'Libri'.
62 Bec, *Les livres*, pp. 62–3.
63 Bresc, *Livre et société*, pp. 84–5.
64 Zorzi, 'La circolazione', pp. 117–30, and 'Le biblioteche', pp. 36–7; see too Palumbo-Fossati, 'Livres et lecteurs'.
65 Lowry, 'Two great Venetian libraries', p. 147 (Grimani); Zorzi, 'La circolazione', pp. 135–6, 149–50 (with an estimate that about 10–20 per cent of books in the largest libraries were manuscript); Harris, 'Marin Sanudo' (1993), p. 27.
66 Geneviève Hasenohr, 'L'essor des bibliothèques privées aux XIVe et XVe siècles', and Jean Vezin, 'Le mobilier des bibliothèques', in Vernet (ed.), *Histoire*, pp. 215–63 (pp. 219–20), 365–71 (pp. 365–6).
67 *Scritti letterari*, pp. 241–3. For an example of 155 books kept in a chest in 1526, see Zorzi, 'La circolazione', p. 118.
68 Clark, *The Care of Books*, pp. 199–205; O'Gorman, *The Architecture*, p. 17.
69 Clark, *The Care of Books*, pp. 207–33, 267–71; Harris, 'Marin Sanudo' (1993), p. 38 n. 31.
70 Clark, *The Care of Books*, p. 316; Zorzi, 'La circolazione', p. 151.
71 Guttiérrez, 'La biblioteca'.

6 PRINTING FOR THE READING PUBLIC: FORM AND CONTENT

1 *Bibliography and the Sociology of Texts*, p. 8.
2 *The Order of Books*, pp. ix–x, 10; see too Chartier's 'Texts, printings, readings'.
3 For an outline, see Febvre and Martin, *L'apparition*, pp. 113–22; Gaskell, *A New Introduction*, pp. 16–25; Hirsch, *Printing, Selling and Reading*, pp. 114–17.
4 Ullman, *The Origin*; Casamassima, 'Litterae gothicae', pp. 116–23, and 'Lettere antiche'; de la Mare, *The Handwriting*, pp. 44–84; Petrucci, '"Anticamente moderni"'.
5 Balsamo, 'I primordi', pp. 257–8.
6 Lowry, *Nicholas Jenson*, pp. 76–81; Mardersteig, 'Aldo Manuzio', pp. 118–37; Lowry, *The World of Aldus Manutius*, pp. 135–7.
7 Casamassima, 'Litterae gothicae'.
8 Scholderer, 'Printing at Venice', pp. 78–81; Lowry, *Nicholas Jenson*, pp. 96, 142–4 and plate 9.
9 Ganda, *I primordi*, pp. 77–8; Rogledi Manni, *La tipografia a Milano*, p. 82.
10 Casciano and others, 'Qualche indicazione', pp. 366–70 and tables 41, 45, 48, 50a, 51b; see too Bühler, 'Roman type'.
11 Fletcher, *New Aldine Studies*, p. 143.
12 Ullman, *The Origin*, pp. 59–77; Wardrop, *The Script of Humanism*, pp. 11–12, 19–35; Mardersteig, 'Aldo Manuzio', pp. 139–43; Balsamo and Tinto, *Origini del corsivo*, pp. 25–41; Lowry, *The World of Aldus Manutius*, pp. 137–41; Fletcher, *New Aldine Studies*, pp. 77–82.
13 Petrucci, 'Scrittura', pp. 168, 173–4, 178–81, 186–7, 195. The *mercantesca* hand is illustrated in Grendler, *Schooling*, p. 326, and in *Letteratura italiana* Einaudi, *Storia e geografia*, vol. II, part 2, plate 49.
14 Adams and Barker, 'A new model', p. 8.
15 *Letters*, V, 2265.
16 Casciano and others, 'Qualche indicazione', p. 366 and table 40.
17 BMC, VII, xxii, 1071; for the Piacenza Bible, see too Rozzo, *Linee*, p. 18.
18 BMC, V, 426; VII, xxiv.
19 Fulin, 'Documenti', docs. 38, 74.
20 A rare case of a classical edition in octavo is the *Satires* of Juvenal issued in Rome by Ulrich Han in about 1468–9 (IGI 5573, where it was wrongly recorded as a quarto). An example of a more popular octavo edition is the translation of Ovid's *De arte amandi* printed by Giovanni Battista Sessa in March 1500.
21 Fulin, 'Documenti', doc. 33.
22 Dionisotti in *Aldo Manuzio editore*, I, xxxix–xlii; Lowry, *The World of Aldus Manutius*, pp. 142–3; Fletcher, *New Aldine Studies*, pp. 88–90; M. Davies, *Aldus Manutius*, pp. 40–50.
23 Needham, 'Aldus Manutius's paper stocks', pp. 302–5.
24 *Aldo Manuzio editore*, I, 152; Clough, 'The library', pp. 308–9; Giannetto, *Bernardo Bembo*, pp. 102–3, 294–5, 296–7, 299–301, 352.
25 *Aldo Manuzio editore*, I, 52, 59, plate XIII.

26 Lowry, *The World of Aldus Manutius*, pp. 143–6; Fletcher, *New Aldine Studies*, pp. 90–1; Wagner, 'Aldo Manuzio'.
27 M. Davies, *Aldus Manutius*, p. 46.
28 Dionisotti in Bembo, *Prose e rime*, p. 14. On the market at which Aldo was aiming, see too Lowry, *The World of Aldus Manutius*, pp. 143–8.
29 Nolhac, 'Les correspondants', no. 24, letter of 24 December 1501.
30 Colantonio's *Saint Jerome* can be compared with that by Antonello da Messina (National Gallery, London). The motif of the reader pausing from casual reading, finger marking his place, is found for instance in portraits by Bronzino (an unknown courtier, Metropolitan Art Gallery, New York) and Pontormo (a cleric identified as Niccolò Ardinghelli, National Gallery of Art, Washington), and in one ascribed to Titian (an unknown man, in the collection of Her Majesty The Queen).
31 Rhodes, *Annali tipografici di Lazzaro de' Soardi*, nos. 81, 82, 95. ISTC records only 14 duodecimo editions among Italian incunables.
32 Nuovo, *Alessandro Paganino*, pp. 36–62, 152–64; Fahy, 'Il formato in 24°'.
33 Richardson, 'Editing Dante's *Commedia*', pp. 255–8.
34 Grendler, *The Roman Inquisition*, pp. 12–13.
35 Fahy, 'The Venetian Ptolemy', p. 91; Bongi, *Annali*, I, 407; Pesenti, 'Il "Dioscoride"', p. 102.
36 Rozzo, *Biblioteche*, p. 201.
37 Fulin, 'Documenti', doc. 23.
38 Parkes, 'The influence', p. 135. Also useful are Lehmann, 'Blätter' (on the numbering of leaves etc.), and Rouse and Rouse, 'La naissance des index'.
39 Bussi, *Prefazioni*, pp. xli–xlii, 25; Smith, 'Printed foliation', p. 58.
40 Scholderer, 'Red printing'; Gaskell, *A New Introduction*, pp. 137–8.
41 For what follows, see especially Smith, 'Printed foliation'.
42 Smith, 'Printed foliation', pp. 61–2 (rubrication); Fletcher, *New Aldine Studies*, p. 97 (apparent insertion of manuscript folio numbers in the Aldine press). For the example of the growth of indexing and foliation in editions of Petrarch, see Richardson, *Print Culture*, p. 36.
43 Smith, 'Printed foliation', pp. 68–70.
44 Cox, *The Renaissance Dialogue*, p. 104.
45 Ong, *Orality and Literacy*, pp. 123–9; Eisenstein, *The Printing Press*, I, 88–107.
46 Kernan, *Printing Technology*, pp. 48–55 (p. 54).
47 Febvre and Martin, *L'apparition*, pp. 122–8; Barberi, *Il frontespizio*; Veneziani, 'Il frontespizio'. For a case in which a fifteenth-century manuscript has a title page, see Eisenstein, *The Printing Press*, I, 52 n. 35.
48 See H. Davies, *Devices*; Zappella, *Le marche*; Nuovo, *Il commercio librario nell'Italia del Rinascimento*, pp. 199–208. On the Aldine device, see Fletcher, *New Aldine Studies*, pp. 43–59.
49 Bongi, *Annali*, II, 273–4, 295, 341, 388.
50 On the topic in general, see Febvre and Martin, *L'apparition*, pp. 133–6; Sander, *Le livre à figures*, IV, ix–lxxxvii; Hind, *An Introduction* and *Early Italian Engraving*. For the statistics, see Bühler, *The Fifteenth-Century Book*, p. 92

(Bologna and Naples); Casciano and others, 'Qualche indicazione', pp. 368–9 and table 42 (Rome).

51 Hind, *An Introduction*, II, 465; Ganda, *Niccolò Gorgonzola*, pp. 72–4. For a similar example, see Ferrari, 'Dal Boccaccio illustrato', pp. 123–4.

52 Infelise, 'Gli editori veneziani', p. 33.

53 Mortimer, *Italian 16th Century Books*, no. 177. On the techniques used, see Gaskell, *A New Introduction*, pp. 154–9, and Woodward, *Maps*, pp. 23–7, 47–52; on the press, see Landau and Parshall, *The Renaissance Print*, pp. 28–30.

54 Donati, 'Escorso', suggests that the date 1467 is fictitious, but his interpretation is debatable.

55 P. Kristeller, *Early Florentine Woodcuts*; Ridolfi, *La stampa in Firenze*, pp. 23–4.

56 Hind, *An Introduction*, II, 464–83; Donati, 'Il mistero'; Ferrari, 'Dal Boccaccio illustrato', pp. 118–23; Bologna, 'Il libro', pp. 116–17; Dillon, 'Sul libro illustrato'.

57 Fowler, *Catalogue*, pp. 79–80.

58 Bühler, *The Fifteenth-Century Book*, p. 80; Donati, 'I fregî' and 'Le iniziali'; Lowry, *Nicholas Jenson*, pp. 86–7; Abrams, 'Venetian xylography'.

59 Books 'are printed, so they are no longer illuminated' ('si fanno in forma che non si miniano più'): quoted in Bühler, *The Fifteenth-Century Book*, pp. 92–3.

60 Hofer, 'Early book illustration'.

61 Dreyer, 'Botticelli's series'.

62 Fahy, 'The Venetian Ptolemy'. On engraved title pages, see Barberi, *Il frontespizio*, pp. 138–41.

63 See in general Eisenstein, *The Printing Press*, II, 520–74.

64 BMC, v, 285–6 (Ratdolt); Donati, 'Leonardo da Vinci', pp. 118–19 (with bibliography), Mortimer, *Italian 16th Century Books*, no. 346, and Nuovo, *Alessandro Paganino*, pp. 15–21, 141–3 (Pacioli).

65 On the Dante illustrations, see Donati, 'Il Manetti'; Parker, *Commentary and Ideology*, pp. 142–3.

66 Cox, *The Renaissance Dialogue*, pp. 104–5.

67 The *Gesamtkatalog der Wiegendrucke*, a detailed catalogue of all known incunables, had in 1994 reached the letter G. The *Incunable Short-Title Catalogue* (ISTC) gives less detail but is available on CD-ROM. The catalogue of sixteenth-century holdings in Italian libraries, *Le edizioni italiane del XVI secolo*, reached the end of the letter C in 1996.

68 On factors affecting survival rates, see Harris, 'Marin Sanudo' (1993), pp. 12–37.

69 On these trends, see Febvre and Martin, *L'apparition*, pp. 349–455, and Hirsch, *Printing, Selling and Reading*, pp. 125–53. For individual cities, I have used statistics from the following sources: Scholderer, 'Printing at Venice', pp. 87–9, and 'Printing at Milan', pp. 103–5; Quondam, 'La parte', pp. 141–4 (Brescia); Bühler, *The University and the Press*, p. 34 (Bologna); Trovato, 'Il libro toscano', pp. 532–9.

70 Cited in Hirsch, *Printing, Selling and Reading*, p. 133.
71 For the fifteenth century, see Quondam, 'La letteratura in tipografia', pp. 588–9; for the sixteenth century, see Marazzini, *Storia . . . il secondo Cinquecento*, pp. 29–41.
72 Cited in Hirsch, *Printing, Selling and Reading*, pp. 128–9.
73 For Rome, I have combined 'religious literature' with the four strictly religious categories used by Casciano and others; for Venice, Milan and Bologna, I have combined vernacular and Latin religious works. On religious incunables, see Rozzo, *Linee*, pp. 7–20.
74 Casciano and others, 'Qualche indicazione', tables 34 and 35.
75 Scholderer, 'Printing at Venice', pp. 75–8; Lowry, *Nicholas Jenson*, pp. 106–11.
76 Rozzo, *Linee*, pp. 69–80.
77 Grendler, *The Roman Inquisition*, pp. 131–3.
78 Quondam, '"Mercanzia d'onore"', p. 89; see too Grendler, *The Roman Inquisition*, pp. 133–4.
79 *Nicholas Jenson*, pp. 98–9.
80 Bussi, *Prefazioni*, p. 83 and plate XXVIII.
81 Hellinga, 'The codex', pp. 81, 83.
82 Lucchi, 'La Santacroce', pp. 613–16 (Tagliente, Verini, Manzoni), and 'Leggere', pp. 115–19 (Manzoni); Grendler, *Schooling*, pp. 100–1 (Tagliente and Manzoni), 158–9 (Tagliente), 306–19 (*abbaco* texts), 325–7 (writing manuals); Petrucci, 'Insegnare a scrivere' (writing manuals). Manzoni requested a privilege for a work of his own on bookkeeping, *L'opera di quaderno*, in 1539 (ASV, ST, reg. 30, f. 139r). In 1525 Tagliente registered with the Florentine guild to which booksellers and stationers belonged: Bertoli, 'Librai', p. 149.
83 On this character, see Stäuble, *'Parlar per lettera'*, pp. 9–130.
84 Dionisotti, 'Niccolò Liburnio'.
85 Lucchi, 'La Santacroce', p. 615.
86 On the acceleration of manuscript production of letters, see Petrucci, 'Introduzione', pp. 550–4.
87 A bibliography of this European genre is found in Kelso, 'The doctrine', pp. 165–277; see too the section 'Libri sulla corte' in Ossola and Prosperi (eds.), *La corte e il 'Cortegiano'*, II, 13–169.
88 Bertoni, *La Biblioteca Estense*, p. 92; Leonardo da Vinci, *Scritti letterari*, pp. 241, 254; Verde, *Lo Studio*, II, 333, 342 (Giovanni Buongirolami); Ginzburg, *Il formaggio*, pp. 35, 62, 92–3; Zardin, *Donna e religiosa*, pp. 159–68.
89 Grendler, 'Francesco Sansovino'.
90 Fioravanti, *Dello specchio*, ff. 61v–63v; Garzoni, *La piazza*, pp. 847–9. On both authors, see Fahy, 'Descrizioni', pp. 57–64, 70–6. On Garzoni's 'rewriting' of works by others, see Cherchi, *Enciclopedismo*. On recipe books, see Marazzini, *Storia . . . il secondo Cinquecento*, pp. 46–7, and Trovato, *Con ogni diligenza corretto*, p. 259 n. 14. Bec notes that in 1570–1608 'technical' books (including law, medicine, mathematics, science, military matters) became

the leading category in the Florentine book inventories studied by him (*Les livres*, pp. 67–73, 97).

91 A general survey is Burke, *Popular Culture*; for France, see Davis, 'Printing and the people'.

92 H. Brown, *The Venetian Printing Press*, pp. 209–10.

93 See for example the definitions of Angeleri, *Bibliografia*, p. 15; Braida, 'Les almanachs', p. 183; Bertoli, 'Nuovi documenti'. Elementary schooltexts in Latin could also be considered 'popular' books because of their form and their widespread use.

94 Grendler, 'Form and function'. See too, on the printing of the *Fior di virtù*, Bühler, 'Studies', and Donati, 'Le vicende', and on the use of italic in romances, Harris, 'Nicolò Garanta', pp. 110–11 and n. 29. For an example of the use of gothic in popular and liturgical books, see Ganda, *Niccolò Gorgonzola*, pp. 69–71.

95 Harris, 'L'avventura', pp. 54–8. See too Medin and Frati (eds.), *Lamenti*.

96 Three versions of the 1517 letter written by Bartolommeo da Villa Chiara: one printed by Simeone di Niccolò dei Nardi, Siena (quarto, 2 leaves, gothic text, woodcut of battle on title page, on which see Rhodes, 'A mysterious Italian newsletter'), one by Gabriele di Bologna, Rome (octavo, 4 leaves, gothic title page and roman text), and another listed in Sander, *Le livre à figures*, no. 911 (Sanudo recorded in his diaries that Venice was abuzz with this story on 29 December 1517); *El gran prodigio de tre soli* (Rome: Albertin Zanelli, 1536); *Lachrimoso e compassionevol caso ... occorso nell'alma città di Roma* (Venice: Marco Claseri, 1599). For other examples of printed letters, speeches etc., see EDIT16, C6265–403, C6407–11. An important study of a French example of the genre of tracts on calamities, crimes and the supernatural is Chartier, 'The hanged woman'.

97 Rozzo, *Linee*, pp. 104–5.

98 Castronovo, 'I primi sviluppi', pp. 6–14.

99 Marucci and others (eds.), *Pasquinate*; Firpo, 'Pasquinate'.

100 Braida, 'Les almanachs'; Garzoni, *La piazza*, p. 116.

101 Schutte, 'Printing, piety', especially p. 17.

102 Dionisotti, 'Leonardo', pp. 185–8; Farenga Caprioglio, 'Indoctis viris'.

103 Quondam, 'La parte', p. 204.

104 Zarri, 'La vita religiosa'. Her sample is selected from the 3,678 editions listed in Schutte, *Printed Italian Vernacular Religious Books*. Studies of books read by nuns include Zardin, 'Mercato librario', and Gehl, 'Libri per donne'.

105 Rusconi, '"Confessio generalis"', pp. 211–15.

106 Lowry, *Nicholas Jenson*, pp. 59–60.

107 *Decor*, I, ff. 7r–v, 13r–v; *Palma*, I. 6 and II. 7–8. On this distinction, see Saenger, 'Books of Hours'.

108 Verde, 'Libri'; see too Bertoni, *La Biblioteca Estense*, p. 47 n. 1, for the copies of Eleonora d'Aragona.

109 Grendler, *Schooling*, pp. 353–4, and 'Form and function', pp. 467–70; L. Miglio, 'Leggere e scrivere', pp. 360–1.

110 Sabadino, *Gynevera*, p. 376.

111 Other examples include some of Raphael's Madonnas, the Mary Magdalenes of Piero di Cosimo, Correggio and Alessandro Allori, and a woodcut of Saint Catherine of Siena surrounded by books and handing two books to laywomen kneeling before her, in her *Dialogo della divina provvidenza* (Venice: Matteo Capcasa, 1494), reproduced in *Letteratura italiana* Einaudi, II (1983), plate 11. See Bell, 'Medieval women book owners', pp. 760–3; Zarri, 'La vita religiosa', pp. 157–8.

112 *Epistola* XXII, in *Tutte le opere*, V, I, 704.

113 *Le vite*, II, 473–4, 499.

114 Cox, 'Women as readers'; Ariosto, *Lettere*, pp. 157–8. Castiglione recognized women's interest in the vernacular in general: *Il libro del cortegiano*, I. 44. For the growth of a specifically female English-speaking readership in this period, see Hull, *Chaste, Silent*, and Caroline Lucas, *Writing for Women.*

115 See also Mortimer, *Italian 16th Century Books*, nos. 47, 368, 470, 519, 520.

116 Editions of Petrarch's verse in 1533, 1539, 1548, 1562; Boccaccio's *Decameron* in 1516, 1538, 1542, 1546 (and in 1535 to 'valorous youths and women in love'); his *Fiammetta* in 1481, 1524 and 1542; his *Comedia delle ninfe fiorentine* (*Ameto*) in 1545.

117 See Laura Terracina's reading of Ariosto's *proemi*, the *Discorso sopra il principio di tutti i canti d'Orlando furioso* (1559), f. 59v, cited in Cox, 'Women as readers', p. 137.

118 Bertoni, *La Biblioteca Estense*, pp. 227–33 (Eleonora), 46–7 (Anna), 92 n. 1 (Lucrezia).

119 Palumbo-Fossati, 'Livres et lecteurs', p. 509–10.

120 Bresc, *Livre et société*, doc. 239.

121 Zorzi, 'La circolazione', pp. 128, 171 n. 22; the case of Bellocchio is cited in Rosenthal, *The Honest Courtesan*, p. 330 n. 89.

122 *Gynevera*, p. 365.

123 On Renaissance translations, see Dionisotti, *Geofrafia e storia*, pp. 103–44 (pp. 123–6 on Landino's Pliny); Fahy, 'love and marriage', p. 121 on Piccolomini), Trovato, *Storia . . . il primo cinquecento*, pp. 149–60.

124 Quondam, '"Mercanzia d'onore"', p. 79.

125 Tinto, *Annali.*

126 Cited in Rozzo, *Biblioteche*, pp. 68–9. See too Schutte, 'Irene di Spilimbergo'.

127 Barbieri, *Le Bibbie*; Trovato, *Storia . . . il primo Cinquecento*, pp. 48–57 (p. 49 for Brucioli's comment).

128 Barbieri, *Le Bibbie*,pp. 155–7 (fra Filippo); Marazzini, *Storia . . . il secondo Cinquecento*, pp. 91–5. On fra filippo's views, see, too Filippo de Strata, *Polemic against Printing*; Lowry, *The World of Aldus Manutius*, pp. 26–7.

129 Rozzo, *Linee*, p. 25.

130 On editors, and for further details on points discussed below, see Trovato, *Con ogni diligenza corretto*, and Richardson, *Print Culture.* A third, occasional editorial function from the 1540s onwards was the compilation of an-

thologies, especially of contemporary letters and verse, one of the purposes of which was to offer texts for imitation.

131 For examples, see Richardson, *Print Culture*, pp. 33 (Petrarch, 1500), 71 (Benvieni, 1522), 123–4 (Machiavelli, 1554).

132 For Borghini, see the *Lettera intorno a' manoscritti antichi.*

133 Diacritic accents were first used in print in a literary text by Aldo Manuzio in a Latin work of Bembo (*De Aetna*, 1496); an exceptional precendent was a guide to the pronunciation of the Latin of religious texts, entitled *Casselina* (1487), in which the stressed syllable had an acute accent. On the development of punctuation and accentution in printing, see Parkes, *Pause and Effect*, especially pp. 50–61; Trovato, 'Serie di carratteri'.

134 For the example of Trissino's use of the printers Arrighi and Zanetti to promote his spelling reforms, together with his own status as an author, see G. Castellani, 'Da Tolomeo Ianiculo' and 'Da Bartolomeo Zanetti'. On Ariosto, see Harris, 'Filologia e bibliologia', pp. 121–2.

135 An index might be provided by a person other than the editor, as when Bernardo Machiavelli compiled a list of geographical names in Livy's Roman history in 1475 in return for a copy of the work (see his *Libro di ricordi*, pp. 14, 35), or when the Greek Mattio Devarris indexed the edition of the commentary of Eustathius sponsored by Cardinal Cervini (1542–50) and was rewarded with 25 copies of the work (Dorez, 'Le cardinal Marcello Cervini', pp. 292–3).

136 Genette, *Palimpsestes.*

137 Guidi, 'Reformulations', p. 145–50; Burke, *The Fortunes*, pp. 42–5.

138 Biagiarelli, 'Il privilegio', p. 348–9.

139 Thus Marcantonio Flaminio made abbreviated versions (printed in 1521 and 1569 respectively) of Fortunio's *Regole grammaticali* and Bembo's *Prose della volgar lingua.*

140 Bongi, *Annali*, II, 219–25; Di Filippo Bareggi, *Il mestiere*, pp. 86–7; Grendler, *Schooling*, pp. 222–9 (on Toscanella's method for studying Cicero's letter); Bolzoni, 'Alberi del sapere e machine retoriche', in *La stanza*, pp. 26–86, especially pp. 53–75.

141 Bolzoni, *La stanza*, pp. 253–4 (on memory); Grendler, 'Francesco Sansovino', p. 179 (on history).

142 *Letilogia* (Milan: Antonio Zarotto, [after 10 March 1488], F. CIV.

143 Darnton, 'History of reading', pp. 148–9, using proposals of Rolf Engelsing and David Hall.

144 Ibid. p. 148.

Bibliography

PRIMARY SOURCES

Alberti, Leon Battista, *De cifris*, in *Opera inedita et pauca separatim impressa*, ed. G. Mancini (Florence: Sansoni, 1890)

Aldo Manuzio editore: dediche, prefazioni, note ai testi, intro. by Carlo Dionisotti, ed. and trans. Giovanni Orlandi, 2 vols. (Milan: Il Polifilo, 1976)

Aretino, Pietro, *Lettere: il primo e il secondo libro*, ed. Francesco Flora with notes by Alessandro Del Vita (Milan: Mondadori, 1960)

Il primo (–sesto) libro delle lettere, 6 vols. (Paris: Matteo il Maestro, 1609)

Ariosto, Ludovico, *Lettere*, ed. Angelo Stella, in *Tutte le opere*, ed. Cesare Segre, vol. III (Milan: Mondadori, 1984), 109–562

Bembo, Pietro, *Lettere*, ed. Ernesto Travi, 4 vols. (Bologna: Commissione per i testi di lingua, 1987–93)

Prose e rime, ed. Carlo Dionisotti, 2nd edn (Turin: UTET, 1966)

Benedetti, Alessandro, *Diaria de bello Carolino (Diary of the Caroline War)*, ed. and trans. Dorothy M. Schullian (New York: Frederick Ungar for the Renaissance Society of America, 1967)

Boccaccio, Giovanni, *Tutte le opere*, ed. Vittore Branca (Milan: Mondadori, 1967–)

Borghini, Vincenzio, *Lettera intorno a' manoscritti antichi*, ed. Gino Belloni (Rome: Salerno, 1995)

Bussi, Giovanni Andrea, *Prefazioni alle edizioni di Sweynheim e Pannartz prototipografi romani*, ed. Massimo Miglio (Milan: Il Polifilo, 1978)

Calmeta, Vincenzo, *Prose e lettere edite e inedite*, ed. Cecil Grayson (Bologna: Commissione per i testi di lingua, 1959)

Caro, Annibal, *Commento di ser Agresto da Ficaruolo sopra la prima ficata del padre Siceo* (Bologna: Romagnoli, 1861)

Castiglione, Baldesar, *Il libro del cortegiano con una scelta delle Opere minori*, ed. Bruno Maier, 2nd edn (Turin: UTET, 1964)

Cherubino da Siena [but da Spoleto], fra, *Regole della vita matrimoniale*, ed. Francesco Zambroni and Carlo Negroni (Bologna: Romagnoli, 1888)

Chesterfield, Lord (Philip Donner Stanhope), *Letters*, ed. Bonamy Dobrée, 6 vols. (London: Eyre and Spottiswoode, 1932)

Del Sera, Beatrice, *Amor di virtù*, ed. Elissa Weaver (Ravenna: Longo, 1990)

Erasmus, Desiderius, *Opus epistolarum*, ed. P. S. Allen, 12 vols. (Oxford: Clarendon Press, 1906–58)

Filippo de Strata, *Polemic against Printing*, trans. Shelagh Grier, ed. Martin Lowry ([Birmingham]: Hayloft Press, 1986)

Fioravanti, Leonardo, *Dello specchio di scientia universale* (Venice: Vincenzo Valgrisi, 1564)

Fratta, Giovanni, *Della dedicatione de' libri, con la corretion dell'abuso, in questa materia introdotto* (Venice: Giorgio Angelieri, 1590)

Garzoni, Tomaso, *La piazza universale di tutte le professioni del mondo, e nobili et ignoranti: nuovamente formata, e posta in luce* (Venice: Giovanni Battista Somasco, 1585)

Giovio, Paolo, *Lettere*, ed. G. G. Ferrero, 2 vols. (Rome: Libreria dello Stato, 1956–8)

Landoni, Teodorico (ed.), *Lettere scritte a Pietro Aretino*, 2 vols. (Bologna: Romagnoli, 1873–5)

Larivaille, Paul (ed.), *Lettere di, a, su Pietro Aretino nel Fondo Bongi dell'Archivio di Stato di Lucca* (Paris: Université Paris X – Nanterre, 1980)

Leonardo da Vinci, *Scritti letterari*, ed. Augusto Marinoni, new edn (Milan: Rizzoli, 1974)

Machiavelli, Bernardo, *Libro di ricordi* (Florence: Le Monnier, 1954)

Machiavelli, Niccolò, *De principatibus*, ed. Giorgio Inglese (Rome: Istituto storico italiano per il Medio Evo, 1994)

Marucci, Valerio, Marzo, Antonio, and Romano, Angelo (eds.), *Pasquinate romane del Cinquecento*, 2 vols. (Rome: Salerno, 1983)

Medin, Antonio, and Frati, Ludovico (eds.), *Lamenti storici dei secc. XIV, XV e XVI*, 4 vols. (Bologna: Romagnoli, 1887–94)

Morales, Cristóbal de, *Missarum liber primus (–secundus)*, in *Opera omnia*, ed. Higinio Anglés (Rome: Consejo superior de investigaciones científicas), vols. I (1952), III (1954), VI (1962)

Petrarca, Francesco, *Letters of Old Age: Rerum senilium libri I–XVIII*, vol. I, books I–IX, trans. Aldo S. Bernardo and others (Baltimore: Johns Hopkins University Press, 1992)

Letters on Familiar Matters: Rerum familiarum libri XVII–XXIV, trans. Aldo S. Bernardo (Baltimore: Johns Hopkins University Press, 1985)

Poliziano, Angelo, *Della congiura dei Pazzi*, ed. Alessandro Perosa (Padua: Antenore, 1958)

Sabadino degli Arienti, Giovanni, *Gynevera de le clare donne*, ed. Corrado Ricci and A. Bacchi della Lega (Bologna: Romagnoli, 1887)

Sabellico, Marcantonio, *Opera* (Venice: Albertino da Vercelli, 1502)

Tasso, Bernardo, *Delle lettere . . . volume primo (–terzo)*, 3 vols. (Padua: Comino, 1733–51)

Tasso, Torquato, *Le lettere*, ed. Cesare Guasti, 5 vols. (Florence: Le Monnier, 1852–5)

Trissino, Giovan Giorgio, *Scritti linguistici*, ed. Alberto Castelvecchi (Rome: Salerno, 1986)

Vespasiano da Bisticci, *Le vite*, ed. Aulo Greco, 2 vols. (Florence: Istituto Nazionale di Studi sul Rinascimento, 1970–6)

SECONDARY SOURCES

Abrams, George, 'Venetian xylography at the John Rylands University Library', *GJ*, 1995, 66–82

Accademico Rozzo, 'Vita di Pietro Andrea Mattioli raccolta dalle sue opere da un Accademico Rozzo di Siena', in *Memorie istoriche per servire alla vita di più uomini illustri della Toscana*, 2 parts (Livorno: Anton Santini e compagni, 1757–8), part II, 169–222

Adams, Thomas R., and Barker, Nicolas, 'A new model for the study of the book', in Barker (ed.), *A Potencie of Life*, pp. 5–43

Adda, Girolamo d', *Indagini storiche, artistiche e bibliografiche sulla libreria visconteo-sforzesca del Castello di Pavia*, 2 parts (Milan, 1875–9)

Agee, Richard J., 'The Venetian privilege and music-printing in the sixteenth century', *Early Music History*, 3 (1983), 1–42

Alexander, Jonathan J. G. (ed.), *The Painted Page: Italian Renaissance Book Illumination 1450–1550* (Munich: Prestel Verlag, 1994)

Alhaique Pettinelli, Rosanna, 'Elementi culturali e fattori socio-economici della produzione libraria a Roma nel '400', in *Letteratura e critica: studi in onore di Natalino Sapegno*, 3 vols. (Rome: Bulzoni, 1976), III, 101–43

Allen, P. S., 'Erasmus' relations with his printers', *Transactions of the Bibliographical Society*, 13 (1913–15), 297–321

Altieri Biagi, Maria Luisa, '"Vile meccanico"', *Lingua nostra*, 26 (1965), 1–12

Andrews, Richard, 'Written texts and performed texts in Italian Renaissance comedy', in J. R. Dashwood and J. E. Everson (eds.), *Writers and Performers in Italian Drama from the Time of Dante to Pirandello: Essays in Honour of G. H. McWilliam* (Lewiston, NY: Edwin Mellen Press, 1991), pp. 75–94

Angeleri, Carlo, *Bibliografia delle stampe popolari a carattere profano dei secoli XVI e XVII conservate nella Biblioteca Nazionale di Firenze* (Florence: Sansoni Antiquariato, 1953)

Aquilecchia, Giovanni, 'Pietro Aretino e altri poligrafi a Venezia', in *Storia della cultura veneta*, vol. 3/II (Vicenza: Neri Pozza, 1980), pp. 61–98

Armstrong, Elizabeth, *Before Copyright: the French Book-Privilege System 1498–1526* (Cambridge University Press, 1990)

Armstrong, Lilian, 'The hand-illumination of printed books in Italy 1465–1515', in Alexander (ed.), *The Painted Page*, pp. 35–47

Ascarelli, Fernanda, and Menato, Marco, *La tipografia del '500 in Italia* (Florence: Olschki, 1989)

Balduino, Armando, 'Petrarchismo veneto e tradizione manoscritta', in Giorgio Padoan (ed.), *Petrarca, Venezia e il Veneto* (Florence: Olschki, 1976), pp. 243–70

Balsamo, Luigi, 'Commercio librario attraverso Ferrara fra 1476 e 1481', *LB*, 85 (1983), 277–98

'Una iniziativa editoriale-tipografica fra Bologna e Parma (1474)', in Anna Laura Lepschy, John Took and Dennis E. Rhodes (eds.), *Book Production and Letters in the Western European Renaissance: Essays in Honour of Conor Fahy* (London: Modern Humanities Research Association, 1986), pp. 7–16

'I primordi della tipografia in Italia e Inghilterra', *LB*, 79 (1977), 231–62

Produzione e circolazione libraria in Emilia (XV–XVIII sec.): studi e ricerche (Parma: Casanova, 1983)

'Tecnologia e capitali nella storia del libro', in Biagiarelli and Rhodes (eds.), *Studi offerti a Roberto Ridolfi*, pp. 77–94

Balsamo, Luigi, and Tinto, Alberto, *Origini del corsivo nella tipografia italiana del Cinquecento* (Milan: Il Polifilo, 1967)

Barberi, Francesco, *Il frontespizio nel libro italiano del Quattrocento e del Cinquecento*, 2 vols. (Milan: Il Polifilo, 1969)

Paolo Manuzio e la Stamperia del Popolo Romano (1561–1570) (Rome: Ministero dell'Educazione Nazionale, 1942)

Tipografi romani del Cinquecento: Guillery, Ginnasio mediceo, Calvo, Dorico, Cartolari (Florence: Olschki, 1983)

Barbieri, Edoardo, *Le Bibbie italiane del Quattrocento e del Cinquecento*, 2 vols. (Milan: Editrice Bibliografica, 1991–2)

Barker, Nicolas (ed.), *A Potencie of Life: Books in Society. The Clark Lectures 1986–1987* (London: British Library, 1993)

Baruchson-Arbib, Shifra Z., 'The prices of Hebrew printed books in Cinquecento Italy', *LB*, 97 (1995), 149–61

Baschet, Armand, 'Documents inédits tirés des Archives de Mantoue', *Archivio storico italiano*, 3rd ser., 3 (1866), 105–30

Bataillon, Louis Jacques, Guyot, Bertrand G., and Rouse, Richard H. (eds.), *La production du livre universitaire au Moyen Age: exemplar et pecia* (Paris: Editions du CNRS, 1991)

Bec, Christian, *Les livres des florentins (1413–1608)* (Florence: Olschki, 1984)

'Lo statuto socio-professionale degli scrittori (Trecento e Cinquecento)', in *Letteratura italiana* Einaudi, II (1983), 229–67

Beer, Marina, *Romanzi di cavalleria: il 'Furioso' e il romanzo italiano del primo Cinquecento* (Rome: Bulzoni, 1987)

Bell, Susan Groag, 'Medieval women book owners: arbiters of lay piety and ambassadors of culture', *Signs*, 7 (1982), 742–68

Bellettini, Pierangelo, 'La stamperia camerale di Bologna', *LB*, 90 (1988), 21–53

Bellingeri, Luca, 'Editoria e mercato: la produzione giuridica', in *Il libro italiano del Cinquecento*, pp. 155–85

Bentley, Jerry H., *Politics and Culture in Renaissance Naples* (Princeton University Press, 1987)

Bernstein, Jane A., 'Financial arrangements and the role of printer and composer in sixteenth-century Italian music printing', *Acta musicologica*, 63 (1991), 39–56

Bertola, Maria, 'Incunaboli esistenti nella Biblioteca Vaticana durante il secolo XV', in *Miscellanea Giovanni Mercati*, vol. VI (Vatican City: Biblioteca Apostolica Vaticana, 1946), 398–408

Bertoli, Gustavo, 'Una bozza di stampa del Cinquecento: problemi e ipotesi', *LB*, 88 (1986), 279–95

'Librai, cartolai e ambulanti immatricolati nell'Arte dei medici e speziali di Firenze dal 1490 al 1600', *LB*, 94 (1992), 125–64, 227–62

'Nuovi documenti sull'attività di John Wolf a Firenze (1576–1577), con alcune considerazioni sul fenomeno delle stampe popolari', *Archivio storico italiano*, 153 (1995), 577–89

'Organizzazione del lavoro tipografico, lettura in piombo e correzione nei preliminari del contratto fra Scipione Ammirato e Filippo Giunti per la stampa delle *Istorie fiorentine*', *LB*, 97 (1995), 163–86

Bertolo, Fabio Massimo, 'Nuovi documenti sull'edizione principe del *Cortegiano*', *Schifanoia*, 13/14 (1992), 133–44

Bertoni, Giulio, *La Biblioteca Estense e la coltura ferrarese ai tempi del Duca Ercole I (1471–1505)* (Turin: Loescher, 1903)

Biagiarelli, Berta Maracchi, 'Editori di incunaboli fiorentini', in *Contributi ... Donati*, pp. 211–20

'Incunabuli fiorentini "sine notis"', *LB*, 67 (1965), 153–61

'Il privilegio di stampatore ducale nella Firenze Medicea', *Archivio storico italiano*, 123 (1965), 304–70

Biagiarelli, Berta Maracchi, and Rhodes, Dennis E. (eds.), *Studi offerti a Roberto Ridolfi direttore de 'La Bibliofilia'* (Florence: Olschki, 1973)

Bianca, Concetta, Farenga, Paola, Lombardi, Giuseppe, Luciani, Antonio G., and Miglio, Massimo (eds.), *Scrittura, biblioteche e stampa a Roma nel Quattrocento: aspetti e problemi. Atti del seminario 1–2 giugno 1979*, vol. I (Vatican City: Scuola Vaticana di Paleografia, Diplomatica e Archivistica, 1980)

Blackburn, Bonnie J., 'The printing contract for the *Libro primo de musica de la salamandra* (Rome, 1526)', *Journal of Musicology*, 12 (1994), 345–56

Blasio, Maria Grazia, *Cum gratia et privilegio: programmi editoriali e politica pontificia, Roma, 1487–1527* (Rome: Roma nel Rinascimento, 1988)

Bloy, C. H., *A History of Printing Ink, Balls and Rollers 1440–1850* (London: Wynkyn de Worde Society, 1967)

Bologna, Giulia, 'Il libro come oggetto di visione: l'attività grafico-illustrativa a Brescia nel Rinascimento', in Sandal (ed.), *I primordi della stampa a Brescia*, pp. 107–19

Bolzoni, Lina, *La stanza della memoria: modelli letterari e iconografici nell'età della stampa* (Turin: Einaudi, 1995)

Bongi, Salvatore, *Annali di Gabriel Giolito de' Ferrari da Trino di Monferrato stampatore in Venezia*, 2 vols. (Rome: Ministero della pubblica istruzione, 1890–5)

Bonifacio, Achille, *Gli annali dei tipografici messinesi del Cinquecento* (Vibo Valentia: Grafica Meridionale, 1977)

Bonora, Elena, *Ricerche su Francesco Sansovino imprenditore librario e letterato*, Classe di Scienze morali, lettere ed arti, 52 (Venice: Istituto Veneto di scienze, lettere ed arti, 1994)

Borrelli, Luciano, Groff, Silvano, and Hausbergher, Mauro, *Edizioni per i Madruzzo (1540–1659): dedicatari, committenti e autori nella famiglia dei principi vescovi di Trento* (Trento: Società di studi trentini di scienze storiche, 1993)

Bourgain, Pascale, 'L'édition des manuscrits', in *Histoire de l'édition française*, I, 49–75

Braida, Lodovica, 'Les almanachs italiens: évolution et stéréotypes d'un genre (XVIe–XVIIe siècles)', in Roger Chartier and Hans-Jürgen Lüsebrink (eds.), *Colportage et lecture populaire: imprimés de large circulation en Europe, XVIe–XIXe siècles. Actes du colloque des 21–24 avril 1991, Wolfenbüttel* (Paris: Institut Mémoires de l'édition contemporaine / Maison des Sciences de l'Homme, 1996), pp. 183–207

'Quelques considérations sur l'histoire de la lecture en Italie: usages et pratiques du livre sous l'Ancien Régime', in Roger Chartier (ed.), *Histoires de la lecture: un bilan des recherches* (Paris: IMEC, 1995), pp. 23–49

Brand, Peter, *Ludovico Ariosto: a Preface to the 'Orlando furioso'* (Edinburgh University Press, 1974)

Breitenbruch, Bernd, 'Ein Fragment einer bisher unbekannten Buchhändleranzeige', *GJ*, 1987, 138–45

Bresc, Henri, *Livre et société en Sicile (1299–1499)* (Palermo: Centro di studi filologici e linguistici siciliani, 1971)

Briquet, Charles-Moïse, *Les filigranes: dictionnaire historique des marques du papier*, 2nd edn, 4 vols. (Leipzig: Hiersemann, 1923)

Brown, Alison, *Bartolomeo Scala, 1430–1497, Chancellor of Florence: the Humanist as Bureaucrat* (Princeton University Press, 1979)

'The humanist portrait of Cosimo de' Medici, Pater Patriae', *Journal of the Warburg and Courtauld Institutes*, 24 (1961), 186–221

Brown, Horatio F., *The Venetian Printing Press 1469–1800* (London, 1891; repr. Amsterdam: van Heusden, 1969)

Bruni, Roberto, and Zancani, Diego, *Antonio Cornazzano: la tradizione testuale* (Florence: Olschki, 1992)

Bühler, Curt F., *The Fifteenth-Century Book: the Scribes, the Printers, the Decorators* (Philadelphia: University of Pennsylvania Press, 1960)

'Manuscript corrections in the Aldine edition of Bembo's *De Aetna*', *Papers of the Bibliographical Society of America*, 45 (1951), 136–42

'Roman type and Roman printing in the fifteenth century', in Joost (ed.), *Bibliotheca docet*, pp. 101–10

'Studies in the early editions of the *Fiore di virtù*', *Papers of the Bibliographical Society of America*, 49 (1955), 315–39

The University and the Press in Fifteenth-Century Bologna (Notre Dame, IN: Medieval Institute, University of Notre Dame, 1958)

Bullock, Walter Ll., 'Some notes on the circulation of lyric poems in sixteenth-century Italy', in *Essays and Studies in Honor of Carleton Brown* (New York University Press, 1940), pp. 220–41

Burke, Peter, *The Fortunes of the 'Courtier': the European Reception of Castiglione's 'Cortegiano'* (Cambridge: Polity Press, 1995)

Popular Culture in Early Modern Europe (London: Temple Smith, 1978)

Tradition and Innovation in Renaissance Italy: a Sociological Approach (London: Fontana/Collins, 1974)

'The uses of literacy in early modern Italy', in *The Historical Anthropology of Early Modern Italy* (Cambridge University Press, 1987), pp. 110–31

Camerini, Paolo, *Annali dei Giunti*, vol. 1, parts 1–2 (Florence: Sansoni, 1962–3)

Carosi, Gabriele Paolo, *Da Magonza a Subiaco: l'introduzione della stampa in Italia* (Busto Arsizio: Bramante, 1982)

Carpanè, Lorenzo, 'Libri, librai, tipografi nella Verona del Cinquecento: note', *Bollettino della Biblioteca Civica di Verona*, 1 (Spring 1995), 203–34

Carter, Harry, *A View of Early Typography up to about 1600* (Oxford: Clarendon Press, 1969)

Carter, Tim, 'Another promoter of the 1582 "rassettatura" of the *Decameron*', *Modern Language Review*, 81 (1986), 893–99

'Music-printing in late sixteenth- and early seventeenth-century Florence: Giorgio Marescotti, Cristofano Marescotti and Zanobi Pignoni', *Early Music History*, 9 (1989), 27–72

Casadei, Alberto, 'Sulle prime edizioni a stampa delle "Rime" ariostesche', *LB*, 94 (1992), 187–95

Casamassima, Emanuele, 'Ancora su Ludovico degli Arrighi vicentino', *GJ*, 1965, 35–42

'Lettere antiche: note per la storia della riforma grafica umanistica', *GJ*, 1964, 13–26

'Litterae gothicae: note per la storia della riforma grafica umanistica', *LB*, 62 (1960), 109–43

Casciano, Paola, Castoldi, Giustina, Critelli, Maria Pia, Curcio, Giovanni, Farenga Caprioglio, Paola, and Modigliani, Anna, 'Qualche indicazione per la tipologia del libro', in Bianca and others (eds.), *Scrittura*, pp. 363–70

Casella, Maria Teresa, and Pozzi, Giovanni, *Francesco Colonna: biografia e opere*, 2 vols. (Padua: Antenore, 1959)

Castellani, Carlo, *La stampa in Venezia dalla sua origine alla morte di Aldo Manuzio seniore* (Venice: Ongania, 1889; repr. Trieste: LINT, 1973)

Castellani, Giordano, 'Da Bartolomeo Zanetti a Tolomeo Ianiculo via Guillaume Pellicier', *LB*, 96 (1994), 1–13

'Da Tolomeo Ianiculo a Bartolomeo Zanetti via Giovangiorgio Trissino', *LB*, 94 (1992), 171–85

Castronovo, Valerio, 'I primi sviluppi della stampa periodica fra Cinque e Seicento', in Valerio Castronovo, Giuseppe Ricuperati and Carlo Capra, *La stampa italiana dal Cinquecento all'Ottocento* (Bari: Laterza, 1976), pp. 1–66

Catalano, Michele, *Vita di Ludovico Ariosto*, 2 vols. (Geneva: Olschki, 1930–1)

Cavaciocchi, Simonetta (ed.), *Produzione e commercio della carta e del libro: secc. XIII–XVIII* (Florence: Le Monnier, 1992)

Ceccarelli, Patrizia, 'Il "Zornale" di Francesco de' Madiis e i romanzi di cavalleria', in *I libri di 'Orlando innamorato'*, pp. 101–3

Charon-Parent, Annie, 'Le monde de l'imprimerie humaniste: Paris', in *Histoire de l'édition française*, 1, 237–53

Chartier, Roger, 'The hanged woman miraculously saved: an *occasionel*', in Chartier (ed.), *The Culture of Print*, pp. 59–91

The Order of Books: Readers, Authors, and Libraries in Europe between the Fourteenth and Eighteenth Centuries, trans. Lydia G. Cochrane (Cambridge: Polity Press, 1994)

'Texts, printings, readings', in Lynn Hunt (ed.), *The New Cultural History* (Berkeley and Los Angeles: University of California Press, 1989), pp. 154–75

Chartier, Roger (ed.), *The Culture of Print: Power and the Uses of Print in Early Modern Europe*, trans. Lydia G. Cochrane (Cambridge: Polity Press, 1989)

Chavasse, Ruth, 'The first known author's copyright, September 1486, in the context of a humanist career', *Bulletin of the John Rylands University Library of Manchester*, 69 (1986–7), 11–37

Cherchi, Paolo, *Enciclopedismo e politica della riscrittura: Tommaso Garzoni* (Pisa: Pacini, 1980)

Cherubini, Paolo, Esposito, Anna, Modigliani, Anna, and Scarcia Piacentini, Paola, 'Il costo del libro', in M. Miglio and others (eds.), *Scrittura*, pp. 323–553

Cian, Vittorio, *Un decennio della vita di M. Pietro Bembo* (Turin: Loescher, 1885)

Cipolla, Carlo M., *Literacy and Development in the West* (Harmondsworth: Penguin, 1969)

La moneta a Firenze nel Cinquecento (Bologna: Il Mulino, 1987) (*Money in Sixteenth-Century Florence* (Berkeley and Los Angeles: University of California Press, 1989))

Cittadella, Luigi Napoleone, *La stampa in Ferrara* (Rome: Fratelli Bocca, 1873)

Clark, John Willis, *The Care of Books: an Essay on the Development of Libraries and Their Fittings, from the Earliest Times to the End of the Eighteenth Century* (Cambridge University Press, 1901)

Clough, Cecil H., 'The library of Bernardo and of Pietro Bembo', *Book Collector*, 33 (1984), 305–31

Clubb, Louise George, and Black, Robert, *Romance and Aretine Humanism in Sienese Comedy: Pollastra's 'Parthenio' at the Studio di Siena* (Florence: La Nuova Italia, 1993)

Colla, Angelo, 'Tipografi, editori e libri a Padova, Treviso, Vicenza, Verona, Trento', in Pozza and others, *La stampa degli incunaboli*, pp. 37–80

Connell, Susan, 'Books and their owners in Venice: 1345–1480', *Journal of the Warburg and Courtauld Institutes*, 35 (1972), 163–86

Contò, Agostino, 'Notes on the history of printing in Treviso in the 15th century', in Reidy (ed.), *The Italian Book*, pp. 21–9

Contributi alla storia del libro italiano: miscellanea in onore di Lamberto Donati (Florence: Olschki, 1969)

Costabile, Patrizia, 'Forme di collaborazione: ri-edizioni, coedizioni, società', in *Il libro italiano del Cinquecento*, pp. 127–54

Cox, Virginia, *The Renaissance Dialogue: Literary Dialogue in Its Social and Political Contexts, Castiglione to Galileo* (Cambridge University Press, 1992)

'Women as readers and writers of chivalric poetry in early modern Italy', in Gino Bedani, Zygmunt Barański, Anna Laura Lepschy and Brian Richardson (eds.), *Sguardi sull'Italia: miscellanea dedicata a Francesco Villari* (Leeds: Society for Italian Studies, 1997), pp. 134–45

Da Pozzo, Giovanni (ed.), *La ragione e l'arte: Torquato Tasso e la Repubblica Veneta* (Venice: Il Cardo, 1995)

Darnton, Roger, 'History of reading', in Peter Burke (ed.), *New Perspectives on Historical Writing* (Cambridge: Polity Press, 1991), pp. 140–67

Davies, Hugh William, *Devices of the Early Printers 1457–1560: Their History and Development* (London: Grafton, 1935; repr. London: Dawsons, 1974)

Davies, Martin, *Aldus Manutius: Printer and Publisher of Renaissance Venice* (London: British Library, 1995)

'Two book-lists of Sweynheym and Pannartz', in Istituto di Biblioteconomia (ed.), *Libri, tipografi, biblioteche*, I, 25–53

Davis, Nathalie Z., 'Beyond the market: books as gifts in sixteenth-century France', *Transactions of the Royal Historical Society*, 5th ser., 33 (1983), 69–88

'Printing and the people', in *Society and Culture in Early Modern France* (London: Duckworth, 1975), pp. 189–226

De Frede, Carlo, *Ricerche per la storia della stampa e la diffusione delle idee riformate nell'Italia del Cinquecento* (Naples: De Simone, 1985)

de la Mare, Albinia, *The Handwriting of Italian Humanists*, vol. I, fasc. I (Oxford: Association Internationale de Bibliophilie, 1973)

'The library of Francesco Sassetti (1421–1490)', in Cecil H. Clough (ed.), *Cultural Aspects of the Italian Renaissance: Essays in Honour of Paul Oskar Kristeller* (Manchester University Press and New York: Zambelli, 1976), pp. 160–201

'New research on humanistic studies in Florence', in Annarosa Garzelli (ed.), *Miniatura fiorentina del Rinascimento 1440–1525: un primo censimento*, 2 vols. (Florence: La Nuova Italia, 1985), I, 393–600

'Script and manuscripts in Milan under the Sforzas', in *Milano nell'età di Ludovico il Moro: atti del Convegno internazionale 28 febbraio–4 marzo 1983*, 2 vols. (Milan: Archivio storico civico e Biblioteca Trivulziana, 1983), pp. 399–408

'The shop of a Florentine "cartolaio" in 1426', in Biagiarelli and Rhodes (eds.), *Studi offerti a Roberto Ridolfi*, pp. 237–48

Del Re, Niccolò, 'Prospero Farinacci giureconsulto romano (1544–1618)', *Archivio della Società romana di storia patria*, 98 (1975), 135–220

Destrez, Jean, *La pecia dans les manuscrits universitaires du XIIIe et du XIVe siècle* (Paris: Vautrain, 1935)

Di Filippo Bareggi, Claudia, *Il mestiere di scrivere: lavoro intellettuale e mercato librario a Venezia nel Cinquecento* (Rome: Bulzoni, 1988)

Dillon, Gianvittorio, 'Sul libro illustrato del Quattrocento: Venezia e Verona', in Pozza and others, *La stampa degli incunaboli*, pp. 81–96

Dionisotti, Carlo, 'Amadigi e Rinaldo a Venezia', in Da Pozzo (ed.), *La ragione e l'arte*, pp. 13–25

Geografia e storia della letteratura italiana (Turin: Einaudi, 1967)

'Leonardo uomo di lettere', *IMU*, 5 (1962), 183–216

'Niccolò Liburnio e la letteratura cortigiana', in *Appunti su arti e lettere* (Milan: Jaca Book, 1995), pp. 81–109

Donati, Lamberto, 'Escorso sulle Meditationes Johannis de Turrecremata (1467)', *LB*, 76 (1974), 1–34

'I fregî xilografici stampati a mano negl'incunabuli italiani', *LB*, 74 (1972), 157–64, 303–27; 75 (1973), 125–74

'Le iniziali stampate a mano', *GJ*, 1978, 37–42

'Leonardo da Vinci ed il libro illustrato', in Joost (ed.), *Bibliotheca docet*, pp. 117–38

'Il Manetti e le figure della Divina Commedia', *LB*, 67 (1965), 273–96

'Il mistero della Bibbia italica (Venezia, 1490, 1492, 1494)', *LB*, 77 (1975), 93–105

'Le vicende del *Fior di virtù*', *LB*, 76 (1974), 175–207

Dondi, Giuseppe, 'Apprendisti librai e operai tipografici in tre officine piemontesi del sec. XVI', in *Contributi ... Donati*, pp. 107–18

'Giovanni Giolito editore e mercante', *LB*, 69 (1967), 147–89

Dorez, Léon, 'Le cardinal Marcello Cervini et l'imprimerie à Rome (1539–1550)', *Ecole française de Rome, Mélanges d'archéologie et d'histoire*, 12 (1892), 289–313

Dreyer, Peter, 'Botticelli's series of engravings "of 1481"', *Print Quarterly*, 1 (1984), 111–15

Duggan, Mary Kay, *Italian Music Incunabula: Printers and Type* (Berkeley and Los Angeles: University of California Press, 1992)

Durling, Robert M., *The Figure of the Poet in Renaissance Epic* (Cambridge, MA: Harvard University Press, 1965)

Eisenstein, Elizabeth L., *The Printing Press as an Agent of Change: Communications and Cultural Transformations in Early-Modern Europe*, 2 vols. (Cambridge University Press, 1979)

Essling, Prince d' (V. Masséna), *Les livres à figures vénitiens de la fin du XVe siècle et du commencement du XVIe*, 3 parts (Florence: Olschki, and Paris: Leclerc, 1907–14)

Fahy, Conor, 'La carta nell'analisi bibliografica', in Alessandro Scarsella (ed.), *Sul libro antico. Bibliografia – filologia – catalogo: spazi della funzione bibliografica* (Viterbo: BetaGamma, 1995), pp. 3–19

'La carta nel libro quattrocentesco e nelle edizioni aldine', *LB*, 98 (1996), 55–7

'Descrizioni cinquecentesche della fabbricazione dei caratteri e del processo tipografico', *LB*, 88 (1986), 47–86

'Il formato in 24° di Alessandro Paganino', *LB*, 98 (1996), 59–63

'Introduzione alla bibliografia testuale', in Fahy, *Saggi di bibliografia testuale*, pp. 33–63

L'"Orlando furioso" del 1532: profilo di una edizione (Milan: Vita e Pensiero, 1989)

'Love and marriage in the *Institutione* of Alessandro Piccolomini', in *Italian Studies Presented to E. R. Vincent* (Cambridge: Heffer, 1962), pp. 121–35

'Per la vita di Ortensio Lando', *GSLI*, 142 (1965), 243–58

Saggi di bibliografia testuale (Padua: Antenore, 1988)

'The Venetian Ptolemy of 1548', in Reidy (ed.), *The Italian Book*, pp. 89–115

Farenga, Paola, 'Le prefazioni alle edizioni romane di Giovanni Filippo De Lignamine', in M. Miglio and others (eds.), *Scrittura*, pp. 135–74

'Il sistema delle dediche nella prima editoria romana del Quattrocento', in Quondam (ed.), *Il libro a corte*, pp. 57–87

Farenga Caprioglio, Paola, 'Indoctis viris ... mulierculis quoque ipsis: cultura in volgare nella stampa romana?', in Bianca and others (eds.), *Scrittura*, pp. 403–15

Fattori, Daniela, 'Per la storia della tipografia veronese: Giovanni da Verona', *LB*, 92 (1990), 269–81

Fava, Domenico, 'Libri membranacei stampati in Italia nel Quattrocento', *GJ*, 1937, 55–78

Fava, Mariano, and Bresciano, Giovanni, 'I librai ed i cartai di Napoli nel Rinascimento', *Archivio storico per le province napoletane*, 43 (1918), 89–104, 253–70; 45 (1920), 228–50; 59 (1934), 324–73

Febvre, Lucien, and Martin, Henri-Jean, *L'apparition du livre*, 2nd edn (Paris: Albin Michel, 1971) (*The Coming of the Book: the Impact of Printing, 1450–1800*, trans. David Gerard (London: Verso, 1990))

Fenlon, Iain, *Music, Print and Culture in Early Sixteenth-Century Italy* (London: British Library, 1994)

Ferrari, Mirella, 'Dal Boccaccio illustrato al Boccaccio censurato', in Gilbert Tournoy (ed.), *Boccaccio in Europe* (Leuven University Press, 1977), pp. 111–33

Fiorato, Charles Adelin, 'François Guichardin: un auteur sans public?', in Fiorato and Margolin (eds.), *L'écrivain face à son public*, pp. 155–71

Fiorato, Charles Adelin, and Margolin, Jean-Claude (eds.), *L'écrivain face à son public en France et en Italie à la Renaissance* (Paris: Vrin, 1989)

Firpo, Massimo, 'Pasquinate romane del Cinquecento', *Rivista storica italiana*, 96 (1984), 600–21

Fletcher, Harry George, III, *New Aldine Studies: Documentary Essays on the Life and Work of Aldus Manutius* (San Francisco: Rosenthal, 1988)

Foffano, Francesco, 'L'"Amadigi di Gaula" di Bernardo Tasso', *GSLI*, 25 (1885), 249–310

Folena, Gianfranco, 'La tradizione delle opere di Dante', in *Atti del Congresso internazionale di studi danteschi (20–27 aprile 1965)* (Florence: Sansoni, 1965), pp. 1–76

Fowler, Mary, *Catalogue of the Petrarch Collection Bequeathed by Willard Fiske* (London: Oxford University Press, 1916)

Frajese, V., 'Regolamentazione e controllo delle pubblicazioni negli antichi stati italiani (sec. XV–XVIII)', in Cavaciocchi (ed.), *Produzione*, pp. 677–724

Franceschini, Adriano, 'Codici e libro a stampa nella società e nelle biblioteche private ferraresi del secolo XV', *LB*, 85 (1983), 321–39

Frasso, Giuseppe, 'Appunti sul "Petrarca" aldino del 1501', in Rino Avesani,

Mirella Ferrari, Tino Foffano, Giuseppe Frasso and Agostino Sottili (eds.), *Studi in onore di Giuseppe Billanovich* (Rome: Edizioni di Storia e Letteratura, 1984), pp. 315–35

Frey, K. (ed.), *Der literarische Nachlass Giorgio Vasaris*, vol. I (Munich: Müller, 1923)

Frova, Carla, and Miglio, Massimo, 'Dal ms. Sublacense XLII all'*editio princeps* del "De civitate Dei" di sant'Agostino (Hain 2046)', in Bianca and others (eds.), *Scrittura*, pp. 245–73

Fulin, Rinaldo, 'Documenti per servire alla storia della tipografia veneziana' and 'Nuovi documenti ...', *Archivio veneto*, 23 (1882), 84–212, 390–405

Ganda, Arnaldo, *Niccolò Gorgonzola editore e libraio in Milano (1496–1536)* (Florence: Olschki, 1988)

I primordi della tipografia milanese: Antonio Zarotto da Parma (1471–1507) (Florence: Olschki, 1984)

'Vicende editoriali della *Patria Historia* di Bernardino Corio', *LB*, 96 (1994), 217–32

Gaskell, Philip, *A New Introduction to Bibliography*, 2nd edn (Oxford: Clarendon Press, 1974)

Gehl, Paul, 'Libri per donne: le monache clienti del libraio fiorentino Piero Morosi (1588–1607)', in Gabriella Zarri (ed.), *Donna, disciplina, creanza cristiana dal XV al XVII secolo: studi e testi a stampa* (Rome: Edizioni di Storia e Letteratura, 1996), pp. 67–82

Genette, Gérard, *Palimpsestes: la littérature au second degré* (Paris: Editions du Seuil, 1982)

Ghinassi, Ghino, 'L'ultimo revisore del "Cortegiano"', *Studi di filologia italiana*, 21 (1963), 217–64

Giannetto, Nella, *Bernardo Bembo umanista e politico veneziano* (Florence: Olschki, 1985)

Ginzburg, Carlo, *Il formaggio e i vermi: il cosmo di un mugnaio del '500* (Turin: Einaudi, 1976)

Goldthwaite, Richard A., *The Building of Renaissance Florence: an Economic and Social History* (Baltimore: Johns Hopkins University Press, 1980)

Grafton, Anthony, 'The Vatican and its library', in Anthony Grafton (ed.), *Rome Reborn: the Vatican Library and Renaissance Culture* (Washington, DC: Library of Congress, and New Haven: Yale University Press, 1993), pp. 3–45

Grendler, Paul F., *Critics of the Italian World (1530–1560): Anton Francesco Doni, Nicolò Franco & Ortensio Lando* (Madison: University of Wisconsin Press, 1969)

'Form and function in Renaissance popular books', *Renaissance Quarterly*, 46 (1993), 457–85

'Francesco Sansovino and Italian popular history 1560–1600', *Studies in the Renaissance*, 16 (1969), 139–80, and in his *Culture and Censorship in Late Renaissance Italy and France* (London: Variorum, 1981)

'Printing and censorship', in Charles B. Schmitt (general ed.), *Cambridge History of Renaissance Philosophy* (Cambridge University Press, 1988), pp. 25–53

The Roman Inquisition and the Venetian Press, 1540–1605 (Princeton University Press, 1977)

Schooling in Renaissance Italy: Literacy and Learning, 1300–1600 (Baltimore: Johns Hopkins University Press, 1989)

Guidi, José, 'Reformulations de l'idéologie aristocratique au XVIe siècle: les différentes rédactions et la fortune du "Courtisan"', in *Réécritures I: commentaires, parodies, variations dans la littérature italienne de la Renaissance* (Paris: Université de la Sorbonne Nouvelle, 1983), pp. 121–84

Guttiérrez, D., 'La biblioteca agostiniana di Cremona alla fine del secolo XVI', *Analecta augustiniana*, 24 (1961), 313–30

Haebler, Konrad, *Handbuch der Inkunabelkunde* (Leipzig: Hiersemann, 1925)

Hankins, James, 'Cosimo de' Medici as a patron of humanistic literature', in Francis Ames-Lewis (ed.), *Cosimo 'il Vecchio' de' Medici, 1389–1464: Essays in Commemoration of the 600th Anniversary of Cosimo de' Medici's Birth* (Oxford: Clarendon Press, 1992), pp. 69–94

Harris, Neil, 'L'avventura editoriale dell'"Orlando innamorato"', in *I libri di 'Orlando innamorato'*, pp. 35–100

Bibliografia dell'"Orlando Innamorato', 2 vols. (Modena: Panini, 1988–91)

'Filologia e bibliologia a confronto nell'*Orlando furioso* del 1532', in Istituto di Biblioteconomia (ed.), *Libri, tipografi, biblioteche*, I, 105–22

'Marin Sanudo, forerunner of Melzi', *LB*, 95 (1993), 1–38, 101–45; 96 (1994), 15–42

'Nicolò Garanta editore a Venezia 1525–30', *LB*, 97 (1995), 99–148

'Una pagina capovolta nel *Filocolo* veneziano del 1472', *LB*, 98 (1996), 1–21

Hellinga, Lotte, 'The codex in the fifteenth century: manuscript and print', in Barker (ed.), *A Potencie of Life*, pp. 63–88

'Peter Schoeffer and the book trade in Mainz: evidence for the organization', in Dennis E. Rhodes (ed.), *Bookbindings and Other Bibliophily: Essays in Honour of Anthony Hobson* (Verona: Edizioni Valdonega, 1994), pp. 131–83

'Press and text in the first decades of printing', in Istituto di Biblioteconomia (ed.), *Libri, tipografi, biblioteche*, I, 1–23

'Three notes on printers' copy: Strassburg, Oxford, Subiaco', *Transactions of the Cambridge Bibliographical Society*, 9 (1987), 194–204

Hill Cotton, Juliana, 'Alessandro Sarti e il Poliziano', *LB*, 64 (1962), 225–46

Hind, Arthur M., *Early Italian Engraving: a Critical Catalogue with Complete Reproduction of All the Prints Described*, 7 vols. (London: Quaritch, 1938–48)

An Introduction to a History of Woodcut with a Detailed Survey of Work Done in the Fifteenth Century, 2 vols. (New York: Houghton Mifflin, 1935; repr. New York: Dover Press, 1963)

Hindman, Sandra, and Farquhar, J. D., *Pen to Press: Illustrated Manuscripts and Printed Books in the First Century of Printing* (College Park: University of Maryland Art Department; Baltimore: Johns Hopkins University Department of the History of Art, 1977)

Hirsch, Rudolf, *Printing, Selling and Reading, 1450–1550* (Wiesbaden: Harrassowitz, 1967)

Histoire de l'édition française, 4 vols. (Paris: Promodis, 1982–6): vol. 1, *Le livre conquérant: du Moyen Age au milieu du XVIIe siècle*

Hobson, Anthony, 'Booksellers and bookbinders', in Robin Myers and Michael Harris (eds.), *A Genius for Letters: Bookselling and Bookbinding from the 16th to the 20th Century* (Winchester: St Paul's Bibliographies, and New Castle, DE: Oak Knoll Press, 1995), pp. 1–14

Hofer, Philip, 'Early book illustration in the intaglio medium', *Print Collector's Quarterly*, 21 (1934), 203–27, 295–316

Hoyoux, Jean, 'Les moyens d'existence d'Erasme', *Bibliothèque d'humanisme et Renaissance*, 5 (1944), 7–59

Hull, Suzanne, *Chaste, Silent and Obedient: English Books for Women 1475–1640* (San Marino, CA: Huntington Library, 1982)

Ianziti, Gary, *Humanistic Historiography under the Sforza: Politics and Propaganda in Fifteenth-Century Milan* (Oxford: Clarendon Press, 1988)

'Patronage and the production of history: the case of Quattrocento Milan', in Kent and Simons (eds.), *Patronage, Art, and Society*, pp. 299–311

Infelise, Mario, 'L'editoria veneta tra XVI e XIX secolo: una base di dati', *La fabbrica del libro*, 1 (1995), 5–8

'Gli editori veneziani del secondo Cinquecento', in Da Pozzo (ed.), *La ragione e l'arte*, pp. 27–33

Istituto di Biblioteconomia e Paleografia, Università degli Studi, Parma (ed.), *Libri, tipografi, biblioteche: ricerche storiche dedicate a Luigi Balsamo*, 2 vols. (Florence: Olschki, 1997)

Joost, Siegfried (ed.), *Bibliotheca docet: Festgabe für Carl Wehmer* (Amsterdam: Erasmus-Buchhandlung, 1963)

Kallendorf, Craig, 'In search of a patron: Anguillara's vernacular Virgil and the print culture of Renaissance Italy', *Papers of the Bibliographical Society of America*, 91 (1997), 294–325

Kelso, Ruth, 'The doctrine of the English gentleman in the sixteenth century', *University of Illinois Studies in Language and Literature*, 14 (1929), 1–288

Kent, F. W., and Simons, Patricia (eds.), *Patronage, Art, and Society in Renaissance Italy* (Oxford: Clarendon Press, 1987)

Kernan, Alvin, *Printing Technology, Letters & Samuel Johnson* (Princeton University Press, 1987)

Kettering, Sharon, *Patrons, Brokers, and Clients in Seventeenth-Century France* (Oxford: Oxford University Press, 1986)

Klapisch-Zuber, Christiane, 'Le chiavi fiorentine di Barbablù: l'apprendimento della lettura a Firenze nel XV secolo', *Quaderni storici*, no. 57 (December 1984), 765–92

Kolsky, Stephen, *Mario Equicola: the Real Courtier* (Geneva: Droz, 1991)

Kristeller, Paul, *Early Florentine Woodcuts* (London, 1897; repr. London: Holland Press, 1968)

Kristeller, Paul Oskar, *Supplementum ficinianum*, 2 vols. (Florence: Olschki, 1937)

Landau, David, and Parshall, Peter, *The Renaissance Print, 1470–1550* (New Haven: Yale University Press, 1994)

Larivaille, Paul, *Pietro Aretino fra Rinascimento e Manierismo* (Rome: Bulzoni, 1980)
'Poeta, principe, pubblico dall'"Orlando innamorato" all'"Orlando furioso"', in Marianne Pade, Lene Waage Petersen and Daniela Quarta (eds.), *La corte di Ferrara e il suo mecenatismo, 1441–1598* (Copenhagen: Museum Tusculanum, and Modena: Panini, 1990)
Laufer, Roger, 'L'espace visuel du livre ancien', in *Histoire de l'édition française*, I, 579–601
Ledos, E.-G., 'Lettre inédite de Cristoforo Landino à Bernardo Bembo', *Bibliothèque de l'Ecole des Chartes*, 54 (1893), 721–4
Lehmann, Paul, 'Blätter, Seiten, Spalten, Zeilen', in *Erforschung des Mittelalters: ausgewählte Abhandlungen und Aufsätze*, vol. III (Stuttgart: Anton Hiersemann, 1960), 1–59
Letteratura italiana, directed by Alberto Asor Rosa (Turin: Einaudi, 1982–91)
I libri di 'Orlando innamorato' (Modena: Panini, 1987)
Il libro italiano del Cinquecento: produzione e commercio. Catalogo della mostra, Biblioteca Nazionale Centrale, Roma, 20 ottobre–16 dicembre 1989 (Rome: Istituto Poligrafico e Zecca dello Stato, 1989)
Lopez, Pasquale, *Sul libro a stampa e le origini della censura ecclesiastica* (Naples: Regina, 1972)
Love, Harold, *Scribal Publication in Seventeenth-Century England* (Oxford: Clarendon Press, 1993)
Lowry, Martin, 'Aldus Manutius and Benedetto Bordon: in search of a link', *Bulletin of the John Rylands University Library of Manchester*, 66 (1983), 173–97
Nicholas Jenson and the Rise of Venetian Publishing (Oxford: Blackwell, 1991)
'La produzione del libro', in Cavaciocchi (ed.), *Produzione*, pp. 365–87
'Two great Venetian libraries in the age of Aldus Manutius', *Bulletin of the John Rylands University Library of Manchester*, 57 (1974–5), 128–66
The World of Aldus Manutius: Business and Scholarship in Renaissance Venice (Oxford: Blackwell, 1979)
Lubkin, Gregory, *A Renaissance Court: Milan under Galeazzo Maria Sforza* (Berkeley and Los Angeles: University of California Press, 1994)
Lucas, Caroline, *Writing for Women: the Example of Woman as Reader in Elizabethan Romance* (Milton Keynes: Open University Press, 1989)
Lucas, Corinne, 'Vers une nouvelle image de l'écrivain: *Della dedicatione de' libri* de Giovanni Fratta', in Fiorato and Margolin (eds.), *L'écrivain face à son public*, pp. 85–104
Lucchi, Piero, 'Leggere, scrivere e abbaco: l'istruzione elementare agli inizi dell'età moderna', in *Scienze, credenze occulte, livelli di cultura: Convegno internazionale di studi (Firenze, 26–30 giugno 1980)* (Florence: Olschki, 1982), pp. 101–19
'La Santacroce, il Salterio e il Babuino: libri per imparare a leggere nel primo secolo della stampa', *Quaderni storici*, no. 38 (May–August 1978), 593–630
Luzio, Alessandro, *Pietro Aretino nei primi suoi anni a Venezia e la corte dei Gonzaga* (Turin: Loescher, 1888)

Mackenney, Richard, *Tradesmen and Traders: the World of the Guilds in Venice and Europe, c. 1250–c. 1650* (London: Croom Helm, 1987)

McKenzie, Donald F., *Bibliography and the Sociology of Texts* (London: British Library, 1986)

McQuail, Denis, *Mass Communication Theory: an Introduction*, 3rd edn (London: Sage, 1994)

Manzi, Pietro, *La tipografia napoletana nel '500: annali di Giuseppe Cacchi, Giovanni Battista Cappelli e tipografi minori (1566–1600)* (Florence: Olschki, 1974)

La tipografia napoletana nel '500: annali di Mattia Cancer ed eredi (1529–1593) (Florence: Olschki, 1972)

La tipografia napoletana nel '500: annali di Sigismondo Mayr, Giovanni A. de Caneto, Antonio de Frizis, Giovanni Pasquet de Sallo (1503–1535) (Florence: Olschki, 1971)

Marazzini, Claudio, *Storia della lingua italiana: il secondo Cinquecento e il Seicento* (Bologna: Il Mulino, 1993)

Marciani, Corrado, 'Il commercio librario alle fiere di Lanciano nel '500', *Rivista storica italiana*, 70 (1958), 421–41

'Editori, tipografi, librai veneti nel Regno di Napoli nel Cinquecento', *Studi veneziani*, 10 (1968), 457–554

Marcon, Susy, 'Una aldina miniata', in Marcon and Zorzi (eds.), *Aldo Manuzio e l'ambiente veneziano*, pp. 107–33

Marcon, Susy, and Zorzi, Marino (eds.), *Aldo Manuzio e l'ambiente veneziano 1494–1515* (Venice: Il Cardo, 1994)

Mardersteig, Giovanni, 'Aldo Manuzio e i caratteri di Francesco Griffo da Bologna', in *Studi di bibliografia e di storia in onore di Tammaro De Marinis*, vol. III (Vatican City: Biblioteca Apostolica Vaticana, 1964), pp. 105–47

'La singolare cronaca della nascita di un incunabolo: il commento di Gentile da Foligno stampato da Pietro Maufer nel 1477', *IMU*, 8 (1965), 249–67

Marotti, Arthur F., *Manuscript, Print, and the English Renaissance Lyric* (Ithaca: Cornell University Press, 1995)

Martani, Margherita, 'Librerie a Parma nella seconda metà del XV secolo', *LB*, 97 (1995), 211–44

Martin, Henri-Jean, *Le livre français sous l'Ancien Régime* (Paris: Promodis, 1987)

Martines, Lauro, 'Love and hate in Renaissance patronage', *Italianist*, 14 (1994), 5–31

Martini, Giuseppe Sergio, 'La bottega di un cartolaio fiorentino della seconda metà del Quattrocento: nuovi contributi biografici intorno a Gherardo e Monte di Giovanni', *LB*, 58 (1956), supplement

Masetti Zannini, Gian Ludovico, *Stampatori e librai a Roma nella seconda metà del Cinquecento: documenti inediti* (Rome: Fratelli Palombi, 1980)

Mazzoldi, Leonardo, 'I primi librai bresciani', *Commentari dell'Ateneo di Brescia*, 172 (1973), 29–44

Menato, Marco, Sandal, Ennio, and Zappella, Giuseppina (eds.), *Dizionario dei tipografi e degli editori italiani: il Cinquecento*, vol. I (Milan: Editrice Bibliografica, 1997)

Michelini Tocci, Luigi, 'La formazione della biblioteca di Federico da Montefeltro: codici contemporanei e libri a stampa', in Giorgio Cerboni Baiardi, Giorgio Chittolini and Piero Floriani (eds.), *Federico di Montefeltro: lo stato, le arti, la cultura*, 3 vols. (Rome: Bulzoni, 1986), *La cultura*, pp. 9–18

Miglio, Luisa, 'Leggere e scrivere il volgare: sull'alfabetismo delle donne nella Toscana tardo medievale', in *Civiltà comunale: libro, scrittura, documento: atti del Convegno, Genova, 8–11 novembre 1988* (Genoa: Società ligure di storia patria, 1989), pp. 355–83

Miglio, Massimo, Farenga, Paola, and Modigliani, Anna (eds.), *Scrittura, biblioteche e stampa a Roma nel Quattrocento: atti del 2º seminario 6–8 maggio 1982* (Vatican City: Scuola Vaticana di Paleografia, Diplomatica e Archivistica, 1983)

Modigliani, Anna, *Tipografi a Roma prima della stampa: due società per fare libri con le forme (1466–1470)* (Rome: Roma nel Rinascimento, 1989)

Monfasani, John, 'The first call for press censorship: Niccolò Perotti, Giovanni Andrea Bussi, Antonio Moreto, and the editing of Pliny's *Natural History*', *Renaissance Quarterly*, 41 (1988), 1–31

Montecchi, Giorgio, *Aziende tipografiche, stampatori e librai a Modena dal Quattrocento al Settecento* (Modena: Mucchi, 1988)

Il libro nel Rinascimento: saggi di bibliologia (Milan: Editrice La Storia, 1994)

Moro, G., 'Insegne librarie e marche tipografiche in un registro veneziano del Cinquecento', *LB*, 91 (1989), 51–80

Mortimer, Ruth, 'The author's image: Italian sixteenth-century printed portraits', *Harvard Library Bulletin*, new ser., 7, no. 2 (Summer 1996)

Harvard College Library, Department of Printing and Graphic Arts: Catalogue of Books and Manuscripts. Part II: *Italian 16th Century Books*, 2 vols. (Cambridge, MA: Belknap Press of Harvard University Press, 1974)

Motta, Emilio, 'Demetrio Calcondila editore', *Archivio storico lombardo*, 20 (1893), 143–66

'Di Filippo di Lavagna e di alcuni altri tipografi-editori milanesi del Quattrocento', *Archivio storico lombardo*, 25 (1898), 28–72

Needham, Paul, 'Aldus Manutius's paper stocks: the evidence of two uncut books', *Princeton University Library Chronicle*, 55 (1994–5), 287–307

'ISTC as a tool for analytical bibliography', in Lotte Hellinga and John Goldfinch (eds.), *Bibliography and the Study of 15th-Century Civilisation*, British Library Occasional Papers 5 (London: British Library, 1987), pp. 39–54

Nelson, William, 'From "Listen, lordings" to "Dear Reader"', *University of Toronto Quarterly*, 46 (1976–7), 110–24

Niero, Antonio, 'Decreti pretridentini di due patriarchi di Venezia su stampa di libri', *Rivista di storia della Chiesa in Italia*, 14 (1960), 450–2

Noakes, Susan, 'The development of the book market in late Quattrocento Italy: printers' failures and the role of the middleman', *Journal of Medieval and Renaissance Studies*, 11 (1981), 23–55

Nolhac, Pierre de, 'Les correspondants de Alde Manuce: matériaux nouveaux d'histoire littéraire (1483–1514)', *Studi e documenti di storia e diritto*, 8 (1887),

247–99, and 9 (1888), 203–48 (repr. Turin: Bottega d'Erasmo, 1967)

Nuovo, Angela, *Alessandro Paganino (1509–1538)* (Padua: Antenore, 1990)

Il commercio librario a Ferrara tra XV e XVI secolo: la bottega di Domenico Sivieri (Florence: Olschki, 1998)

Il commercio librario nell'Italia del Rinascimento (Milan: FrancoAngeli, 1998)

O'Gorman, James F., *The Architecture of the Monastic Library in Italy, 1300–1600* (New York University Press, 1972)

Omont, Henri, 'Inventaire de la bibliothèque de Ferdinand Ier d'Aragon roi de Naples (1481)', *Bibliothèque de l'Ecole des Chartes*, 70 (1909), 456–70

Ong, Walter, *Orality and Literacy: the Technologizing of the Word* (London: Methuen, 1982)

Ossola, Carlo, and Prosperi, Adriano (eds.), *La corte e il 'Cortegiano'*, 2 vols. (Rome: Bulzoni, 1980)

Palumbo-Fossati, Isabelle, 'Livres et lecteurs dans la Venise du XVIe siècle', *Revue française d'histoire du livre*, 15 (1985), 481–513

Parenti, Giuseppe, 'Prezzi e salari a Firenze dal 1520 al 1620', in Ruggiero Romano (ed.), *I prezzi in Europa dal XIII secolo a oggi* (Turin: Einaudi, 1967), pp. 203–58

Parker, Deborah, *Commentary and Ideology: Dante in the Renaissance* (Durham, NC: Duke University Press, 1993)

'Women in the book trade in Italy, 1475–1620', *Renaissance Quarterly*, 49 (1996), 509–41

Parkes, Malcolm B., 'The influence of the concepts of *ordinatio* and *compilatio* on the development of the book', in J. J. G. Alexander and M. T. Gibson (eds.), *Medieval Learning and Literature: Essays Presented to Richard William Hunt* (Oxford: Clarendon Press, 1976), pp. 115–41

Pause and Effect: an Introduction to the History of Punctuation in the West (Aldershot: Scolar Press, 1992)

Pastorello, Ester, 'Di Aldo Pio Manuzio: testimonianze e documenti', *LB*, 67 (1965), 163–220

Perosa, Alessandro, 'Contributi e proposte per la pubblicazione delle opere latine del Poliziano', in *Il Poliziano e il suo tempo* (Florence: Sansoni, 1957), pp. 89–100

Pesenti, Tiziana, 'Il "Dioscoride" di Pier Andrea Mattioli e l'editoria botanica', in Decio Gioseffi, Vincenzo Fontana, Salvatore Ciriacono, Tiziana Pesenti, Adriana Chemello and Giovambattista Gasparini, *Trattati di prospettiva, architettura militare, idraulica e altre discipline* (Venice: Università Internazionale dell'Arte, 1985), pp. 61–103

Petrucci, Armando, '"Anticamente moderni e modernamente antichi"', in Armando Petrucci (ed.), *Libri, scrittura e pubblico nel Rinascimento: guida storica e critica* (Bari: Laterza, 1979), pp. 21–36

'Insegnare a scrivere imparare a scrivere', in Petrucci and others, 'Pratiche di scrittura', pp. 611–30

'Introduzione alle pratiche di scrittura', in Petrucci and others, 'Pratiche di scrittura', pp. 549–62

'Scrittura, alfabetismo ed educazione grafica nella Roma del primo Cinquecento: da un libretto di conti di Maddalena pizzicarola in Trastevere', *Scrittura e civiltà*, 2 (1978), 163–207

'La scrittura del testo', in *Letteratura italiana* Einaudi, IV, 283–308

'Storia e geografia delle culture scritte (dal secolo XI al secolo XVIII)', in *Letteratura italiana* Einaudi, *Storia e geografia*, vol. II, part 2, 1193–292

Writers and Readers in Medieval Italy: Studies in the History of Written Culture (New Haven: Yale University Press, 1995)

Petrucci, Armando, and others, 'Pratiche di scrittura e pratiche di lettura nell'Europa moderna', *Annali della Scuola Normale Superiore di Pisa*, Classe di Lettere e Filosofia, 3rd ser., 23 (1993), 375–823

Pettas, William A., 'The cost of printing a Florentine incunable', *LB*, 75 (1973), 67–85

The Giunti of Florence: Merchant Publishers of the Sixteenth Century (San Francisco: Rosenthal, 1980)

Plaisance, Michel, 'Les dédicaces à Côme Ier: 1546–1550', in Fiorato and Margolin (eds.), *L'écrivain face à son public*, pp. 173–87

Plebani, Tiziana, 'Omaggio ad Aldo grammatico: origine e tradizione degli insegnanti-stampatori', in Marcon and Zorzi (eds.), *Aldo Manuzio e l'ambiente veneziano*, pp. 73–102

Pollak, Michael, 'The daily performance of a printing press in 1476: evidence from a Hebrew incunable', *GJ*, 1974, 66–75

'Production costs in fifteenth-century printing', *Library Quarterly*, 39 (1969), 318–30

Pollard, Graham, 'The *pecia* system in the medieval universities', in M. B. Parkes and Andrew G. Watson (eds.), *Medieval Scribes, Manuscripts and Libraries: Essays Presented to N. R. Ker* (London: Scolar Press, 1978), pp. 145–61

Pollard, Graham, and Ehrman, Albert, *The Distribution of Books by Catalogue from the Invention of Printing to A.D. 1800* (Cambridge: printed for presentation to members of the Roxburghe Club, 1965)

Pozza, Neri, Colla, Angelo, Dillon, Gianvittorio, Gasparini, Giovan Battista, and Mazzariol, Giuseppe, *La stampa degli incunaboli nel Veneto* (Verona: Neri Pozza, 1984)

Pullan, Brian, 'Wage earners and the Venetian economy, 1550–1630', in Brian Pullan (ed.), *Crisis and Change in the Venetian Economy in the Sixteenth and Seventeenth Centuries* (London: Methuen, 1968), pp. 146–74

Quondam, Amedeo, 'Aretino e il libro: un repertorio, per una bibliografia', in *Pietro Aretino nel cinquecentenario della nascita: atti del Convegno di Roma–Viterbo–Arezzo (28 settembre – 1 ottobre 1992), Toronto (23–24 ottobre 1992), Los Angeles (27–29 ottobre 1992)*, 2 vols. (Rome: Salerno, 1995), I, 197–230

'Le biblioteche della Corte estense', in Quondam (ed.), *Il libro a corte*, pp. 7–38

'La letteratura in tipografia', in *Letteratura italiana* Einaudi, II, 555–686

'"Mercanzia d'onore", "mercanzia d'utile": produzione libraria e lavoro intellettuale a Venezia nel Cinquecento', in Armando Petrucci (ed.), *Libri, editori e pubblico nell'Europa moderna: guida storica e critica* (Bari: Laterza, 1977), pp. 51–104

'La parte del volgare', in Sandal (ed.), *I primordi della stampa a Brescia*, pp. 139–205

Quondam, Amedeo (ed.), *Il libro a corte* (Rome: Bulzoni, 1994)

Reeve, M. D., 'Manuscripts copied from printed books', in J. B. Trapp (ed.), *Manuscripts in the Fifty Years after the Invention of Printing* (London: Warburg Institute, 1983), pp. 12–20

Reidy, Denis V. (ed.), *The Italian Book 1465–1800: Studies Presented to Dennis E. Rhodes on His 70th Birthday* (London: British Library, 1993)

Renier, Rodolfo, 'Gaspare Visconti', *Archivio storico lombardo*, 2nd ser., 13 (1886), 509–63, 777–824

Renouard, Antoine Auguste, *Annales de l'imprimerie des Alde*, 3rd edn (Paris: Renouard, 1834)

Rhodes, Dennis E., *Annali tipografici di Lazzaro de' Soardi* (Florence: Olschki, 1978)

Gli annali tipografici fiorentini del XV secolo (Florence: Olschki, 1988)

'Lorenzo Lorio, publisher at Venice, 1514–1527', *LB*, 89 (1987), 279–83

'A mysterious Italian newsletter of 1517', *British Library Journal*, 9 (1983), 185–92

Silent Printers: Anonymous Printing at Venice in the Sixteenth Century (London: British Library, 1995)

Riccò, Laura, 'Testo per la scena – testo per la stampa: problemi di edizione', *GSLI*, 173 (1996), 210–66

Richardson, Brian, 'The debates on printing in Renaissance Italy', *LB*, 100 (1998), forthcoming

'Editing Dante's *Commedia*, 1472–1629', in T. J. Cachey (ed.), *Dante Now: Current Trends in Dante Studies* (Notre Dame, IN: University of Notre Dame Press, 1995), pp. 237–62

'*The Prince* and its early Italian readers', in Martin Coyle (ed.), *Niccolò Machiavelli's 'The Prince': New Interdisciplinary Essays* (Manchester University Press, 1995), pp. 18–39

Print Culture in Renaissance Italy: the Editor and the Vernacular Text, 1470–1600 (Cambridge University Press, 1994)

Richardson, Brian (ed.), *Trattati sull'ortografia del volgare 1524–1526* (University of Exeter, 1984)

Ridolfi, Roberto, *La stampa in Firenze nel secolo XV* (Florence: Olschki, 1958)

Vita di Niccolò Machiavelli, 4th edn, 2 vols. (Florence: Sansoni, 1969)

Rizzo, Silvia, *Il lessico filologico degli umanisti* (Rome: Edizioni di Storia e Letteratura, 1973)

Robin, Diana, *Filelfo in Milan: Writings 1451–1477* (Princeton University Press, 1991)

Rogledi Manni, Teresa, *La tipografia a Milano nel XV secolo* (Florence: Olschki, 1980)

Romano, Vincenzo, 'Predicazioni savonaroliane e attività redattrice dei primi editori', *LB*, 69 (1967), 277–308

Root, Robert K., 'Publication before printing', *PMLA*, 28 (1913), 417–31

Roover, Florence Edler de, 'New facets on the financing and marketing of early printed books', *Bulletin of the Business Historical Review*, 27 (1953), 222–30

'Per la storia dell'arte della stampa in Italia: come furono stampati a Venezia tre dei primi libri in volgare', *LB*, 55 (1953), 107–15

Rose, Mark, *Authors and Owners: the Invention of Copyright* (Cambridge, MA: Harvard University Press, 1993)

Rosenthal, Margaret F., *The Honest Courtesan: Veronica Franco, Citizen and Writer in Sixteenth-Century Venice* (University of Chicago Press, 1992)

Rotondò, Antonio, 'La censura ecclesiastica e la cultura', in *Storia d'Italia*, vol. V, part II (Turin: Einaudi, 1973), 1397–492

Rouse, Mary A., and Rouse, Richard H., *Cartolai, Illuminators and Printers in Fifteenth-Century Italy: the Evidence of the Ripoli Press* (Los Angeles: UCLA Research Library, 1988)

'La naissance des index', in *Histoire de l'édition française*, I, 77–85

'Nicolaus Gupalatinus and the arrival of print in Italy', *LB*, 88 (1986), 221–51

Rozzo, Ugo, *Biblioteche italiane del Cinquecento tra Riforma e Controriforma* (Udine: Arti Grafiche Friulane, 1994)

Linee per una storia dell'editoria religiosa in Italia (1465–1600) (Udine: Arti Grafiche Friulane, 1993)

Rusconi, Roberto, '"Confessio generalis": opuscoli per la pratica penitenziale nei primi cinquanti anni dalla introduzione della stampa', in Società internazionale di studi francescani, *I frati minori*, pp. 189–227

Saenger, Paul, 'Books of Hours and the reading habits of the later Middle Ages', in Chartier (ed.), *The Culture of Print*, pp. 141–73

'Manières de lire médiévales', in *Histoire de l'édition française*, I, 131–41

'Silent reading: its impact on later medieval script and society', *Viator*, 13 (1982), 367–414

Sambin, Paolo, 'Libri in volgare posseduti da Bardo de' Bardi e custoditi da Palla Strozzi', *IMU*, 1 (1958), 371–3

Sandal, Ennio, 'Dal libro antico al libro moderno: premesse e materiali per una indagine. Brescia, 1472–1550: una verifica esemplare', in Sandal (ed.), *I primordi della stampa a Brescia*, pp. 227–307

Sandal, Ennio (ed.), *I primordi della stampa a Brescia 1472–1511: atti del Convegno internazionale (Brescia, 6–8 giugno 1984)* (Padua: Antenore, 1986)

Sander, Max, *Le livre à figures italien depuis 1467 jusqu'à 1530*, 6 vols. (Milan: Hoepli, 1942) (supplement by C. E. Rava, Milan, 1969)

Santoro, Caterina, 'Contributi alla storia dell'amministrazione sforzesca', *Archivio storico lombardo*, new ser., 4 (1939), 27–114

'Due contratti di lavoro per l'arte della stampa a Milano', in Lamberto Donati (ed.), *Miscellanea bibliografica in memoria di don Tommaso Accurti* (Rome: Edizioni di Storia e Letteratura, 1947), pp. 185–92

Sartori, Antonio, 'Documenti padovani sull'arte della stampa nel sec. XV', in

Libri e stampatori a Padova: miscellanea di studi storici in onore di mons. G. Bellini, tipografo editore libraio (Padua: Tipografia Antoniana, 1959), pp. 111–231

Saunders, J. W., 'The stigma of print: a note on the social bases of Tudor poetry', *Essays in Criticism*, 1 (1951), 139–64

Sayce, R. A., 'Compositorial practices and the localization of printed books, 1530–1800', *Library*, 5th ser., 21 (1966), 1–45

Scarpa, Emanuela, 'L'autografo del primo "Decennale" di Niccolò Machiavelli', *Studi di filologia italiana*, 51 (1993), 149–80

Scholderer, Victor, *Fifty Essays in Fifteenth- and Sixteenth-Century Bibliography*, ed. Dennis E. Rhodes (Amsterdam: Hertzberger, 1966)

'The invention of printing', in *Fifty Essays*, pp. 156–68

'The petition of Sweynheym and Pannartz to Sixtus IV', in *Fifty Essays*, pp. 72–3

'Printers and readers in Italy in the fifteenth century', in *Fifty Essays*, pp. 202–15

'Printing at Ferrara in the fifteenth century', in *Fifty Essays*, pp. 91–5

'Printing at Milan in the fifteenth century', in *Fifty Essays*, pp. 96–105

'Printing at Venice to the end of 1481', in *Fifty Essays*, pp. 74–89

'Red printing in early books', in *Fifty Essays*, pp. 265–70

'The shape of early type', in *Fifty Essays*, pp. 106–7

Schutte, Anne Jacobson, 'Irene di Spilimbergo: the image of a creative woman in late Renaissance Italy', *Renaissance Quarterly*, 44 (1991), 42–61

Printed Italian Vernacular Religious Books, 1465–1500: a Finding List (Geneva: Droz, 1983)

'Printing, piety, and the people in Italy: the first thirty years', *Archiv für Reformationsgeschichte*, 71 (1980), 5–19

Shaw, David J., 'The Lyons counterfeit of Aldus's italic type: a new chronology', in Reidy (ed.), *The Italian Book*, pp. 117–33

Sheppard, L. A., 'A fifteenth-century humanist, Francesco Filelfo', *Library*, 4th ser., 16 (1935), 1–26

Sighinolfi, Lino, 'Francesco Puteolano e le origini della stampa in Bologna e in Parma', *LB*, 15 (1913–14), 263–6, 331–44, 451–67

Smith, Margaret M., 'Printed foliation: forerunner to printed page-numbers?', *GJ*, 1988, 54–70

Società internazionale di studi francescani, *I frati minori tra '400 e '500: atti del XII Convegno internazionale, Assisi 18–19–20 ottobre 1984* (Assisi: Centro di studi francescani, 1986)

Solerti, Angelo, *Vita di Torquato Tasso*, 3 vols. (Turin: Loescher, 1895)

Sorrentino, Andrea, *La letteratura italiana e il Sant'Uffizio* (Naples: Perrella, 1935)

Spotti, Alda, 'Il manoscritto nell'officina tipografica', in *Il libro italiano del Cinquecento*, pp. 63–75

Stannard, Jerry, 'P. A. Mattioli: sixteenth century commentator on Dioscorides', *Bibliographical Contributions*, 1 (1969), 59–81

Stäuble, Antonio, *'Parlar per lettera': il pedante nella commedia del Cinquecento e altri saggi sul teatro rinascimentale* (Rome: Bulzoni, 1991)

Steele, Robert, 'The pecia', *Library*, 4th ser., 11 (1931), 230–4

Stevens, Kevin M., and Gehl, Paul F., 'Giovanni Battista Bosso and the paper trade in late sixteenth-century Milan', *LB*, 96 (1994), 43–90

Tavoni, Mirko, 'Scrivere la grammatica: appunti sulle prime grammatiche dell'italiano manoscritte e a stampa', in Petrucci and others, 'Pratiche di scrittura', pp. 759–96

Tenenti, Alberto, 'Luc'Antonio Giunti il giovane stampatore e mercante', in *Studi in onore di A. Sapori*, 2 vols. (Milan: Istituto Editoriale Cisalpino, 1957), II, 1023–60

Tinto, Alberto, *Annali tipografici dei Tramezzino* (Venice: Istituto per la collaborazione culturale, 1968)

Il corsivo nella tipografia del Cinquecento (Milan: Il Polifilo, 1972)

Tompkins, Jane P., 'The reader in history: the changing shape of literary response', in Jane P. Tompkins (ed.), *Reader-Response Criticism: from Formalism to Post-Structuralism* (Baltimore: Johns Hopkins University Press, 1980), pp. 201–32

Tristano, Caterina, 'Economia del libro in Italia tra XV e XVI secolo: il costo del libro "nuovo"', *Bulletin du bibliophile* (1991), 273–98

Trovato, Paolo, *Con ogni diligenza corretto: la stampa e le revisioni editoriali dei testi letterari italiani (1470–1570)* (Bologna: Il Mulino, 1991)

'Il libro toscano dell'età di Lorenzo: schede ed ipotesi', in *La Toscana al tempo di Lorenzo il Magnifico: politica economia cultura arte*, vol. II (Pisa: Pacini, 1996), 525–63

'Per la storia delle *Rime* del Bembo', *Rivista della letteratura italiana*, 9 (1991), 465–508

'Per un censimento dei manoscritti di tipografia in volgare', in Marco Santagata and Amedeo Quondam (eds.), *Il libro di poesia dal copista al tipografo* (Modena: Panini, 1989), pp. 43–81

'Serie di caratteri, formato e sistemi di interpunzione nella stampa dei testi in volgare (1501–1550)', in Emanuela Cresti, Nicoletta Maraschio and Luca Toschi (eds.), *Storia e teoria dell'interpunzione* (Rome: Bulzoni, 1992), pp. 89–110

Storia della lingua italiana: il primo Cinquecento (Bologna: Il Mulino, 1994)

Ullman, B. L., *The Origin and Development of Humanistic Script* (Rome: Edizioni di Storia e Letteratura, 1960)

Urban, Lina Padoan, 'La festa della Sensa nelle arti e nell'iconografia', *Studi veneziani*, 10 (1968), 291–353

Vaglia, Ugo, 'I Da Sabbio stampatori in Brescia', *Commentari dell'Ateneo di Brescia*, 172 (1973), 59–87

Valenti, Tommaso, 'Per la storia dell'arte della stampa in Italia: la più antica Società tipografica (Trevi–Umbria 1470)', *LB*, 26 (1924), 105–27

Varanini, Gian Maria, 'Per la storia della tipografia veronese nel Quattrocento: due schede d'archivio', *IMU*, 25 (1982), 407–15

Veneziani, Paolo, 'Il frontespizio come etichetta del prodotto', in *Il libro italiano del Cinquecento*, pp. 99–125

'Introduzione', in *Il libro italiano del Cinquecento*, pp. 13–23

'La marca tipografica di Comin da Trino', *GJ*, 1990, pp. 162–73

'Platone Benedetti e la prima edizione degli "Opera" del Poliziano', *GJ*, 1988, pp. 95–107

'Vicende tipografiche della *Geografia* di Francesco Berlinghieri', *LB*, 84 (1982), 195–208

Venier, Marina, 'Immagini e documenti', in *Il libro italiano del Cinquecento*, pp. 25–61

Verde, Armando F., 'Libri tra le pareti domestiche: una necessaria appendice a *Lo Studio fiorentino 1473–1503*', *Memorie domenicane*, new ser., 18 (1987), 1–225

Lo Studio fiorentino 1473–1503: ricerche e documenti, 4 vols. (Florence: Istituto nazionale di studi sul Rinascimento, 1973–85)

Vernet, André (ed.), *Histoire des bibliothèques françaises: les bibliothèques médiévales, du VIe siècle à 1530* (Paris: Promodis, 1989)

Veyrin-Forrer, Jeanne, 'Fabriquer un livre au XVIe siècle', in *Histoire de l'édition française*, I, 279–301

Vezin, Jean, 'La fabrication du manuscrit', in *Histoire de l'édition française*, I, 25–47

'Manuscrits "imposés"', in Henri-Jean Martin and Jean Vezin (eds.), *Mise en page et mise en texte du livre manuscrit* (Paris: Editions du Cercle de la librairie – Promodis, 1990), pp. 423–5

Villari, Pasquale, *La storia di Girolamo Savonarola e de' suoi tempi*, 2 vols. (Florence: Le Monnier, 1859–61)

Volpati, Carlo, 'Gli Scotti di Monza tipografi-editori in Venezia', *Archivio storico lombardo*, 6th ser., 59 (1932), 365–82

Wagner, Klaus, 'Aldo Manuzio e i prezzi dei suoi libri', *LB*, 77 (1975), 77–82

Wardrop, James, *The Script of Humanism: Some Aspects of Humanistic Script, 1460–1560* (Oxford: Clarendon Press, 1963)

Welch, Evelyn, *Art and Authority in Renaissance Milan* (New Haven: Yale University Press, 1995)

Wickham Legg, J., 'An agreement in 1536 between certain booksellers of Rome and Venice to bring out the second text of the reformed breviary of Cardinal Quignon', *Transactions of the Bibliographical Society*, 13 (1913–15), 323–48

Wilkins, Ernest H., 'On the earliest editions of the *Morgante* of Luigi Pulci', *Papers of the Bibliographical Society of America*, 45 (1951), 1–22

Woodward, David, *Maps as Prints in the Italian Renaissance: Makers, Distributors & Consumers* (London: British Library, 1996)

Zanelli, Agostino, 'Debiti e crediti di un libraio bresciano del secolo XVI', *LB*, 4 (1902–3), 99–101

Zappella, Giuseppina, *Le marche dei tipografi e degli editori italiani del Cinquecento: repertorio di figure, simboli e soggetti e dei relativi motti*, 2 vols. (Milan: Editrice Bibliografica, 1986)

Zardin, Danilo, *Donna e religiosa di rara eccellenza: Prospera Corona Bascapè, i libri e la cultura nei monasteri milanesi del Cinque e Seicento* (Florence: Olschki, 1992)

'Mercato librario e letture devote nella svolta del Cinquecento tridentino:

note in margine ad un inventario milanese di libri di monache', in Nicola Raponi and Angelo Turchini (eds.), *Stampa, libri e letture a Milano nell'età di Carlo Borromeo* (Milan: Vita e Pensiero, 1992), pp. 135–246

Zarri, Gabriella, 'La vita religiosa femminile tra devozione e chiostro: testi devoti in volgare editi tra il 1475 e il 1520', in Società internazionale di studi francescani, *I frati minori*, pp. 125–68

Zorzi, Marino, 'Le biblioteche, tra pubblico e privato', in Da Pozzo (ed.), *La ragione e l'arte*, pp. 35–48

'La circolazione del libro a Venezia nel Cinquecento: biblioteche private e pubbliche', *Ateneo veneto*, 177 (1990), 117–89

Index